T0301179

Jokes, Jokes, Jokes

Jokes, Jokes, Jokes

My Very Funny Memoir

Jenny Eclair

SPHERE

SPHERE

First published in Great Britain in 2024 by Sphere

1 3 5 7 9 10 8 6 4 2

Copyright © Jenny Eclair 2024

The moral right of the author has been asserted.

Extract on page 5 from 'This Be the Verse' from Philip Larkin, *Collected Poems* (London: Faber & Faber, 2003). © Estate of Philip Larkin.

A CIP catalogue record for this book
is available from the British Library.

Hardback ISBN 978-1-4087-3205-2
C format ISBN 978-1-4087-3206-9

Typeset in Goudy by M Rules
Printed and bound in Great Britain by
Clays Ltd, Elcograf S.p.A

Papers used by Sphere are from well-managed forests
and other responsible sources.

MIX
Paper | Supporting
responsible forestry
FSC
www.fsc.org   FSC® C104740

Sphere
An imprint of
Little, Brown Book Group
Carmelite House
50 Victoria Embankment
London EC4Y 0DZ

An Hachette UK Company
www.hachette.co.uk

www.littlebrown.co.uk

For Arlo Jude
In memory of June and Derek, the original and best

Introducing . . .

I make my bloodied, screaming entrance on 16 March 1960, in the Kinrara military hospital in Kuala Lumpur, a hospital originally opened a decade earlier to treat Gurkhas with TB.

There is nothing remotely unusual about my birth. While my mother June huffs and puffs, my father, like all self-respecting fathers-to-be at the time, paces around the golf course.

Derek (a name that has never come back into fashion) Hargreaves is a major, or is it a captain? I think he was demoted once and then promoted again. Whatever, he is an incredibly brave man, but like a lot of chaps of his generation he cannot stomach childbirth.

I am his second daughter: I don't think he is too disappointed! He is a man who smiles a great deal, and he loves my mother.

My father loves my mother so much that almost ten years earlier, in 1951, when June has polio and is in a bad way in the infectious diseases hospital in Blackpool, my soldier dad-to-be begs compassionate leave and hitchhikes back to the UK from Cyprus. He isn't actually going out with my mother at the time – they are on 'a break' and she is in fact seeing someone else. However, my father has other plans.

According to family legend, Derek comes crashing into the

hospital room, where June lies bedbound and smoking therapeutic Balkan Sobranie cigarettes (on medical advice), and tells her that she will walk again. His exact words being, 'Don't worry, June, you will walk again, when you walk down the aisle to marry me.'

Which she does, her calliper hidden under her empire-line white dress, her proud eagle nose accentuated by a terrible haircut, the two of them beaming, beaming, beaming.

With this one passionate declaration of intent in the hospital, my father uses up every last shred of romance that he ever possessed

Despite never having eyes for anyone else, he is not given to soppiness or extravagant gestures, hence caravan holidays. However, every week for many years he buys my mother a Walnut Whip, which he presents to her on Friday evenings, having first bitten the walnut off the top of the whip.

There is also a birthday which involves the gift of an egg-poaching pan and a KitKat, which he insists on sharing, before he coaxes my mother out of bed to poach some eggs.

When my parents are in their eighties, a very dear uncle visits. Unbeknownst to anyone, he is in early stages of Alzheimer's and, a pint of lager in, comments loudly, 'Well done, Derek, you took a cripple woman on when you didn't need to, and made the best of it.'

Ha!

For years I am convinced my mother contracted polio from a trip to the cinema in Blackpool, while my sister insisted she was youth hostelling, but it transpires she had attended a swimming party at a friend's house in Marton, near Blackpool. I have no idea how my mother knew people who had their own swimming pool, but, according to her sister this is what happened.

My mother wears a calliper for the rest of her life, graduating from a knee-length number to a monster thigh-length beast when she gets older. They are all awful, and because the shoe the calliper clips into has to be drilled by the NHS with a metal cylinder, my mother is limited to two pairs of shoes per year. Heels have to be low, solid and not made of rubber. Once, when a pair of shoes is rejected as being unsuitable, the man behind the orthopaedic counter at Blackpool Victoria sneers, 'and we don't do slippers either'.

I rarely see my mother angry, but on that occasion she is furious. She used to play competitive tennis, winning silver cups, her picture regularly in the paper, and now she is being patronised by this complete arsehole.

Post-polio, June is told she probably shouldn't/wouldn't have children and, in typical style, she has three. For many, many years, I couldn't tell you which leg that calliper is strapped to – it is never really mentioned – and I am taken aback when other people stare. The sixties might be swinging, but they are still calling people cripples and spastics.

Many years later, Damien Hirst makes a seven-metre-high sculpture, called *Charity* (2003), which is a replica of a sixties Spastics Society collection box, depicting a disabled young girl in a calliper clutching a teddy bear and a collection tin. These used to be a common sight outside supermarkets; teenagers used to shove chips into the money slot in the top of the collection box. At the time I didn't realise how offensive they were, but years later, despite being a fan of Hirst's, when I first see *Charity* at the Yorkshire Sculpture Park, I cringe.

I have no clear recollections of our time spent in KL. I wish that, when I got older, I had asked my parents, both raised in Lancashire, how it felt to be in their thirties and so far away from a fish and chip shop.

I'm not sure, either, what my father is up to at this point in his career; these details are often vague, especially later, when we are stationed in Berlin, but I know my mother helped local girls get contraception and did a course in making Malaysian curries.

My mother continues to make curries throughout her life, until she is ninety: prawn and egg and chicken are her specialities. In the seventies, when we are back in the UK and everyone is experimenting with Asian-inspired Vesta ready meals, my mother continues to make hers from scratch, served up with fluffy rice, a pile of poppadoms and little side dishes of desiccated coconut, mango chutney and chopped peanuts.

I think life 'out East' possibly sounds slightly more exotic than the reality; my parents certainly weren't living some Happy Valley expat lifestyle. I hat said, we did have a nanny, a wash amah and a gardener.

Once, while I am lying on a rug on the grass outside our home in KL, a big black mamba snake begins to slither towards little baby me, and while everyone else freezes in horror, my father arrives home from the golf club, sees it and knocks its head off with a nine iron.

Details of this incident may well be exaggerated. I am sixty-four years old now and not really to be trusted. I'll check with my sister.

Note from Sara: I'm not sure it was a mamba, Jenny.

Early photographs show me in a terry towelling nappy, as white as a maggot and as bald as a potato. Not much has changed since. I still have the skin tones of a jellyfish but have learned to cheat with fake tan; consequently I always smell like old biscuits. As for my hair, it is short and bleached and I am waiting for the silver to invade entirely before I can give up the peroxide for good.

The crap straight, fine (aka limp) hair is inherited from my mother, who perms and rollers her own skimpy locks for years, until she opts for a silver pixie crop in her sixties and never looks back.

From my father I inherit my appalling knees. Seriously, this is a terrible piece of genetic unfairness. My sister has dainty knees but my brother and I have knees that look like they belong on an allotment. They are massive, swollen turnip affairs, hence the gag 'I once wore shorts to a fruit and produce show and won first prize for my giant cauliflowers'. I find this joke works best if I am actually showing my knees at the time: basically, if in need of a laugh I can always get my knees out. Thanks, Pa.

My parents are extremely happy together, which obviously makes my life very difficult, so much so that I have no one to blame for anything. I am never neglected, shoved to one side or traumatised by any marital fighting, death or divorce. In fact, years later, when I am receiving some psychiatric help, one therapist suggests that my idyllically happy childhood and my loving and secure family background had ill prepared me for the real world. So, yeah, in some respects I can blame them. 'They fuck you up, your mum and dad.' In my case by tucking me up, reading me stories and kissing me goodnight.

Funny Bones

I know from an early age that I am funny, and my sister isn't; she is clever, that is her role. I am her fool.

When my brother comes along seven years after me (an afterthought, a terrible accident, IMO) he shifts the balance. I now have competition from someone who has the potential to be funny. I try never to laugh at him, possibly I dent his confidence. Good. The truth is, had he pursued a comedy career I have no doubt he would be *quite* good (haha).

To this day I insist I am still the funniest of the three of us. My sister doesn't really 'do' jokes, whereas my brother retains the promise he had as a child, which is possibly why, as a criminal barrister, he has never made silk. Their loss, in my opinion.

My brother is good with dogs: he likes those whippets that can walk through an antique shop without knocking anything over and don't bark. He is green-fingered and is the only one of the three of us who can really cook, although my sister would argue this.

Both my brother and I understand social media, my sister can't see the point; she doesn't get *Taskmaster* either. She watched the first episode of the series I did in 2023 and was left stone cold. Our phone conversation went like this:

Sara: 'Was that it?'

Me: 'No, there are nine more episodes.'

Sara: 'Jesus Christ.'

Two and a half years older than me, my sister is also a qualified barrister (and the youngest female ever to qualify back in 1981). Both my siblings own those grey horsehair wigs which they keep in tins. My daughter borrows my sister's when she co-writes a very camp play about Oscar Wilde and needs one for a court scene.

I think this sums the family up. There's quite a lot of showing off and dressing up involved in our everyday lives. My brother is like a better-looking, younger Rumpole, whereas my sister, having left her chambers, is an adjudicator (no, me neither. I keep meaning to ask, but I fear the answer will be long-winded.) My sister is the most academic of the three of us and does history degrees for fun. During Covid, she gets a first in 'blah blah' from Birkbeck. She also belongs to a book club which to my knowledge has never ever chosen a readable book. I think my sister can be amusing but she is too clever to be funny, whereas my brother and I aren't.

Our father is funny, he has funny bones. I suspect he was funny from birth. The middle one of three sons, as a small boy he has the blond curls of a Pears soap baby. His older brother Stanley is also funny: funny in a much broader 'funny man telling jokes in a pub' way. My Uncle Stanley retains his Blackpool accent all his life; my father doesn't. My father becomes plummy in the army; after all, he is an officer.

His younger brother, Tom, is a stranger, really. He marries a woman called Easter, moves to the States and works for Mattel, which means our cousins, Carole and David, have better toys than us. Eventually, Tom becomes a part-time figure skater in New Zealand (seriously) and is a very early adoptee of the word processor. He sends us printed-off computer-typed annual Xmas round robins which are always a bit 'showy off'.

My mother is always a bit anti Uncle Tom, especially after he insists on having their dead mother's grandfather clock transported out to New Zealand, against everyone else's better judgement. By the time it arrives, it is, inevitably, all smashed up.

'I could have told you,' snaps my mother.

Meanwhile, Stanley works in cars and marries Dorothy, who is lovely and has a glass eye, and together they raise a good-looking and rather glamorous family in Oxford.

My cousin Lesley is a rather sexy girl and Lord Lichfield, the famous royal photographer, ends up taking topless photographs of her, which Uncle Stanley is very proud of. We are all shown the contact sheets.

My Uncle Stanley makes me laugh. He comes to stay with us and spends hours in the toilet, reading the *Sun* and smoking. He is deliberately 'very common'. Years later, back in the north and a widower, he decides to buy a little terrace cottage in the centre of Lytham, and when he views a likely property the sixty-something owner, herself a widow, is greeted with the words 'I'll take the house and I'll take you with it'. Stanley and Brenda live very happily together for years, until Stanley smokes a leg off, catches one of those horrific flesh-eating illnesses in hospital and dies. He was good fun.

My father is not really suited to civvy street. When he first comes out of the army after the war he goes to Africa to sell bicycles to the natives, catches malaria and has to come home, whereupon, having walked in and out of a bank interview, he rejoins the army. During his military career, he works in intelligence, pilots one-man submarines and jumps out of aeroplanes.

The parachuting screws up his knees, and at some point in the eighties he has them replaced. I think the new ones are made of plastic, because whenever he sits near a fire he jokes that he can smell them burning. Occasionally the malaria also flares up and he spends several days bright yellow and shaking in bed.

Once I am old enough to tell the difference, I realise my father isn't like other fathers, who rarely speak to their daughters or their daughters' friends, men who disappear behind newspapers and choose what to watch on the television. Despite being an army major, my father is not a disciplinarian. He likes fart jokes and made-up stories and in the summer he wears a sarong in bed. My mates sleeping over have never seen anything like it.

'Comedy Roots'

The first time I ever laugh so hard I think I am going to be sick, I am on my father's shoulders and he is walking us home from the corner shop in Blackpool where we have bought broken biscuits for half-price. I am probably about three and for now we are 'home' from the Far East (as people used to say). The reason for my hysterics is that my daddy pretends he can't remember where we live. 'Is it this one?' he asks, actually opening a strange gate and proceeding to walk up the path. 'Nooooo,' I squeal. 'Noo, not this one,' until eventually he finds the right gate and the right path, and I am weak with laughter and relief.

It is 1963 and at the time he is briefly home from doing a tour of Arabia with the peacekeeping Trucial Oman Scouts, which btw, according to the internet, were 'a highly respected impartial paramilitary armed security and rural police force, regarded as a well-trained, well paid and efficient military unit'. I'm not sure how well paid my mother thought they were.

As a Trucial Oman Scout my father wears an Arab-style red and white headdress and rides around on camels, living from one desert camp to another. In some respects, the Oman Scouts are the last of the Lawrence of Arabia style of soldiering.

My father has a touch of the Boy Scout about him: he likes

opening a tin with a knife and whittling a stick. Because of his peacekeeping duties I don't see my father much between the ages of two and four, when he is recommissioned and we are packed off to Berlin.

While Pa is in Arabia, my mother, my sister Sara and I live in a thirties house in Blackpool quite close to our maternal grandparents, Tommy and Jenny 1.

By this time, Tommy (orphaned tragically young) has done very well for himself, and my grandparents reside in a large detached house on Preston New Road, complete with a rose garden and a poodle called Mitzi. My grandmother isn't very imaginative when it comes to names: neither of her daughters have middle names and, after Mitzi dies, another Mitzi takes her place.

I have never owned a dog myself. My parents buy my brother a Westie called Humphrey after my sister and I leave home (spoilt), but I have always been very drawn to poodles – poodles and dachshunds, they're the only dogs for me. In the absence of both, I have a fifties porcelain poodle on my bedside table – just the one: any more and I'd be in danger of turning into one of those women who 'collects china poodles'. You've got to watch it. Humphrey the Westie eventually develops doggy dementia, starts weeing in the wardrobe and has to be put down. I hope if I start weeing in the wardrobe someone will put me down, too.

I remember my grandparents' big house on Preston New Road well, because when I am very little and we are home from Singapore for Xmas (I spend the first two years of my life in KL and Singapore), I fall down the toilet in their massive black and green art deco-style bathroom, and none of the grown-ups revelling downstairs (all cigar smoke, cheese straws and trifle in a cut-glass dish) can hear me cry. I think my sister can, but she pretends to be asleep.

My grandfather Tommy is mostly humourless. He is missing the septum to his nose and only has half a little finger on one hand. I believe he lost the top half in an incident involving one of the first electric garage doors on the north-west coast.

He is also a Freemason, which is odd, but I think it may stem from needing to feel accepted, having been brought up in a children's home.

As a young man Tommy works on Blackpool Pleasure Beach, taking money for rides, but one of the bosses spots his potential and helps him into the legal profession. Possibly a lot of funny handshakes are involved?

A fully qualified solicitor, he has an office in the centre of town, with a secretary who sits outside the inner sanctum typing letters on a proper clickety-clack typewriter.

My grandfather is very, very dark. When he visits us in Singapore he is frequently mistaken for a local. Tommy Hesmondhalgh is an unusual-looking man, not handsome, but extremely charismatic, a bit like Humphrey Bogart.

By contrast, my grandmother is very fair-skinned. As a young woman she has a long auburn plait, which for a while is kept in a tin in the attic. But by the time I come into her life, she is sixty and her hair is silver-white. Tommy is very thin on top and he wears what little hair is left slicked back with Brylcreem, hence the antimacassars on the backs of their chairs.

Tommy and Jenny are very dressy: Tommy wears three-piece suits with braces, sock suspenders, tie clips and cufflinks. His collars are studded. My grandfather comes home from work and changes into a red satin Chinese smoking jacket and a pair of those lozenge-shaped leather slippers. Once in his smoking garb he proceeds to sit in an upright wing-backed chair, smoking. Tommy smokes Players or Senior Service through a silver cigarette holder and drops ash into one of those magical ashtrays which swallow down the ash when you press a knob. Inevitably he dies of lung cancer, which my nana refuses to believe has anything to do with the fags.

Tommy and Jenny keep their large television hidden behind the doors of a teak cabinet. My grandmother likes nothing better than sitting on the sofa, eating Pontefract cakes and knitting, while simultaneously watching the television. Her favourite programmes are *Coronation Street*, *Come Dancing* (the original *Strictly*) and, to my burning shame, *The Black and White Minstrel Show*. She is a little woman and when I picture her sitting on that sofa, her feet don't touch the carpet.

Tommy and Jenny also have an oriental black and gold lacquered drinks cabinet which is mirrored on the inside and houses golden cockerel-headed cocktail sticks and jars of maraschino cherries. It smells divine.

I cannot remember my grandfather ever really laughing or telling a joke. When my father asks my mother to marry him, Tommy goes to bed for a week with a bottle of champagne. He isn't celebrating, he is sulking; he doesn't want my mother to marry my father on account of the fact that Derek is a soldier and, worse, he wears a duffle coat! This coming from a man whose older sisters had been working girls in Preston. Not street-walkers, you understand; they might have been sex workers, but they were carriage trade only, no street-corner blowjobs for them.

My grandmother is light to Poppa's dark. She is originally a mill girl, working in one of the cotton mills in nearby Preston. These mills were notoriously loud and, as a consequence, my grandmother went deaf very young. 'I never heard a bird sing after the age of fourteen,' she repeats frequently.

Jenny comes from poor stock: there is boozy Welsh blood on her father's side, a mother who looks like a witch and a number of siblings: Ida, who lives for a long time in Florida and famously never set foot in the sun – 'lovely skin' – and Emily, who is one of the original women football players on the famous Dick, Kerr Ladies team founded in 1917. She also has a number of brothers, most of whom seemed to be called Bert.

My grandmother is so northern that for years I think she has a cousin called Armoury Jane. Turns out she is saying 'our Mary Jane'.

Once Tommy starts to do well, my grandmother enjoys spending his money, and goes to Blackpool shopping most days. She is the type to match her handbag to her shoes and always wears a hat when going 'out out'.

Hats in the sixties and seventies remain on the head, even when sitting indoors. She is also partial to a brooch, and her jewellery box is a constant trove of delight for me, my sister and our cousin Elizabeth, or 'the Three Graces' as she nicknames us.

I once catch sight of her getting dressed. It's the seventies but she still wears a corset with a suspender belt attached. She has lovely legs and tiny feet.

In the huge matching his and hers mahogany wardrobes, my grandmother stashes her many pairs of shoes, leather, patent and suede, in all colours and all with a heel. Her furs are zipped into plastic and stored in the upstairs attic space. Me, Sara and Elizabeth spend hours snooping through Nana's old treasures, marvelling over the oil paintings my mother did in hospital while recovering from polio. They are amazing, especially the one of the nun. Many years later I am told it was a painting by numbers kit.

Tucked away in a drawer is a miniature salt and pepper cruet set, a sachet of mustard and a serviette saved from a Pan Am flight to Majorca in 1965. As a child, this souvenir represents the highest level of sophistication and we are allowed to 'look, but not touch'. It is the most glamorous thing I've ever seen, only to be beaten some years later by my Aunty Aileen and Uncle Richard having an avocado bathroom suite installed, complete with a semi-circular corner bath.

As a result of doing well and coming up in the world, my grandmother is a terrible snob. She reads the *Daily Mail* religiously, but occasionally she forgets who she is and licks her plate.

Jenny 1 is a good, plain cook. When my grandfather dies, we all go back to their house in Poulton where she has made a large meat and potato pie. Cutting into the crust, revealing the bubbling gravy beneath, she announces, 'Eee, Tommy would have loved this.' It is served with red cabbage, obviously.

My mother doesn't inherit Jenny 1's dressiness, but her older sister Aileen does. Aileen is ninety-eight now and registered blind but can still pull an outfit together better than the rest of us combined.

Other things I remember about visiting my maternal grandparents include tinned peaches and Carnation milk for 'afters', the smell of tomatoes growing in my grandfather's greenhouse and the insane habit my grandmother has of putting Lux soap flakes in my bathwater, regardless of the fact that, just like her, I am massively allergic to anything perfumed.

My grandmother is regularly given residential coal tar treatment for psoriasis (literally bathed in tar and bandaged) but she refuses to believe that I might have similarly sensitive skin. When I come up in hives, she accuses me of 'showing off and giving myself rashes on purpose'. 'Attention-seeking,' she tells my mother. 'She's a giddy kipper, that one.'

In the Blood?

Be it a blessing or a curse, I believe in being born funny. I can spot a funny child from a distance. It doesn't happen often, and I'm delighted when it turns out to be a girl.

I think we're used to seeing boys fooling around, pulling faces, being physically idiotic. Little girls being overtly funny are a rarity, but when I see them my heart races. I imagine it's like having red hair and spotting another redhead, that instant recognition.

I have spotted them all over the world, on buses and an Australian tram. I saw one in a fruit and veg shop in Camberwell, another in an airport. Of course, there are millions more, but some will know it and hide it like a birthmark.

The entertainment blood in my family can be traced back to only one person: my father's mother.

Lilian, or Daisy as she is sometimes known, is a peculiar character, and by the time I know her, my paternal grandmother is an unattractive woman, with dramatic eye bags, a wobbling throat and filthy, inch-thick prescription lenses, behind which watery, pale blue eyes bulge foggily.

It is hard to imagine she has ever trodden the boards, that once upon a time she was a dancer, some kind of high-kicking

Tiller Girl-cum-chorine, who performed in Blackpool, but where I'm not sure.

Blackpool is and always has been a mecca of entertainment venues. My father never talks about his mother's show business career because he is embarrassed by her. Pa, having made his own way in the world, and reinvented himself as a jolly, slightly posh type, is mortified by his mother and yet, as the only son who has returned to live on the north-west coast, while she is still alive he remains resignedly dutiful, until she finally goes into a home and dies.

I don't go to the funeral, I'm not that fussed. I remember seeing the relief on my father's face, but also the sadness.

I never see any physical affection between my father and his mother. He wears a slightly pained expression whenever she is around. I think she triggers his migraines. But after Berlin, when we are back living locally, he offers to help her with any house repairs and religiously invites her for lunch every other Sunday.

My mother dreads these dates, but, equally dutifully, and with gritted teeth, roasts a chicken and makes lemon meringue pies.

The general consensus is that Nana Hargreaves has given up and refuses to move with the times. Lilian hasn't updated any-thing since 1949 and, in stark contrast to my other grandmother, adopts a strange old-fashioned style of clothing. This includes pleated woollen skirts, thick nylon tights the colour of dead salmon and cardigans which reek of mothballs.

She lives on Woodland Road, near Stanley Park in Blackpool, in a dingy Victorian red-brick two-up two-down with a scullery at the back. Compared to my maternal grandparents' homes, the huge house on Preston New Road, followed later by their pin-neat retirement home in Poulton, visiting it is a shocking experience.

Nana Hargreaves is to all intents and purposes chairbound and lives with a shadowy, lank-haired woman named Mrs Cree, who walks with a stick and has teeth like crooked yellow tombstones. Cree sleeps upstairs, while my grandmother beds down in the front parlour, next to a piano that is never opened. The place is full of clutter but contains nothing you ever feel like picking up or touching.

And yet, this is not the full picture, because there is sepia photographic evidence of a once lithe young woman, captured in a coquettish dance pose with what looks like a toy Scottie dog at her feet.

My grandmother is a young woman in this photograph: what on earth is the act and what part does the dog play?

By the time we come along, she has long stopped dancing and her husband has dropped down dead on the street soon after the war, his head riddled with shrapnel. His name was Leonard and once upon a time his family owned a shop selling prams and baby accessories in Leicester.

How they met and how she transformed from Little Miss Twinkle Toes to hunched toad is not something I ever bother to ask.

I am embarrassed about her, too. I hate visiting her house and I hate her coming to ours: she is smelly and gives you thruppences wrapped up in handkerchiefs crusted with dried snot. When she gets older, my mother makes her sit on newspaper when she visits, because she has given up attempting to get to the bathroom. On these occasions my mother wields the electric carving knife with an extra degree of ferocity.

I think my mother's frustration with her mother-in-law stems from an incident she tells me about when I am old enough to understand its significance.

My parents had been stationed in Cyprus. It is the mid-fifties, before any of us three were born, June and Derek are coming home on leave and this time it is Lilian's turn to be visited first. My father is scrupulously fair about things like this, and so my exhausted mother agrees. Arriving back late and starving from the journey, my parents turn up at Nana Hargreaves's horrible house, only to find that her idea of a welcome home meal is to open a tin of Spam. 'I was going to buy a tomato,' she remarks, 'but I forgot.'

Over at Jenny and Tommy's, my maternal grandmother would have killed the fatted calf, in the form of a nice roast with all the trimmings and a trifle to follow.

My biggest phobia growing up is turning into the wrong grandmother. People often comment on how similar our hands and fingernails are and I feel hot with the worry of it.

What if I turn into a dreadful fairy-tale grotesque, too? After all, I have her blood. Maybe living in a horrible house with an equally petrifying 'companion' and allowing budgerigars to kiss me on the lips is my destiny, too?

As it happens, I do take after her in some respects. I, too, am a crap cook, but if my child was coming all the way home from foreign climes, I'd at least make an effort and go to Marks!

Otherness

U nsurprisingly, show business is littered with army brats. There is something about changing schools frequently that gives you the chance to reinvent yourself, to make a new impression and be a slightly more exciting version of yourself: 'Look at me, look at me, look at me.'

It also means that sometimes my father is absent for long periods of time.

I first realise that I don't really know my dad when my mother, sister and I go to a railway station to meet him from leave. This is in the early sixties, I am around three years old and have already moved three times, from Malaya, where I was born, to Singapore and back to the UK. On our return from Singapore we are living in Blackpool while Pa is on camel duty in Arabia and we don't see him for months on end. The fact that he is coming home is very exciting. In a scene that makes watching *The Railway Children* years later slightly triggering, I remember waiting on the platform and Sara suddenly running at what to me looks like a complete stranger, shouting gleefully, 'My daddy, my daddy', while I, a confused but crafty three-year-old, quickly suss the situation and decide to copy her. 'My daddy, my daddy,' I parrot, running at this man's legs and clasping him around the knees.

Luckily, my father is an easy man to get to know again, and by the time we are home we feel like old mates.

My mother doesn't work, unlike her sister who studied science at university and worked in a lab with Margaret Thatcher, experimenting with ice-cream flavours, before teaching chemistry (with mixed results) at the school I later attend. June didn't really find her 'thing' until she married my father and became a full-time army wife, either following him around the world or single parenting when the posting wasn't family-friendly.

Naively, I decide that polio may have had something to do with my mother's lack of career, but she later tells me she was just 'bone idle'. Instead of seeking further education, June attends a typing course for young ladies at an academy in Manchester's exclusive St Ann's Square and after marrying my father joins him in Cyprus as a secretary. Here she works in an office where the previous occupant had his head blown off, the bloodstains still visible on the wall.

I'm not sure what is going on politically in Cyprus during the fifties (you can Google that yourselves), but the situation means my father spends his days burrowing along underground tunnels to capture insurgents, and my mother never knowing if he, too, will get his head blown off.

Despite not being the slightest bit sentimental (this is a woman who cut up her wedding dress to make a lampshade), my father is my mother's hero.

When we get older, the two things June forbids my sister and me from doing 'when we grow up' are typing or teaching. She thinks secretarial work would make us miserable, while being teachers would make our pupils miserable. She is probably right.

The fact I do type for a living is beside the point; it's just my own stuff and the spelling and grammar is corrected for me by experts. As for teaching, a few years ago I give a motivational speech to the sixth form at the school where my sister-in-law

teaches drama and halfway through I call one of the boys a cunt
for yawning in my face, so she was right about teaching.

I never manage to be in the right place at the right time to
go to nursery school, but by the time we pack up the Blackpool
house and leave for Berlin my sister has completed a term at
primary school and already been labelled 'bright'. I don't recall
any trauma over yet another move; my wicker rocking horse from
Singapore comes with me and so does my sister, my mummy and,
of course, my daddy, who will be living with us full-time, apart
from when he has to go away on 'manoeuvres' and sleep outside
in a special sleeping bag and eat out of tins with no labels. Is it
Spam? Is it sponge pudding? Some of these tins end up in our
kitchen cupboards.

Arriving in Berlin, we are put in temporary accommodation
for a couple of weeks, and Edinburgh House is my first experience
of hotel life. I am very much taken by the lifts; in fact I still get
excited in a lift, unless it's small, liable to break down and stinks
of piss.

Our eventual address in the Charlottenburg district of Berlin
is 32 Kiplingweg, which is at one end of a meandering cul-de-sac
of semi-detached purpose-built houses, next to a row of garages.
Our house, like all the other houses, is a pale grey pebbledash
with parquet floors, a sitting room, dining room, kitchen and
cloakroom downstairs and four bedrooms and a bathroom upstairs. There is a loft, too. I remember seeing my father carrying
our Christmas presents down the metal ladder one Xmas Eve
when I am about seven and thinking I must never tell my sister
(who is ten by now and, being 'bright', probably knows).

Thus, the tricky 'idyllic childhood' that is to blight my life
begins in Berlin. The first thing that goes wrong is that we are
enrolled in the best school in the world, a school against which
all other educational establishments fall horribly short. Five minutes from the Olympic Stadium, the modern, single-storey school

is a celebration of sixties progressiveness combined with a touch of old-fashioned quaintness. We have an adventure playground featuring lifelike trains and folded cotton napkins on the dinner tables.

The food is delicious, the teachers are kind, next to my coat peg is a picture of three ducklings, my sister is in a classroom up the corridor, everything smells of new wood and there is no uniform. We spend a lot of time at this school drawing round each other while we lie on the floor; formal maths is ignored, although there are boxes of what look like false teeth to count if you fancy, which I don't.

I draw pictures and write stories as soon as I can form letters.

I like drawing and I like reading; there isn't much else to do. We don't have a telly, we have Forces Radio and when I turn six my sister's request for my favourite tune is played on my birthday. The song is that old classic 'Three Wheels on My Wagon'. Originally written in 1961 with music by Burt Bacharach and lyrics by Bob Hilliard, it was released as a novelty record in the UK both in '65 and '66. What can I say? I also like the one about the mouse with clogs on. My musical tastes remain dubious to this day.

A Trip Down Memory Lane

I go back to the Charlottenburg school many years later to make a TV programme. Despite it having shrunk, the sight, sound and smell of it are so familiar I want to lie down on the floor and cry. If I had done, I hope one of the kids would have drawn round me.

When we finish filming inside the school, the cameras follow me as I retrace the steps I took forty-odd years ago to walk home. At the corner of a big road, I freeze. My body won't allow me to cross, the road is too big and dangerous, I need my mother's hand in mine. I am knocking on fifty at the time of filming this show.

Once I manage to cross the road, the cameras follow me back to number 32. All the houses have been painted white. Back in the sixties, the fences down our road were wooden and designed in a simple double-height criss-cross style. They are still there. I've never seen them anywhere else.

On the way, I pass the house where the nasty dog lived, leaving me with a distrust of Alsatians ever since, and the house where I used to read really outdated *Bunty* comics with a girl who may have been called Deborah. Deborah (or was it Belinda?) has relatives who send them over from England. She also teaches me how to do French knitting on a wooden doll with pins sticking out of its head.

My best mates are mostly boys, though, the Goldstein boys, JonJon (who once bounced on his bed and straight out of the window) and Marcus, and the Backhouse brothers, Nicholas, Timothy and Jeremy. One summer, Jeremy is a page boy at a wedding and takes to wearing the patent buckled shoes until they fall off his feet.

Back in my old garden, I search for the slope we used to toboggan down, but it has disappeared. I presume the old bombsite which bordered our back fence encroached on our land when it was redeveloped. It hasn't: the garden is just tiny with only the slightest of inclines.

My sister and I play on that bombsite and I'm not sure my mother knows how far we go or what we get up to. These are the days of children 'going out to play' and sometimes we go 'out out'. Once we climb into a hole and see the slither of a pale green snake; another time, in the rubble of what had been someone's home, we find an intact set of Christmas tree decorations.

We are too young to know about a war that ended twenty years ago. We make a den on the bombsite, with sticks and plastic sheeting, and furnish it with wooden crates. When it is vandalised, we blame a German boy called Wolfgang, who is the local twelve-year-old thug.

We are priggish little English children, miles from home but educated at an English-speaking school and raised on a diet of Enid Blyton. There are goodies and baddies, and we are on the goodies' side.

Our housekeeper is German, however. She is called Frau Hermann, and we love her. She is in her late fifties/early sixties at the time and has problems 'mit meinen Gallensteinen' (with my gallstones), her skin is very yellow, which I presume is a result of the 'Gallensteinen' or the fags. There is a streak at the front of her hair the colour of nicotine.

Looking back, I cannot think of anything more insane than

my mother being provided with a housekeeper when we are living in what is essentially a bog-standard council house. But as far as I can remember, Frau Hermann comes every day and starts by laying the table for breakfast. This involves curling the butter with a hot spoon until it is shaped into a small palace. I know, right, in a four-bedroom council house backing onto a bombsite.

Frau Hermann's husband, Herr Hermann, makes us a puppet theatre, and for some reason I get it into my head that their own children were all killed in the war and now he finds solace from his grief in carpentry. I have no idea if this storyline is true; as a child with a vivid imagination I will often weave fantasy around fact and, as time passes, lose sight of the original story. I have never been a trustworthy narrator of my own story, but the truth is always buried somewhere, like a plain wall underneath an abundance of Virginia creeper. In this case, the Hermanns, the decorative butter and the puppet theatre definitely existed. As for the tragically killed children, I doubt it.

Our parents populate the puppet theatre with locally bought puppets: some have wooden heads and some are rubber, some are grotesque and, looking back, possibly antisemitic. Some are characters from German children's literature, including Max and Moritz, two supposedly mischievous little boys who got up to comical pranks, such as strangling an old widow woman's chickens. Mischief, my arse, they were psychopaths.

Thus equipped, my sister and I start putting on shows in the basement of our house. These are performed during the summer when there is plenty of space due to no coal delivery. All the local kids gather round while Sara and I embark on interminably long-winded shows that bore our audience to the point of such tedium that they escape the torture by climbing up the coal chute and crawling out into the garden. I blame Sara. My bits are hilarious.

By the time I am six, my comedy appetite comprises scatological gags about farting and poo, and practical jokes involving putting washing-up liquid and white pepper in the grown-ups' drinks. Black pepper has yet to be invented.

I also like getting out of bed and coming downstairs when my parents are having drinks parties, on one occasion wearing just my pants and my father's military hat. Look at me, look at me, look at me.

I love the smell of my parents' drinks parties, the combination of fags, booze and cigars, the little bowls of nuts and crisps, the rigmarole, my mother dabbing scent behind her ears, the bursts of laughter, women shrieking, men chuckling. I sit on the stairs and listen. Sometimes my sister joins me and we creep into the kitchen to get a midnight feast. Both of us have woollen long-tailed Wee Willie Winkie hats that we wind around the bottom half of our faces to stifle the giggling and prevent recognition. We aren't the children of a British intelligence officer for nothing.

At this point in Pa's career, he is a member of BRIXMIS, which, if you look it up, is described as follows: 'Brixmis (the British Commander-in-Chief's Mission to the Group Soviet Forces of Occupation in Germany) is one of the least-known elite spying units of the British Army.'

I'll leave it there for now. It is a strange sort of spying if you ask me; it seems to be done with the complete consent of the Russians, who even send us a weekly 'Russian rations' box containing butter and a big chicken. If I was making this up, I'd add more weird stuff, but everything is very ordinary, only sometimes it isn't.

BRIXMIS has a mission house in Potsdam, a city that was bombed down to 20 per cent of its existence during the Second World War, sort of like Coventry, but not.

The mission house is a white Palladian mansion, overlooking a lake which divides East from West Berlin. On occasional Friday afternoons, my sister and I are picked up from school in an olive-green BRIXMIS car with a badge on the front and driven with our mother to the mission house. Here we have a posh weekend break with breakfast served under silver cloches and all that jazz. It is infinitely grand and, every Xmas, Santa turns up at the annual children's party, which is on this ludicrous scale, complete with a Trafalgar Square-sized tree. One year I win a black and white soft toy in the raffle. I presume it's a squirrel but it turns out to be a skunk. I am rather embarrassed of my skunk. No one wants a toy skunk.

My parents buy us wooden toys from Potsdam. They have a very individual smell: whenever we unwrap a wooden toy, we inhale its scent and then exclaim, 'Ah, Potsdam.' I swear I would still recognise that smell today.

The BRIXMIS mission house is eventually sold to the German fashion designer Wolfgang Joop (a different Wolfgang, I presume) and again, thanks to the power of that telly job, I am allowed inside to snoop. Gone is all the traditional posh if threadbare pomp, the white linen and silverware. Joop has modernised the fuck out of the place and it's magnificent. The man has made a fortune out of flogging his fashion wares around the world and as a result has one of the best private collections of art I've ever been in gawping distance of.

In the garden, perched on a little jetty over the lake, is a familiar piece, a miniature version of Antony Gormley's *Angel of the North* looking out over the water.

We used to swim in that lake. Once it got dark, searchlights from the 'other side' would swing across its inky darkness, and, rumour had it, if you dipped your fingers too far over, the soldiers manning the lookout towers would shoot you. They certainly had the machine guns to prove it.

Swimming is a big thing for me and my sister. We both learn very young in the officers' club in Singapore, which again conjures up this rarefied lifestyle which is in stark contrast with my parents' Lancashire roots. My father is totally at ease with this weird straddling of two very different worlds. He is a man who fits in and makes friends wherever he goes.

Neither of my parents sound northern any more. My father's accent is incredibly convincing, my mother's occasionally strays into 'posh telephone voice', especially if she's been hobnobbing with the very gentrified, which occasionally they do. My father is an officer: there are certain expectations, social gatherings, dinners and receptions, and my mother is an officer's wife. She knows the drill and occasionally has to wear long evening gloves up to her elbows and keep smiling.

In Berlin we swim in the huge local Olympic pool, which is exhausting for a six-year-old. Even the walk from the changing room is a bit of a trek.

Returning to the area with my partner for my fiftieth birthday in 2000, and doing all the tourist things, I am slightly overwhelmed by the Olympic Stadium. It is such a thrusting monument to Nazism, I find it extraordinary but chilling.

I swim a lot in my twenties and thirties, but get lazy in my forties. My sister doesn't; she keeps going. She swam around Greece a couple of years ago. This is very typical of Sara. She is a very small but determined woman, like a miniature lady Jack Russell.

The night before her first marriage, she pops to a local indoor pool for a relaxing forty-length swim and is offered a child's ticket.

We attend ballet classes, too, in a dark basement where a fat German woman barks orders and a thin man plays the piano. I want so desperately to be good, but sadly neither Sara nor I show much promise and neither of us is ever chosen for solo roles.

However, I'm grateful to the fat dance teacher for lowering her massive arse onto my lap when I sit cross-legged, thus forcing my knees to the floor and consequently rendering my hips flexible for life. Unfortunately, it doesn't work for Sara: she is as flexible as a frozen leg of lamb.

It is in Berlin that I develop a taste for Bratwurst with sauer-kraut. I enjoy the squeak the sausage makes against my teeth and the way the skin pops when I bite down on it. I still do. There was a Bratwurst chain in London for a short while about ten years ago, called Herman Ze German. I loved their slogan, 'Our Wurst is Ze Best', and I loved their sausages. Mmmm, Bratwurst.

I genuinely believe living in Berlin affected my taste buds. As an adult I much prefer a European breakfast to a disgusting English fry-up. I like smoked hams and waxy cheeses, hardboiled eggs, pumpernickel, pretzels and strong German lager (not necessarily for breakfast).

The Usurper

During the summer of 1967 my mother is pregnant with her third child. We are caravanning in the Italian Lakes. Our tiny Sprite 400, the smallest caravan in the world, parked up by Lake Como, famous now for being where George Clooney has a house.

Back in '67 something has gone wrong with the water in the lake and all the fish are dying. Unknowingly, my sister and I float out on our blue and red lilo and find ourselves surrounded by bloated dead fish, lying belly-up. My sister, typically, remains tight-lipped. I, typically, fall instantly to pieces.

A young kitchen porter from a nearby hotel rescues us, swimming through the water, batting away the corpses and towing us back to land. As he drags us to safety, I notice half the fingers on one hand are missing: horror is always in the detail, so is comedy.

Dead fish still upset me, and I'm not relaxed around a fishmonger's. Fortunately, I live with a similarly fish-phobic man, which makes life easier as I'm not likely to open the fridge and encounter a dead trout.

Geof (aka the old man) was traumatised by a fish incident as a child, too, having choked on a fish bone, which resulted in him and his family missing a holiday-bound ferry.

Consequently, we both have a bone-free fish policy in the house and our favourite piscine treat is a cod loin that has been breadcrumbed and baked (aka big fish fingers for neurotic adults).

Other memories of this pre-new baby holiday include daily ice-cream excursions with our out-of-uniform 'holiday Daddy', as glamorous as a film star in his sunglasses, while Mummy rests her vast bump.

On the long drive home, our shoulders peeling (Factor 50 is yet to be a 'thing'), we pass a roadside stall selling fancy porcelain dolls. They have painted faces, flouncy silk petticoats and lacy bloomers. I want one desperately, but my mother thinks they are 'common'. Years later she won't let me watch *Magpie* on ITV for the same reason. Sadly, I have always been slightly drawn to the common.

I do have dolls. I have ugly Damas, with her waxy yellow face, and Potsy, a black porcelain baby doll, who cracks her head open falling down the stairs and is sent to the dolls' hospital to be re-paired. When she comes back, Potsy is no longer a baby: they've fixed her head by gluing a black curly wig over the hole and she looks a great deal older, like a toddler, I decide. Her transition unnerves me.

My brother Benjamin Thomas is born on 9 August 1967, bringing the number of Leos in the family to three; my mother (Taurus) and me (Pisces) are outnumbered.

He is an accident. My mother is thirty-eight, I am seven, my sister almost ten. We might still suck our thumbs, but we are out of nappies. Who needs another baby? My mother is offered a termination, but she bottles it, that insistent voice in her head, 'What if it's a boy, what if it's a boy?'

I think my mother presumes my father really wants a boy, but I don't think Derek is fussed one way or another, not until Ben arrives and they are both smitten.

The day my mother gives birth in yet another military hospital, my sister is invited to Diana Greenleaves's tenth birthday party and, for want of anyone to look after me (Frau Hermann is on annual leave), I am dragged along.

In the sixties, children's parties are a sadistic mix of competitive fun (e.g. musical statues and pass the passive aggressive parcel) and upsetting memory games, including that old blood-chilling favourite, the tray game. This involves being given a piece of paper, a pencil and a minute to look at twenty items arranged on a tray, before it's whisked away, and you must quickly write down as many items you can remember. Spoiler alert: safe bets include an egg cup, a teaspoon and a safety pin.

On this occasion, after Diana's birthday tea, all the little girls in their sticky-out party frocks and patent shoes settle down for a nice general knowledge quiz. Great: what could be more fun for a seven-year-old?

The look my sister gives me when I say the capital of England is Paris stays with me for a long time. It is powerfully withering, considering it comes from a buck-toothed kid who is still only nine. Having a 'bright' sister is a curse, I decide.

At this point my father turns up: we have a new baby brother. I try very hard to sound pleased and excited. The cuckoo has landed and is safely in the nest.

In actual fact, he is still in hospital. We visit the tiny miracle the next day and make all the right noises over a little bald head, until my mother decides to do a nappy change, only to discover her son's penis is missing. The wrong swaddled baby has been brought in from the nursery.

Drat. If only she'd kept quiet, I could have had a younger sister to boss about.

Recovering from the birth of this brother, my parents send Sara and me to England as unaccompanied minors, to stay with our grandparents (Tommy and Jenny, not the Spam-eating toad).

We travel with labels around our necks, and, as part of our

special treatment, we're offered a tour of the cockpit. All the other children stare at us. I love it. Immediately, I wonder if anyone thinks we are orphans and experiment with looking sad.

On the way 'home' we hit very bad turbulence, which coincides with the lunch service. In 1967 you get a proper hot meal with every flight, and as the plane bucks about the sky, peas and Yorkshire puddings roll up and down the aisle and my sister is sick into a paper bag. Somehow, she manages to regurgitate an entire Yorkshire pudding.

So now I have two things that frighten me – fish and turbulence. I am starting to learn that bad things can happen without any warning.

Once we are safely landed, Nana and Poppa take us to Poulton-le-Fylde, where they now live on a neat little cul-de-sac, in a smart little red-brick fifties place with an alpine rockery, crazy paving and a terracotta rabbit.

A terracotta rabbit which, I notice recently, now resides in my sister's London garden. How does she do it?!

Once 'home', we play with our cousins. Cousins are useful because they have to play with you. It's one of the rules: you are thrust into each other's company, because your mothers are very obviously sisters with similarly big noses and a matching way about them. My mother and my aunt are mistaken for each other even into their nineties. They certainly aren't identical, Aileen taking after her father, being so much darker than June and calliper-free, but there is something about them. They are a pair and throughout their lives people refer to them as the 'Hesmondhalgh Girls'. Their love for each other and their increasing reliance on each other, especially in old age when both are widowed, still makes me cry.

My Aunty Aileen also has three children, Nigel (bright), Elizabeth (strong-willed and dimpled) and Jonathan (like Ben, just a boring baby).

My sister and I compete for Elizabeth's affections: she is dark and bonny, younger than Sara but older than me.

I get a lot of her hand-me-downs. Sara isn't ever really big enough to pass me down her clothes. At sixty-six she still wears a white T-shirt which once formed part of her second son's prep-school PE uniform. His name tag is sewn into the neck. Jasper last wore it when he was twelve.

By the time we return to Berlin for the autumn school term the baby brother is still there, taking up carpet space, his shitty terry nappies soaking in a bucket of hot water and Milton sterilising tablets, my mother and father putty in his tiny hands.

All Change

After four years of the best time of my life so far, our Berlin bubble bursts.

It is time to say goodbye to the place where we learned to ride our bikes, roller skate and hang out with our mates who live down the same road.

In Berlin, I even have a sworn enemy called Nigel, whose teeth I can still picture. I throw snowballs at him in a weird Mills & Boon/slightly over-excitable way. I hate him, I love him.

Obviously, I know the rules. I am used to people leaving. People leave all the time. There is always a new girl or boy that we have to be 'especially nice' to. I just never thought we would be the ones doing the leaving.

It happens quite fast, and the details are blurred. It may have had something to do with my dad being caught taking photographs of Russian tanks; it may not have had anything to do with that at all. Maybe our time was naturally up and a new posting simply inevitable.

At least we are coming back to the UK, but not to the Lancashire coast. My father is summoned to the other side of the country, to County Durham, and, obviously, we go with him, to Barnard Castle, to another pebbledash house that somehow never feels entirely like home.

In line with army regulations, my mother packs up 32 Kiplingweg. As an army wife, you are counted in and counted out of your quarters: every teaspoon is accounted for, everything belongs to the army, the furniture is not yours, you must only take what you actually own.

In my parents' case, this includes the wicker laundry basket from KL which survives to this day and is the same age as me, ditto my wicker rocking horse, imaginatively named Horsey, a red Sellotape dispenser that still dispenses Sellotape, and some pictures.

Among these is a seascape in oils that now hangs on the wall of my study, and a Modigliani print of a long-nosed woman. This was bought by my father because it reminded him of my mother, who tried not to get upset.

By far the most newspaper goes on wrapping my parents' bewildering collection of Meissen porcelain figures. Meissen is a weird one. I once heard Fiona Bruce say she hates the stuff on *Antiques Roadshow*, which made me laugh. Some of it is incredibly collectable and worth a fortune; some of it isn't. Sadly, my parents' collection is the latter. A great deal of it is white Meissen, animals and birds mostly. But there are also shelves of colourful birds, soldiers and – the stuff of nightmares – a monkey band, around twelve small figurines of hideous monkeys dressed up as musicians. Sadly, if this was the real thing and dated back to the 1890s, it would buy me a new kitchen. Ours is sixties repro.

Other things that 'belong to us' include our toys and clothes and the clothes that belong to our toys. My mother makes outfits for our Sindys, Tressys and Barbies. Her sewing machine will come, too. 'What fun,' we are promised.

Stainton Camp Primary School is a series of gloomy barrack huts in a muddy field. Unlike Charlottenburg, there is no adventure playground, but there is a barbed-wire perimeter fence.

The thick blunt yellow and black lead pencils that pupils use for everything are strictly rationed and you have to stick your hand up and ask for toilet paper should you feel the urge. Consequently, everyone knows when you are going for a poo, and hold their noses while you exit. To make matters worse, the toilet paper issued is that useless Izal stuff that can double up as tracing paper. It is mortifying. Children are beaten for crimes such as not eating maggoty potatoes, a punishment I see with my own eyes. It is the freezing polar opposite of everything we are used to.

On my first day at this new school we do a times tables test. At the end of this test, we swap papers with the person next to us and mark each other's answers. The girl sitting next to me tries not to snigger when she hands back my paper. I have scored one out of ten. The humiliation isn't over yet. The teacher asks us to stand on our chairs; those who got ten out of ten can sit down, and so it goes on. I am the last girl standing, shame burning, fighting back the tears, loathing my new life.

Later, I try to draw a 'good' picture. I draw an African woman sitting under a coconut tree. No one is impressed. I've tried too hard, it isn't very good, there are better artists in the class, I want to die.

My sister has a similarly hideous experience, and at the end of the day is weirdly kind to me. I'm not used to this, because I haven't really needed it before. It teaches me something about our relationship that has never changed: my sister and I can be very antagonistic towards each other, but when the chips are really down there is no one else I'd rather have in my corner.

In a peculiar echo of Aileen and June, we have ended up living very near each other in south-east London. Dammit, we live on the same bloody road. I've got the keys to her house. If I feel like it, I could let myself in and take that terracotta rabbit from her back garden and bring it back to mine.

Sara, at ten years old, deals with the Barnard Castle situation in the same pragmatic and practical way she will deal with all her adult traumas, including a tricky divorce from her first husband and the death of her second. She copes with it. She hangs a drawstring bag filled with proper toilet paper brought from home under her coat on her peg, so that, instead of suffering the indignity of putting up our hands and begging for shitty Izal, we can help ourselves on the way to the horrible smelly toilets.

Looking back, although our time at this unforgivably shit school is short, I think it is necessary for both of us. Up until Barnard Castle we really only know what it is like to have a nice time, with nice people, in nice places.

In Barnard Castle, we experience something else. It teaches us that not everyone has the same kind of luck.

My brother is too young to be affected by this, but my sister is in the last year of her primary education, and let's not forget she is 'bright'. I think it instils in her a great sense of injustice, and as far as I know she has never once fallen foul of the law.

In fact, she is the only teenager I know to vomit after celebrating the end of her A levels not because she is pissed, but because, having an August birthday and therefore not legally allowed to drink alcohol, she has downed fifteen Britvic Oranges, before yipping them all back up in our downstairs toilet.

That'll teach her, I think, by then aged fifteen and already a seasoned drinker.

Other memories of Barnard Castle are vague. I remember my father taking us to an art gallery and Sara, standing in front of a particularly lurid painting, loudly asking Pa what *The Rape of the Sabine Women* meant.

I remember a van coming to our bleak housing estate every week and my mother buying groceries and sweets from it. I don't remember her having a car; instead, an army private would drive us to school in a military Land Rover, a vehicle that still stirs my

loins today. If I'm honest, there's something about an army truck
full of squaddies that mushes my ancient heart.

I first kiss a girl in Barnard Castle – take that, Katy Perry – she
is another Sara but with an h. She has blonde hair but surprisingly
dark eyebrows. She initiates it, we kiss in her garden among the
raspberry canes. It is summer and the place isn't quite so miserable. There is a waterfall nearby which you can stand under, and
rocks you can jump off into a pool of crystal-clear water. Things
that give you moments of sheer happiness. I am also introduced
to the taste sensation that is lettuce and Marmite sandwiches by
a neighbour who has loads of kids and one of those open houses
that everyone runs in and out of.

I'm not sure my mother ever gets used to this posting. In Berlin
she had her friend Mavis (born Lady something or other), mother
of the three Backhouse boys, to drink gin and gossip with. There
was also Maureen Southwood, wife of scary Angus and mother
of Clive and naughty Anne, an adorably cheeky, freckled little
madam who will get me into awful trouble some years later, when
my mother finds a letter I was in the middle of writing to her,
describing my sordid teenage antics, which included the word
'fingered'.

Maureen Southwood is a beauty. She has the face of Gina
Lollobrigida crossed with Sophia Loren. My mother's other best
mate, and my godmother, is the uber-posh Diana, never to be
seen without an Alice band and more commonly known as Wha
(apparently Indian for baby elephant). Diana, and her husband
Peter, had been on the boat to Cyprus with my parents all those
years ago, and they remained friends forever.

In fact, my mother is packing to see Wha in 2020 when her
mind unravels and everything that could possibly go wrong goes
wrong.

But here we are in 1967 and, as far as I recall, the silver lining
to the whole Barnard Castle debacle is our first telly.

The last time I was able to watch telly regularly had been in 1963, post-Singapore and pre-Berlin postings, when I remember vividly sitting on Horsey in our house in Blackpool, watching *Bill and Ben The Flowerpot Men*, *Andy Pandy* and *The Woodentops*. It is 1963, the TV is in black and white, but I remember these programmes in colour.

I first watched *Top of the Pops* in BC, sitting on the carpet. I am completely transfixed by Herman's Hermits and inch my way over to the television until I am close enough to the screen to kiss the preternaturally boyish lead singer Peter Noone.

I am not yet eight and already I have kissed a girl and a pop star. Well done me.

Coming Out

I have no clear memory of being told that my father is leaving the army, but I realise now it must have been a massive wrench for him. I think his decision is partly due to the fact that he doesn't want us to go to boarding school and another foreign posting would make this inevitable.

I'm a teeny bit gutted. I am besotted with all Enid Blyton boarding school stories, Darrell at Malory Towers, the twins at St Clare's; in fact, when I hit sixty during the 2020 lockdown I binge the entire BBC *Malory Towers* series, which is quite brilliant, thank you very much.

Whatever the reasons, and I know my father felt slighted by those higher up the ranks – and, who knows, Barnard Castle may have felt like the last straw – like it or not, the decision is made. It is time to return to civvy street, to swap one uniform for another. For the first time in his life, my father is facing the prospect of a suit and tie. Derek is only forty-three; there is plenty of time for him to do something else, whatever that might be.

Decades on, I'm still not sure it was the right choice, although it makes life much easier for the rest of us and it means my mother can finally stop counting teaspoons.

We move across the country to Lytham St Annes, close to the

cousins and the grandparents and close to the sea which ebbs muddily in the distance.

19 Rossall Road will be our first home for a while that isn't pebbledash army property.

We all go to look at the house and my parents make an offer of about six bob, which is accepted because this is 1968 and in those days you can buy a house for less than the price of one of Victoria Beckham's handbags.

On that first viewing I am transfixed by a kidney-shaped dressing table with frilly chintz skirts in the large bedroom at the front of the house and can't wait to claim it as my own, to sit on its little upholstered stool and stare at myself in a triple set of mirrors from every angle, like a film star. I have no idea that the house won't come with the furniture that is already in situ and am gutted to find the dressing table gone when we finally move in.

The large front bedroom is designated mine and Sara's to share; my parents will sleep in the middle room and my little brother in the smallest bedroom at the back of the house. 'Not fair,' my sister and I mutter. 'Why do we have to share?' 'Because,' my mother answers and that is that. Parents don't negotiate with their children in the sixties. Their job is to tell them what to do. It's quite simple, really.

Sara, being 'bright', has passed her eleven-plus at Stainton Camp, so is accepted into the local girls' grammar, Queen Mary School Lytham, a wide, two-storey thirties job, with well-tended lawns and a general air of smugness.

I, meanwhile, with the jury still out on whether I am 'bright' or not, get a place at the same school as my cousin Elizabeth.

Ansdell County Primary is a ten-minute walk from home. On my first day, my cousin points out three girls whom she deems suitable playmates. Elizabeth's match-making skills are faultless: Jane, Gill and Susan became my very best friends for a long time. Each of them offers something different and, years later, I will use each of their childhood homes as inspiration for interiors in my novels. Susan's big architect-designed fifties modernist number and Gill's dormer bungalow both appear in *Life, Death and Vanilla Slices*, while Jane's forties semi with the weeping willow in the garden crops up as Elaine's home in *The Writing on the Wall*. I don't steal characters when I write, but I do steal houses. Oh, and pets.

From a very early age I am fascinated by the differences in how people live, their individual choice of sofas, rugs, the ornaments on their windowsills, what kind of curtains they draw at night. From having grown up visiting houses that are more or less identical to my own in Berlin and Barnard Castle, suddenly I'm conscious of this world of choice. How on earth do you decide?

My own parents actually have very little choice. With Derek leaving the army, they are financially strapped; furniture is donated, found in sale rooms and handmade. My father cuts up an old wooden packing case, paints it white, sticks Gallery Five psychedelic butterfly stickers on it and transforms it into a coffee table. My sister and I are delighted, not that either of us drink coffee.

We drink orange squash, R. White's lemonade on Saturday nights, Nesquik strawberry shakes for a treat, and I am still getting my little bottle of free school milk delivered daily to its prime spot next to the classroom radiators.

School is trauma-free. After Barnard Castle, I am braced for all kinds of shit, but it doesn't happen. It is less exciting than Berlin, but far kinder than Stainton Camp, a solid, traditional, English primary, with a multi-purpose assembly hall/dining hall and gym and a playground divided by gender, boys on one side, girls on the other. Here I learn how to play complicated games involving skipping ropes and tennis balls, and the art of doing handstands up against the wall, all of us with our skirts over our faces and our knickers on show.

I am with Jane and Gill when a man shows us his willy down at Granny's Bay, a shallow curve of seafront within a mile of our homes. He asks if we want to see his puppy dogs, but all he shows us is his cock. Seriously, I felt sorry for him: he is obviously what people would later call a loser. We cycle back to my house and my mother overhears us sniggering about it and calls the police. She is livid. I overhear her recounting the tale to my aunt on the phone. She says, 'Yes, but what if Jenny's traumatised and ends up failing her eleven-plus because of it?' Ha! An excuse if ever I heard one, and I squirrel this information away in case I should need it come results day.

I am taken out in a police car and we cruise around the promenade for a while, while Jane and Gill are shown photofit pictures of suspects at home. Lucky me, I think, thrilled to be the one riding around in a cop car.

While in transit, I point out to the police where the man had been loitering and less than a hundred yards further along, there he is, the same bloke surrounded by a group of girls even younger than me. Suddenly the girls run screaming away from him; he's just got his cock out again, in full view of the plod. He's an idiot.

As it happens, I do pass my eleven-plus. I've never seen my mother look so relieved: she genuinely doesn't trust me when it comes to academia. I don't blame her. I only really pass because I take the exam sitting behind Melanie Sibborn ('bright'), and by casually looking over her shoulder I can check anything I'm not sure of against what she's written. Basically, the cleverest thing I'd done is wear my glasses for once.

I hate my glasses. I am diagnosed as short-sighted at the age of nine and instantly loathe my hideous specs and, even more, the sight of myself, for once in sharp focus in the optician's mirror. I am plainer than I'd realised, my hair lanker and the puppy fat more obvious. I solve this depressing problem by wearing them only in the direst emergencies, like when I need to cheat.

Monsters under the Bed

I am a happy child, but there are monsters under my bed, and I am scared of something bad happening in real life.

I feel like a bad thing has to happen, it's coming but I'm not sure when or what it will be.

Nothing I know has ever died, except goldfish from the fair and baby hamsters. In Berlin the mummy hamster ate her little jelly baby newborns. Don't think about it, don't think about it.

My brother gets ill. It's not unusual, he's been ill before, really ill; he had gastroenteritis when he was about three, really badly, probably picked it up from the muddy estuary. He is pale for months. This illness coincides with my parents being poor. Having left the army, my father is now a student. None of my friends have student dads, in fact most people don't really know what their dads do, just that they work in an office.

My dad goes to Manchester Polytechnic every day on the train and draws a Ban the Bomb symbol on his pencil case. He wants to do something useful, be a probation officer or something to do with helping young people. My father is kind. I have a memory now of a man coming to our house in Berlin, a soldier who had done something wrong. He was due to be court-martialled; I could hear shouting, my father talking to him in our kitchen, calming him down.

We are a family of five living on my father's student grant.

We eat mostly mince and my mother looks worried. She makes her own cakes and I wish we had shop-bought cakes like my friends. I want mini rolls wrapped in silver and purple; 'Tough,' my mother snaps, she stretches food out, she makes scallops northern-style, which are slices of potato, battered and deep-fried. When I am older, expensive fish scallops confuse me.

In reality she need only ask my grandparents (Tommy and Jenny 1) for a handout, but she doesn't. My mother is proud, proud of my father; she cuts down an old camel jacket and transforms it into a tiny winter coat for my brother. I see him walking home from nursery in it and I am mortified. I am a poor girl, with a sallow-faced brother wearing a cut-down lady's coat.

What can be worse than this? How long before I have no shoes and start to smell? Oh God, what if my mum can't give me the weekly subs for Brownies? Surely nothing can be worse than this . . .

My brother doesn't get better. He is not just off colour, he is properly ill, he doesn't go to nursery, the doctor suspects a virus. I get home from school and my mother asks me to mind him while she nips to Booths, the rather superior northern supermarket on the corner. My brother behaves oddly. He throws himself head-first at the wall, over and over again. I want to run to the shop for my mother, but I wait; when she gets home she calls the doctor. It's 1971: a doctor comes round to the house. He's called Dr McKenna, and he doesn't wait for an ambulance, he drives my brother and my mother to the hospital himself. My brother is four years old and has to be physically restrained in the back of the car. He is thrashing around, trying to knock himself out.

A lumbar puncture confirms that Ben has meningitis; my sister and I are quarantined and my birthday party for all the girls in my class is cancelled. I wish I'd been nicer to my brother. The sadness and fear emanating from my parents is unbearable.

My aunt steps into the breach. Once we are out of quarantine she holds a small birthday tea party for me at her house. Only Gill, Susan and Jane are invited, but at least my aunt is a better cake maker than my mother.

I start doing badly at school, and my father loses so much weight that his trousers fall down. I never see my mother, she lives at the hospital.

It's 'touch and go'. This phrase is bandied about, a constant whisper behind my back, and makes me feel sick. I don't ask Sara how she feels, it's best to bottle this up. He's been no trouble really, this little boy.

My father comes home from the hospital; he is almost physically having to hold his trousers up with one hand, but he is beaming. My brother woke up from a deep, long sleep and asked for a boiled egg.

My brother begins to recover, my father starts whistling again, my mother's face relaxes, and one day when I get home from school, my brother is sitting on the carpet playing with his toys. He is still the colour of porridge and very thin.

It takes me forever to get over this. I creep into his room at night to check he is breathing. It plants a deeply rooted seed of fear and when my own child is born many years later, the fear takes root again and coils itself around my heart like Japanese knotweed. I cannot ever rid myself of the fear; it is always lurking, something bad will someday happen, and sometimes it does.

A few weeks after Ben's recovery, my parents are due to have a parent/teacher evening at my school. They will look through my exercise books and see that I have been flunking my maths coursework, the squared pages are slashed with numerous red crosses and furious 'see me' messages from the teacher, who is a vile old cow with a habit of poking you in the chest.

At my friend Susan's house we draw a picture of Miss Monroe and tape it up behind her wardrobe door and take it in turn to spit in her face. We like spitting at her with half-chewed food in our mouths. The picture begins to stink.

I decide my parents cannot look at my maths book; nothing else must upset them right now. I tear out all the offending pages and bury them in the garden. Fuck Miss Monroe.

To the Palace

The last thing my father does in uniform is receive a medal from the Queen. He gets the official letter while lying on the landing, painting a bedroom door. It's an MBE, which stands for 'Member of the Order of the British Empire', the same medal John Lennon turned down the year before. My father doesn't turn his down.

We are in the Music Room at Buckingham Palace, where these types of events take place. It is as you would expect: well-hoovered red carpets, white and gold folderol. It's my father's turn to receive his MBE, he is beaming, stepping forward, the Queen speaks to him. My father is quite deaf: he cups his ear so that he can hear Her Majesty, my mother tuts, and mutters 'Bloody hell, Derek' through smiling, gritted teeth.

We have driven to London for this event. My parents have splashed out on a hotel room and Ben is left behind, hahaha. My sister and I have new things: I have a beige corduroy Donny Osmond cap, which does precisely zero for me, and my sister is wearing a knitted beret, while my mother is sporting half a fox on her head. My father is in olive green, with a Sam Browne belt, his shoes are very shiny, even though his are the only ones that aren't patent. Sara and my mother carry matching patent bags.

I am deemed too young for a handbag, which makes me livid. The photo I have of this occasion is in black and white, but I'm sure my mother's coat is emerald; Sara's is navy. Mine is tweed; it looks slightly too tight. I am round with puppy fat. All the ladies (including me) are wearing gloves.

We stay in a hotel in Victoria, whose glamour and three-star rating is proven by the shoeshine machines down every corridor. Imagine! The night before the ceremony we see a West End production of *Charlie Girl*, starring Derek Nimmo, who at some point in the musical lies on his back and does something with his toes that makes the audience roar.

I meet him not twenty years later, at a recording of *Just a Minute* for Radio 4. We are recording outside London, necessitating an overnight stay. In the morning, I hide behind a pillar at the railway station until Nimmo is safely on the train and then deliberately sit in another carriage. What with him and the ghastly Clement Freud, I've had enough of old men talking about themselves.

Nicholas Parsons, the host of JAM, on the other hand, I will love 'til he dies. Nicholas is weirdly kind to me, Clement is beastly and says I smell, because I smoke, and consequently won't stand next to me for press photos. I want both to die of shame and to kill the old fucker.

After the ludicrous excitement of seeing *Charlie Girl*, the Hargreaves family, minus Ben (haha) eat out in an Italian restaurant called the Blue Parrot. There is indeed a parrot in a gilt cage hanging by the entrance. I'm not sure now if it was real. Everything is an immense novelty, although I order spaghetti bolognaise, which we have at home every single week.

We rarely eat out with our parents. Meals out are usually by invitation of my grandfather, mostly in celebration of his or Jenny 1's birthdays.

On these occasions we gather for lunch with the cousins at

the Queensway or the Villa in Wrea Green (still selling pimped-up lunches today), where I order prawn cocktail, gammon and pineapple and Black Forest gateau. No wonder that coat of mine is tight. I am just beginning to despair of my fat tummy. It is 1970. I am ten.

The photograph of the investiture is in our local paper. I am asked to stand up and talk about my 'exciting time in London' when I get back to school: marvellous, ten minutes in the 'show and tell' spotlight. It is not my only claim to fame. I also have an essay entitled 'The Killing of a Giant Squid' up on the wall, which the teacher says 'shows evidence of my vivid imagination'. You're not kidding. I've never actually killed a giant squid before, but I manage two sides of paper on the topic, plus a drawing.

My father is now Major Hargreaves, MBE, but he still hasn't got any money.

We never question what the citation is for. It's pretty obvious to me that my father deserves a medal, whether it's for the charity work he does for SSAFA, the armed forces family charity, or the photos of tanks and Russian soldiers that are hidden in the big chest on the landing, or the other more frightening photos buried much deeper, that I cannot tell anyone I have seen. In recent years my sister does some digging and it turns out my father got the MBE for saving another soldier from drowning. No surprise there, of course he did.

When I think back to those few days in the capital, I have a fleeting memory of seeing another slice of London, away from the tradition of the West End and the pomp of the Palace.

I see a street full of young people wearing all the latest groovy fashions.

I think my father must have driven down the King's Road; it's the only feasible explanation for what I see, which is young people in bell bottoms, men with Afros and patchwork waist-coats, splashes of purple and yellow, shop signs in swirling psychedelic writing. I see this vision like a slide in one of those viewfinder toys we all had as children. If it was a slide, it would have belonged to a series entitled 'Swinging London'. Maybe I didn't see it in real life at all, but the memory is so vivid.

I am learning that there is another world going on after Berlin and Barnard Castle, outside Lytham and even beyond Blackpool.

My parents are both Blackpool-bred, but my mother has turned against it. 'It's gone downhill,' she sighs, 'and there are a lot of very common people about.'

But I love it. I love the very common people, the donkeys on the golden sands, and the rock stalls and palm readers, the log flume on the Pleasure Beach, the ice rink and the big carousel with the painted horses. And I love the illuminations which I spoil annually by getting overexcited and puking up in the back of the car.

Big School

Despite the local pervert's worst intentions, the letter comes informing my parents that I have been offered a place at the same school as my sister Sara and my cousin Elizabeth. Susan, Gill and Jane also get into Queen Mary's and we are all kitted out with the same regulation school uniform. Brown skirt, beige and cream striped nylon shirt, sleeveless brown tank top, additional brown cardigan, beige socks, brown shoes, brown blazer and calf-length brown gaberdine mac, all topped off with a brown felt bowler hat. I shit ye not. The uniform is deliberately sexless. Britney Spears would have struggled with it. I'd like to see a remake of ' . . . Baby One More Time' featuring a seventies QMSL uniform and absolutely *no* make-up or jewellery.

The school has since merged with the next-door boys' school, King Edward's, and the original building has been converted into 'luxury flats'.

In a glass exhibition case in the new shared co-ed building, labelled 'Uniforms from the Past', is my uniform.

During lockdown, I write my first YA book, *The Writing on the Wall*, some of which is set in a school that is virtually identical to Queen Mary's. I change its name to Queen Anne's, thinly disguise some of the teachers and have a ball fictionalising my past.

The school is a mix of traditional and modern, new buildings have been tacked on over the years, and when new buildings haven't been completed we are taught in Portakabins. There are eight hundred girls and our school motto is 'Semper Fidelis, Semper Parata'. Always Faithful, Always Ready – hmm. The school emblem is a marigold.

When I first arrive in the upper third, the girls in the sixth form all look like they might be dating a Beatle. They lounge around the radiators, with their long hair and middle partings; in some respects it's very St Trinian's. It's 1971; this is the moment the school peaks. Once this lot leave, the sixth formers become ever more ordinary. Bar the occasional raving beauty, sexpot and glamour puss, it's the usual mix of skinnies, fatties, spotties, smellies, thumb-suckers, creeps, show-offs and bitches.

I'm a wannabe show-off/bitch but I am only eleven, so I am mostly good-natured and biddable. Early school reports reveal nothing much to worry about . . . Yet.

Gill and I are in Upper 3M, Sue and Jane are in Upper 3S. We also know girls in the other forms, Q and L. There's Alison Redfern, Sheona Norris, Annette McKay and Jane Brewster. More than half a century later, Jane Brewster lives round the corner from me. Sometimes we push our grandchildren round the park together. She still looks exactly the same.

I experiment with getting to know other girls who come from other areas and different primary schools, but for most of my first year I stick with my Ansdell County Primary mob. My mother likes this; she likes knowing what people's fathers do and where they live, and which side of the street. My mother is more suspicious about my choice of friends than either of my siblings'. My brother mostly plays with the boy next door who is called Alex and there's some kid called James who comes round, but I ignore them. My brother is still watching *Mary, Mungo and Midge*. It's kind of useless having a younger brother. Both Jane and Susan have older brothers. Jane's is shy and cute, with a thick fringe like a pony. Sue's is at a posh boarding school called Oundle and often smells of garlic. I am invited to an Oundle school dance. My mother makes me a long skirt with a frill on the bottom – all the rage – and I wear it with a scarlet puffed-sleeve blouse.

A boy called Bill, who also smells of garlic, asks me to dance and we do some half-hearted jigging about, surrounded by beady-eyed parents, which means the most he can get out of me is my address. Bill writes to me for the rest of the term. I've still got a couple of letters: he mostly says he doesn't know what to write but that he has played hockey. As soon as he gets an exeat (I told you it was a posh school) he takes me to see Dr Zhivago at the local cinema in St Annes. My mother has seen the film, and when I get home she quizzes me on performances and plot lines. I tell her I'd forgotten to take my glasses, so it was all a bit of a blur, but in reality we'd spent the entire film snogging. The letters peter out.

I become more interested in boys and make-up and pop music and less interested in school and wearing my hat when I am meant to. I have also started shoplifting, which is exciting. It's mostly sweets and small stuff that I can hide in my hand, but I get caught on a trip to Southport with Gill and her mum. Her mum, Sylvia (tall with a large bosom and a big laugh), leaves us to our own devices which is a shame really, because, left to our own devices, I am arrested for shoplifting in a Co-op.

Having spent the lunch money Gill's mum had given us on tights, I have stolen a chocolate bar and some other bits and bobs. I am taken to a stock room and searched. I give them a false name, but my new Xmas diary is in my bag with my name and address neatly printed on the cover page and they find it. I cry and cry, the police are called, I cry some more, the store detective says she has a niece my age, and if she found her shoplifting she would cut her hands off. I offer her my wrists. She tells me to scarper.

Gill is waiting outside the shop. As we scuttle off, a police car turns up and we leg it. For weeks I am terrified the police will call my mother, but they don't, and many, many years later I tell my parents about it, turning it into an anecdote at the dinner table. The joke backfires: my mother is furious with me and slams a casserole down on the table, snapping, 'Well, you might find it funny, but I don't.'

Throughout my teenage years, my mother always wants to give me the benefit of the doubt, but sometimes I really don't deserve it.

I am thirteen, I have kissed a girl, a pop star, a boy, been shown a flaccid cock on the beach and been arrested for shoplifting. Go me. What next?

19 Blackpool Road

There is a house on the main road between Lytham and St Annes that my father dreams of. It is a large Victorian red-brick detached number, with six bedrooms, two sitting rooms, a breakfast room with walk-in pantry, dining room, two loos and a bathroom. It belongs to a dentist and is in a state of disrepair. The dentist's chair is still firmly rooted in the front room, and in the small back bedroom the dentist makes plaster casts of teeth to fashion into braces and dentures. Despite the whiff of nitrous oxide throughout the place, my father buys it for £7,000.

We sell 19 Rossall Road for £4,500 and move in. I have no idea what gives my father the confidence to do this, but he does.

Pa is now a careers officer rather than a high-ranking army officer. It seems an unlikely move, but he is good-natured about it. He operates from an office in Fleetwood and a lot of the young people he sees are sent to 'blow the shells off prawns' and work on the trawlers. Fleetwood is a fishing port. We are taken on a school trip in the lower fourth, but my raw fish phobia has a massive flare-up and I have to be led, weeping, back to the coach.

One of my father's successful clients gives him a conger eel in gratitude. Christ knows what my mother is supposed to do with a conger eel. She is a good cook but has her limits. My father dutifully keeps it chilled in the large butler's sink in the office kitchen until mid-afternoon, when his secretary starts scream-ing. The conger eel has come back to life, escaped the sink and is thrashing around on the kitchen floor. No doubt my father shoots it or karate chops it down.

He keeps a display cabinet of Xmas cracker novelties in the waiting area of the interview room and pretends his life hasn't shrunk. Inevitably, he takes early retirement.

My mother is happy in the big new house, even though the stairs are hard work. She has recently been issued with a new thigh-length calliper and must pull a catch on the knee mecha-nism in order to walk upstairs. We pay absolutely no attention to this inconvenience and basically let her get on with everything. She shops, cooks and cleans all by herself; consequently, our house is not as manicured as many of my friends'. My mother is fairly relaxed about clutter; in the afternoon she reads books on the sofa and she attends a weekly pottery class. We laugh at her efforts.

In my fifties I will do a pottery taster class and quickly realise my mother's ability to make a teapot, complete with a spout, is bordering on genius and I apologise for being such a dismissive cow. She smirks back at me.

The house is completely redecorated. It's the seventies and Victoriana is in vogue: my parents embrace this, because it's the only way they can afford to fill the house. There is a lot of second-hand, cumbersome 'brown furniture', but it sort of works. It is a house I will always feel smug walking into.

There are many perks to 49 Blackpool Road. For starters, Dr McKenna, the GP who saved my brother's life, *lives next door*. Ah, the sweet relief. He has five children and when their dachshund gives birth to lots of puppies, Dr McKenna trips over one of them on the back steps and accidentally kills it. Fortunately, he is still allowed to practise.

The other attraction for my father is that the house is directly opposite Fylde Rugby Club, which is going through something of a renaissance, mainly due to a brick shithouse of a player called Billy Beaumont. My father realises that he can watch the rugby matches for nothing from his bedroom window and wander over at half-time, when entry is free, to watch the second half.

The downside for me is that the *Sunday Times* sports journalist comes over to our house after the match and files his report to London from our landline. The phone is a fat cream number kept, of course, like all respectable house telephones, on the hall table. I mean, why would anyone want to have a private conversation?

The *Sunday Times* sports journalist is direct from central casting. He is a short, fat man with a moustache, who wears a sheepskin coat and a pork pie hat complete with a pencil tucked into the hatband.

He sits at our hall table, chain-smoking, and monopolises the phone for what seems hours, *on a Saturday afternoon!* Socially the most crucial time of the week, when plans for the evening are being made, cancelled and changed right up until the last minute, and no one can get through to me. We even have our own designated line, unlike my Aunty Aileen who shares her phone line with another family, who occasionally have to be interrupted mid-conversation and reminded that someone else might need to make a call: 'Excuse me, excuse me.' These were called party lines and like capital punishment (at least in this country) no longer exist.

While the journalist hogs the phone, I stomp around upstairs 'getting ready', which basically involves transforming my sixteen-year-old self into a forty-year-old divorcee. There is a lot of make-up going on here, the entire set of my mother's Carmen electric rollers and half a tin of Silvikrin Extreme Hold hairspray dedicated to this task.

I have the second smallest bedroom, bigger than Ben's, which is the ex-false teeth factory, but a great deal smaller than Sara's.

My room has one pink floral- and three purple-papered walls, the carpet is covered in Carmen curler burns, and one night, when I am very drunk, I throw up in the bottom drawer of my chest of drawers where I keep all my *Jackie* magazines. Still pissed, I shut the drawer and have to wait weeks for the coast to be clear enough to get rid of the putrid waste. Every day, I sprinkle the puke-encrusted comics with my precious spherical yellow ball of Xmas Kiku talc to avert suspicion.

When I think what I could have got for a vomit-free collection on eBay now, I could weep.

This is the house I grow up in, where my parents sleep while I get up to all kinds of mischief; where one of my best friends and I spend a night inserting shampoo bottles into each other's vaginas, just to check what works; and where I constantly stare at myself in the mirror.

I have a small single wardrobe, a chest of drawers and a desk with a locked drawer. I begin keeping a diary. Only two survive: they are Biba diaries from 1976 and 1977. My sister bought them for me, *from the actual shop!* Sara has gone to study law at King's College London, clutching her four A-grade A levels and moving into a hall of residence where she shares a room with a girl called Debbie Thrower, who likes Noel Edmonds and Paddington Bear. For a while in the eighties Debbie is on telly, co-presenting on the BBC with everyone's favourite uncle figure, Frank Bough. Inevitably, family-man Frank is the subject of a *News of the World* cocaine and call girl scandal that puts an abrupt end to his telly career. In stark contrast, Debbie finds God.

My teenage diaries show no writerly promise whatsoever; they are both self-obsessed and boring, a lethal combination. My sister also keeps a diary, a little pristine white leather number, like a prayer book. In it she writes that she and her boyfriend have decided to save themselves for their wedding day.

I snigger. I lose my virginity at fifteen.

Sex and the Seventies

I start behaving badly when I am fourteen, not terribly badly, but I am no longer the pink-cheeked, compliant little girl. I think it starts around the time I get my bunches cut off. My parents take us on a caravanning holiday to France and even my sister snogs a boy, a boy with massive French-kissing lips. I am impressed.

On the way home, we visit my uncle and aunt in Oxfordshire and my older teenage cousin Lesley, the one who later gets her kit off for Lord Lichfield, gives me some of her cast-off clothes. I remember exactly what they are: a navy blue A-line needlecord skirt and a rust-coloured jersey top. They seem to be imbued with some kind of magnetic power. I wear them to a party just days before we restart the school term and get off with the host. When I say 'host', it sounds like he might have been wearing a cravat; he isn't, he is wearing a cheesecloth shirt and high-waisted cream Oxford bags. He is fifteen and his mum and dad own a big old hotel in St Annes. It is the end of the season, the paying guests have gone and his parents have vacated the premises. The fools.

Martin has a party that spreads across many floors of this huge Victorian building. There are so many rooms and most of them contain beds; we snog in a room where other couples snog. There is so much snogging, mostly because we are Queen Mary School girls and we don't know how to talk to boys, so we snog.

At school we are taught many useless things. We are taught how to set an appetising lunch tray for an invalid, complete with a tray cloth and maybe a small posy of flowers in a little vase, but we are not taught that boys are human.

When term starts, I am in the girls' toilets and I hear Karen Borsley and Gail Cannel talking about me by the sinks. I hold my breath in the cubicle.

Karen: 'Honestly, are you sure? Only, I mean … ?'

Gail: 'I know, but I saw them, Karen: Martin got off with Jenny Hargreaves.'

Karen can hardly believe it. I am not one of the cool girls, she is a cool girl. Karen is so cool that she has been on telly. Her family are musical, and the three Borsley siblings appear on *Junior Showtime*. Karen plays the clarinet and the melodica. Gail is also cool, even though she has overplucked her eyebrows.

Karen is extremely pretty, possibly the prettiest girl in our year. She is Martin's ex-girlfriend.

I seem to have strayed out of my lane. Go Jenny.

I am Martin's new girlfriend. For my fifteenth birthday he buys me an orange fake leather handbag and a necklace made out of the kind of nails they shoe horses with. This is incredibly exciting. I also have new denim clogs, a collared V-neck T-shirt with a French café scene on the front and some pale blue Oxford bags.

I carry my puppy fat well, although occasionally, encouraged by my mother, I go on a diet, which mostly involves hard-boiled eggs. If I liked grapefruit, I'd eat grapefruit, too. This is the seventies way: hard-boiled eggs, Nimble slimmer's bread and grapefruit, PLJ lemon juice for cystitis. Them's the rules.

But I am greedy. My mother's walk-in pantry calls me. She bakes cakes and loads them into tins stacked on top of a marble slab. My mother is a careless if dutiful cake baker. She knows she should, so she does. She makes flapjacks, which she regularly burns, and fruit cakes, which are frequently dry. My father calls them 'Gobis', as in the desert. My mother couldn't give a shit. She is not easily wounded. In later years, I overhear my father saying to my mother, 'Six years of packed lunches, June, and only three Scotch eggs,' to which she replies, 'Fuck off, Derek.'

I help myself to whatever is in the pantry: a wodge of this, a sliver of that. There is also a Rumtopf pot in the pantry. This is a German ceramic pot contraption, which pickles fruit in alcohol for several months until you have this delicious boozy compote, usually in time for Xmas. Only I prise the lid off to slurp at the booze, and do not put it back on properly. Come Xmas, the Rumtopf is brimming with mould.

I do not own up. My mother keeps giving me the benefit of the doubt; she has absolutely no idea that, on top of the smoking (No. 6) and the drinking (whatever I can get my hands on), I have become a part-time slag.

Most girls at my school have a streak of slag in them; it's something about the time we are living in. The seventies are a very sexual decade. Every advert is an excuse for a pout and a cleavage, young women on the telly flirt with old men and have no objection to being groped in small spaces. There are very few boundaries; girls who say 'no' are frigid bitches, which is a fate worse than death.

We don't have the women's lib in Lytham St Annes, and feminists are considered a hairy, saggy-titted joke.

This is northern seaside territory, the saucy postcard is less of a gag and more of a way of life, there is saltiness in the air and underage girls are being felt up and fingered all over the place.

I go to an all-girls school; my brother is still in primary. I have no idea how to talk to boys, in any case talking to boys, making them laugh, does not make you popular. What makes you popular is squealing a lot, giggling at their jokes and snogging on demand.

In the seventies there are all sorts of subtle rules of behaviour: for example, girls do not eat in front of boys.

Boys have no idea how much we can actually eat. In front of them, we nibble, pinch the occasional chip, lick a lolly and fill ourselves up with nicotine. No wonder when I get home from spending a day hanging round with the opposite sex I am starving and raid the cake tins.

My social life revolves around a couple of cafés in St Annes, several pubs which turn a blind eye to underage drinkers, hotel bars (similarly lax) and the Saturday night discos at the tennis and cricket clubs.

I am a good dancer. I show off on the dance floor, I am not shy, I do not shuffle around my handbag, I wriggle and squirm and tilt my pelvis this way and that.

In the girls' toilets, teenagers try to cover their love bites with toothpaste and swear over laddered tights. We wear clothes from C&A and Chelsea Girl, a poky little shop in Blackpool which my grandmother insists is deliberately kept dark so you can't see how shoddy the seams are. A branch of Miss Selfridge has opened on the top floor of John Lewis. It is an Aladdin's cave of treasure. I want everything.

My friend Gill has more clothes than me; her mother even buys her a pair of massive brown leather lace-up platform wedges. My mother refuses to crumble in the face of these monstrosities. They remind her of the ugly built-up shoes that other polio victims have to wear. She is right. They are hideous, but I still want some.

It's around this time that my mother finds the half-written letter to my old Charlottenburg pal Anne Southwood, when she tremulously asks me what I mean by getting 'fingered'. I cry and tell her I was just showing off and that's why I didn't bother finishing the letter and sending it because I knew Anne would guess I was lying. Once again my mother gives me the benefit of the doubt and swallows the story like a seal eating a sprat.

Goodbye Hymen, Hello Curls

I lose my virginity in fairly squalid circumstances, but feel triumphant. The bloke in question – for he is a bloke not a boy – possibly does not know I am underage. No one really asks: this is the era of extremely blurred lines surrounding the subject of 'consent'. In any case, girls usually cave in under very little pressure.

This man is not entirely at fault. We are both victims of a time and a place. He is gentle, sweet and complimentary during the deflowering, which doesn't entirely make up for the fact that, some weeks later, I discover he had done it for a bet.

On the day I turn sixteen, I start a period. Big relief.

Despite having a feisty live-in girlfriend, the bloke continues to wink and nod at me whenever our paths cross, and he occasionally pops in to where I work to say 'hi'.

I have a Saturday job in Boots the chemist in St Annes. I presume I will be working on the record counter at the back of the store, or, even better, on the make-up counter at the front. I land the make-up counter, which also includes 'feminine hygiene', and I seem to spend most of my Saturday lugging trolleys of Dr

White's sanitary towels from the storeroom down to the shop floor. I spend the rest of the day shelf-stacking and price-tagging period products with a special gun.

Sanitary goods in the seventies have undergone a revolution and towels now have an adhesive strip to attach to your knickers rather than you having to faff about with a plastic belt, loops and safety pins. Tampons are not encouraged for virgins, but even for non-virgins they take quite a lot of practice to find the right angle in order to shove them into a resistant hole, and I spend what seems like hours with one foot up on the lavatory seat, poring over the instructions. I get there in the end and am loyal to Lil-Lets until my last period at the age of fifty-two. My mother does not associate my use of tampons with sex. She just thinks I'm being 'very modern'.

Occasionally at Boots I am promoted to the till, which I like because it means sitting down in my pink and navy cotton overall, praying the till roll doesn't run out. I have a good laugh at Boots: there are plenty of other girls to muck about with and older women to listen in on. They talk about grown-up female things, of making gravy, divorce and hysterectomies. I find them fascinating.

I also clean hotels and holiday flatlets during the long school summer holidays. When I say 'clean', my friend Gill and I do the bare minimum. We put the Hoover on in the hallway to sound willing, and spray the rooms with furniture polish to smell willing, then plonk ourselves down on pleather sofas, to smoke and watch Marc Bolan's Saturday morning show. We love Marc, who is killed in a car crash in 1977, when the car his girlfriend, Gloria Jones, is driving veers off the road in Barnes and hits a tree. Gloria survives, but Marc doesn't. He is only twenty-nine. Hysteria follows this news at school, and we all spend the day crying and repeating 'I just can't believe it'.

So far, I have seen the Bay City Rollers, Mud, Smokey (at a Radio 1 Roadshow), David Essex (in his white suit phase), Diana

Ross and Elton John (but only because a friend of my sister's is ill and can't go). I am massively impressed by Elton John and buy his album *Goodbye Yellow Brick Road*. My father says he wouldn't cross a road to see Elton John do a 'concert'. The word 'gig' is still new and unfamiliar.

Watching bands on stage makes me realise that being in the audience doesn't quite do it for me. I want either to be onstage or backstage. I try and get backstage at the Bay City Rollers' gig but a bouncer picks me up and throws me back into the crowd. I try several more times: by the end of this gig I have rust marks from the metal barriers all over my duck-egg-blue cotton skirt and my friend Rosemary (a pretty girl with fluffy pale hair like a dandelion clock, who married badly and died far too young) has lost her watch. Such an exciting night.

At sixteen I go to a local hairdresser's, which is exotically named Emile of Switzerland, because the salon owner is indeed called Emile and does indeed hail from Switzerland. He is narrow-hipped, dark and moustached with a very heavy accent. In the back of the premises he has a curtained-off area where he privately fits women undergoing cancer treatment with wigs.

I have a perm – a poodle perm to be precise. They are all the rage and once it loosens up it is a triumph: my lank blonde locks are chemically enhanced into springy curls and it gives me Samson-like properties. I become more powerful, the perm is like putting on a wig for a play and becoming a different character. I feel cool and pretty and barely notice that my O level results are extremely mediocre.

My parents are gutted but simultaneously relieved. I have passed enough exams, including the all-important English and Maths, to be able to stay on in the sixth form. The deal is that if I agree to taking my A levels at Queen Mary's, I will be allowed to audition for drama school when I am eighteen.

I cave in, just as easily as I did to losing my virginity. At least in the sixth form we can wear our own version of the uniform, as long as it's equally brown and sexless. We also have our own common room, which is akin to having membership to a private single-sex club. I love the common room and I love not having to do the subjects that I can't be arsed with. I only need two A levels to qualify for a grant to drama school, but considering we have to do three, I choose English, Art and General Studies. Because my timetable is so light, and, unlike my sister, I am not attempting Greek, I am pushed into taking a couple of extra O levels. I choose Latin, because I was pissed off at failing it the first time around, and Domestic Science, because ... well, how hard can it be? Inevitably, I fail it.

Some of my friends leave school at sixteen to attend the local technical college. I feel I am left to play with the children, but deep down I am very comfortable with this.

I love my Art A level class. The teacher takes us to a gallery in Manchester and lets us smoke all the way there and all the way back. We also see some paintings. I am a big, smoking, sexually active child.

My friend Jane gets pregnant in the lower sixth. It's a shock because we both wag off school one day when her period is late and take a bus to a clinic in Blackpool. Her urine is tested and the test comes back negative. Oh, the blessed relief. We laugh and laugh and have egg and chips to celebrate. Only something has gone wrong. The test might be negative but the foetus has other ideas. Jane doesn't tell me until many months later. She tries some of the old housewives' remedies, hot baths and tripping down the stairs, but the baby is a barnacle and refuses to budge. I suspect nothing. I have no idea that she has taken to wearing strapping beneath her clothes to disguise the bulge.

I phone her one weekend to tell her that Gill and I are planning a trip to London to stay in my sister's flat, and, very calmly, she says that we might miss the wedding.

The eighteen-year-old mother and father-to-be get married in a register office. The bride wears pale blue cheesecloth and allows her tummy to breathe out into its natural bulge. We meet up after the ceremony in Jane's back garden to toast the happy couple. As we drink sherry (I know, right) and eat fruit cake, it seems only minutes since Jane was playing in that same garden, training Big Bun, her oversized Belgian hare, to jump over a set of increasingly difficult equestrian-style jumps. I also remember the stick insects that she used to keep in her bedroom and the collection of empty Pony bottles ('The Little Drink with the Big Kick') that she displayed on the pelmet above her bedroom window.

Big Bun and the jumps and Jane's back garden also feature in *The Writing on the Wall*. Sorry, everyone I have ever known, I am a magpie when it comes to how you live. I don't steal people, but I do steal their possessions and their surroundings.

My mother decides to be demonstrably supportive by purchasing a wedding gift: she buys the teenage newly-weds a set of kitchen scales. Because obviously the switch to motherhood will instantly require such kit.

A beautiful big blond nine-pound, five-ounce baby boy is born, and they all live in a small terrace house out by the mushroom farm and, many years later, I steal that little house and set my third novel, *Life, Death and Vanilla Slices*, under its roof.

There is a massive Jane-shaped hole in my school life and I miss her every day. Gill now has other friends from college and when I meet her on the street with a girl I don't recognise, I feel sick with jealousy. From the original four musketeers, only Susan and I are left at QMS.

Susan has rightly distanced herself from me. Like my sister before her, she is our new head girl, and I am not even a prefect. Susan also believes in God, which I struggle with.

I have lots of friends, but I am lonely. I miss the uncomplicated fifth form days. Everything is suddenly more serious and grown up.

I cruise the pubs. I know everyone, but I am hunting for something new: a relationship maybe?

Since I was fourteen, I have kissed so many boys. In my cricket club dance heyday I could notch up as many as eight different snoggees a night. We pass each other around like pass the parcel in human form. Sometimes a layer of clothing comes off, but it's kid's stuff.

My relationship with Martin founders after he is seen in broad daylight, walking hand in hand with a busty red-haired seventeen-year-old employed by his parents to help out in the hotel. The utter cheek of it.

I am incensed and finish with him. There are lots of tears, and terrible poems written in my diary. Several weeks later, my friend Jane Brewster (the nana one who now lives round the corner from me – sorry, there are many, many Janes in my year), comes up to me and says, 'I hope you don't mind, Jenny, but I'm going out with Martin now.' You can't really argue with that.

For a while I date a nineteen-year-old with a manual job, involving overalls, who constantly fails his driving test. He smokes a lot of dope and has well-conditioned long hair in a middle parting and pretty big brown eyes. He seems completely harmless but some years later he is caught flashing in Ashton Gardens. I have no idea what possessed him, apart from the fact that he had an enormous cock and quite possibly wanted to show it off. When I talk about this cock onstage many years later, I liken it to my grandmother's draught excluder.

While we are dating, his mother walks in on the two of us in her son's bed. She is so shocked that she just says the same thing over and over and over again: 'I thought you were making my tea, I thought you were making my tea, I thought you were making my tea.' I let myself out, catch the bus home and watch *The Phoenix and the Carpet* on the telly with my little brother, pretending for all the world that I am just a nice girl.

I have always found my internal 'nice girl' and 'slag' quite compatible; my two alter egos are sort of best friends, politely making way for each other when required. I think these two co-existed from a very early age and both are still with me today. Some people are surprised by how civilised I seem, while others are taken aback by quite how filthy my mouth can be. I am easy with both these sides of my personality. I have a wide vocabulary, but occasionally only the word 'cunt' will do.

First Love

My grandfather dies and I start wearing his Chinese smoking jacket over opaque black ballet tights and a cream-coloured raw silk shirt with a Singapore label in the collar that used to belong to my father. I have gold wedge heels with straps that criss-cross around my ankles, and I have that perm. I am ready for battle – I mean love.

I have very few big meaningful relationships with men in my life. I have my fair share of snogs and one-night stands and back-street wanks and blowjobs. But even as a teenager I prefer the chase to the reality. I like to pretend to strangers that I am a more exotic version of myself, then melt away before they discover the dull reality. I know that I can never be as interesting in real life as the fictional version of myself, at her best around 10 p.m. in a bar/pub/party.

I meet G (not G as in Geof, the man I have lived with now for forty-two years – slow down, we haven't got to him yet, this is G1) in the County, another pub full of underage drinkers in Lytham.

I am at my freshly permed summer best, i.e. slightly burnt, I am a black belt flirt and my radar has picked up fresh blood at the bar. I squeeze myself into the line-up, even though I have no intention of buying myself a drink. I catch his eye and we smirk at each other. He mimes 'Would you like a drink?' and I yell back, 'Pint of lager and lime.'

G is five years older than me and, unlike the dope-smoking flasher-to-be, has a driving licence and access to his parents' car. Ahem, he is back living at home after a series of things that have gone tits up. He has been to art school and he's in a band. The band does gigs. This isn't my first role as girlfriend of the band. Martin was the lead singer in a band called Goose, later renamed Objet Da! His sixteen-year-old, twenty-fags-a-day larynx would wrap themselves around Joe Cocker numbers and when he sang 'Hey Joe' he sounded about fifty.

G1 is the guitarist, bass or lead (I can't recall), he wears a sort of Spiders from Mars stage outfit, complete with Inca leg warmers. He is tiny. Together we go to a jeweller's in St Ann's Square, where I get him fitted for a silver ankle chain. It only costs £1.85 as he has such small ankles. Sometimes I worry about the fact that I know I would not be able to get his jeans over my hips. His parents are sweet and his older brother is a well-known actor (*Van der Valk* for starters) living in London. Of course, the proximity of fame increases my desire to be famous, too.

Weirdly, G knows people like Danny La Rue and we get tickets to see him perform. His penis is incredibly tightly tucked and suddenly it dawns on me that G is a magnet for middle-aged gays. The fact that he is straight and has a seventeen-year-old grammar school girlfriend doesn't seem to put them off, and they continue to swarm.

My parents like G: after all, he only lives on the other side of the rugby pitch and his mother shops in Booths. The fact that he is older than my sister's boyfriend doesn't bother them. He speaks nicely and uses an ashtray.

I am now in the upper sixth, my last year at school, and it's time to audition for drama schools. There is no drama department at my school and no such thing as doing Drama for either

O or A level, but I have an English teacher onside and she helps.
I need a Shakespeare and a modern. I go for Lady M's 'Out,
damned spot' speech from *Macbeth* and a passage from a 1961
Keith Waterhouse and Willis Hall play called *Celebrations*, which
revolves around the same people at both a wedding and a funeral.
Years later, Richard Curtis will make a fortune from ripping this
idea off.

I know nothing about either play before I make these choices
and decide that I don't need to actually read them all the way
through to get the gist of what I need to do. As long as I know
the words and perform with enough oomph, surely that will be
enough.

Many, many years later, my niece Daisy will live with us for a
year while she attends LAMDA, and her dedication and the thor-
oughness of her work ethic makes me blush at these memories.

But it is 1977, I am seventeen, I have an older sexy boyfriend
who buys me funny little presents and looks like a pop star in his
skinny drainpipe jeans and those grey leather ankle boots with
the clippy-clop heels.

There is a girl in my year at school who is a vicar's daughter.
Margaret's dad gets first dibs on house clearances and they have
a floor full of what we'd now call vintage clothing for sale in
their big Victorian house. Punk is chewing around the edges of
fashion, but Lytham St Annes can't quite commit, and there is a
vogue for wearing old nighties and silk bed jackets. Graham (for
this is his name) encourages this, and when he comes with me to
Margaret's he buys a big black fur coat to wear onstage. When he
tries it on, I feel like a pop star's girlfriend. I have a pair of snake-
green winkle-picker booties with a kitten heel, and I wear a lot of
silk shawls. My perm is a fabulous artificial lion's mane but I tell
Graham it's natural. He loves my hair – oh Christ.

My first drama school audition is for Manchester Polytechnic.
It's an accredited school, but it's not one of the big London ones.

It's 16 November, my train is delayed in Preston for two hours and I have to use a payphone to call the school who agree to shift the audition to the afternoon. I give Lady Macbeth a great deal of gusto and suspect I hear someone snigger, but punch through. The other auditionees are in the same large room; we all watch each other. Some are fucking awful. I have face ache from smiling encouragingly at my competition while in my head I'm thinking, *No chance, bitch.* I forget my lines during the Waterhouse and Hall piece, swear fluently until I get back on track. This is meant to be the funny piece. I get some laughs, mostly at the swearing.

At the end of the ordeal I am called to a small room, where a tutor in his sixties has a chat. He tells me I have one of the worst school reports they've ever seen. My headmistress has written a complete character assassination, detailing my inability to conform and my lack of team spirit. I try to persuade him that she's talking about hockey. I don't like the way this is going and there's no point in trying to flirt. He's old and gay.

Suddenly he sighs and seems to change his mind. He tells me that he detects a 'whiff of comedy' and that I am to be given another chance, and that I should try not to let him down. Learn the words, he suggests, and next time we'd like to hear you sing.

Cold sick runs through my veins.

My Secret Shame

Somehow, at birth I get lumped with 'funny' rather than 'musical'. Some people have both, which isn't really fair. Other gifts I get lumped with, apart from my mother's thin hair and my father's hideous knees, include a weird map dyslexia, extreme myopia and the inability to tan.

To this day, there are many things I cannot do: eat oysters, make pastry/gravy, draw anything that looks three-dimensional, stand on one leg in a yoga tree pose, use a sewing machine, wear my hair off my face, knit anything more complicated than a blanket square, run for a bus, sit nicely, speak French, or drive on a motorway. None of these things have really affected the course of my life, but the inability to sing has. It definitely narrowed my career choices, down to the point where I didn't really have any choices.

There has only ever been one option, but at seventeen I don't know about stand-up. All I know is that I want to be onstage, therefore I need to be an actress and here I am at the beginning of my dream come true and the only thing standing in the way of me and a place at drama school is a song: shit, bollocks, bugger and fuck.

I smile weakly and agree to returning with a song. 'Of course,

if you want to accompany yourself on the piano, that can be arranged.' Hahahaha. As if.

Not only can I not sing, I have no musical ability whatsoever.
I struggle to clap in time. When I attempt to play the recorder at
primary school, the only thing that comes out of my instrument
is a pool of dribble, turning my tune-a-day book into papier-
mâché. At the end of the class, when everyone else is playing
'London's Burning', I am busy making a vase.

I am too embarrassed to ask my musician boyfriend for help.
I will happily give him a blowjob from the passenger seat of his
parents' car when we are parked up by the lake, but the idea
of letting him hear me sing is so utterly shameful that I would
rather wade into that lake with stones in my pockets.

Somehow, between myself and a music teacher at QMSL, a big
peroxide bee-hived old blonde who keeps a bottle of vodka in the
baby grand, I stumble upon the song 'If My Friends Could See
Me Now' from *Sweet Charity*.

Shirley MacLaine is my kind of performer, the song also contains the word 'stumblebums', which I like, and I've seen the film,
which helps. I practise it by singing into a tape recorder. I have
no musical accompaniment, since no one in my family plays anything. My sister took guitar lessons for a while but developed too
many warts on her fingers to play properly (she had to have them
burnt off in the end!)

The second audition will be held sometime after Xmas;
maybe before then I will get into another drama school?
Preferably RADA, then Manchester Poly can stick their
bloody song.

But before I do any more auditions there is the subject of my
poor health to contend with.

I do not look unhealthy, but every month I am struck down
with tonsilitis and it takes me a week to recover. My parents
are worried about the impact this will have on my upcoming A

levels. Ha! I'd be more worried about the fact that I have yet to open my copy of *Bleak House*, never mind my tonsils.

But who knows, maybe my tonsils, being all swollen and pus-covered, are affecting my singing? We go and see a specialist who tells me to my face that the two small masses of lymphoid tissue at the back of my throat are 'rotting' and that I can have them whipped out privately for £150.

My parents agree to stump up and I am booked into Blackpool Vic for 24 November. This is ideal as I hope to lose a bit of weight before the annual stuffing of my face at Xmas.

My mother takes me up to Blackpool, but leaves before the anaesthetist arrives, so when I walk through the back garden gate at lunchtime and she sees me through the kitchen window, she thinks I am dead and my ghost is walking up the path. To give June her credit, she doesn't collapse; she comes out onto the back step and says, 'What the hell are you doing home?'

I lie. I speak as if my nose is heavily blocked and burble nonsense about having a temperature. 'Well, you didn't have one this morning,' she snaps, her eyes narrowing. My mother is no fool.

I come clean. 'I'm, er, thing is, I'm on the pill.' Earlier, the anaesthetist, on the verge of putting me under, casually asks, 'You're not on any medication, are you?' 'Only the pill,' I respond, equally casually. 'Then you won't be having this operation,' he replies.

I do my usual hysterical crying routine, and by the time I leave the hospital, me and the anaesthetist have cooked up the sudden temp and heavy head cold story between us, and I catch the bus home.

'Why are you on the pill?' asks my mother. For an intelligent forty-eight-year-old, she is being incredibly naive. Fortunately, I've had enough time on the bus to prepare for this scenario.

I tell her that Jane having a baby was a massive shock and, as a result, I promised myself that if I found myself in a serious relationship then I would take the pill as a precaution.

'Just in case I do ever decide to have sex,' I tell my mother. 'Just to be on the safe side, because I don't want anything to ruin my chances of passing my A levels and going to drama school.' Cue tears.

Bingo! My mother is delighted that I have been so mature and sensible about taking precautions. 'Of course nothing's happened yet,' I fib, and she tells me that she is proud of me. Hahahaha. Once more she has given me the benefit of the doubt.

Under the Knife

After the Microgynon 30g incident, I am rescheduled for a tonsillectomy just a fortnight before Xmas. I'm anxious, but it's not the first time I've been under the knife. Back in '74 I had my appendix out, more through sheer willpower than medical necessity.

Obviously, this is all my older sister's fault.

Sara has her appendix out first and everyone makes a massive fuss of her: my grandfather buys her a bottle of blood-red Dubonnet and insists she has a glass before supper every night. Apparently Dubonnet goes really well with beans on toast.

I am so jealous I will my own appendix to grumble and burst, just as my sister's did on the operating table. After all, there is a history of emergency appendix removal in the family. My mother also has the tell-tale scar.

The next time I have a stomach ache, I milk it hard. I am off school, the doctor is called. My sister's appendix turned nasty very quickly and after the operation she lost all the curl in her hair. I don't have any curl to lose (this is pre-perm) but Dr McKenna isn't taking any chances and I am whisked off to Lytham hospital to have the thing removed. This comes as a bit of a shock, especially as I don't really have much of a tummy ache any more and could quite easily play a game of hockey if pushed.

Never mind. I look forward to the Dubonnet, which I don't receive because I am fourteen. Instead, I get grapes and a telling-off from matron for wandering around the ward in a very short nightie without any knickers. I have never worn knickers under a nightie; it's the sort of thing Americans do, and I find it rather unhygienic.

The tonsillectomy turns out to be rather more dramatic. The rotting fleshy masses are removed on 8 December and I eventually exit Blackpool Vic on the 19th.

Turns out I am not a great clotter and, having initially been released from hospital the day after the op, I wake up to find myself haemorrhaging all over my pillow.

My mother drives me back to Blackpool in her little orange Mini at 3 a.m. She swears all the way under her breath and doesn't wait for red lights to fully turn amber. I bleed into a 'good' purple towel and know this is serious because she doesn't tell me off for not having picked up one of the ratty threadbare ones in the laundry cupboard.

I spend ten days on a children's ward and my mother keeps forgetting to bring in my make-up bag. Consequently, when my boyfriend is allowed in to visit he walks straight past me. My perm is on its last legs.

The outcome of the operation is that I stop getting tonsilitis, but I still can't sing.

However, I return to Manchester and belt out my *Sweet Charity* number, people wince visibly, again there are sniggers, but I receive a letter a few weeks later offering me a place. Good job, too, considering I don't get into any of the London schools.

The RADA experience is particularly vile and I don't even get to do my 'modern': they sneer me out of the building as soon as I finish my 'Out, damned spot'. I've kind of resented them ever since.

Twats.

LAMDA are more encouraging, telling me that I have potential but that I am very young and maybe I should apply when I'm a bit older and have a little more life experience. Obviously, I proceed to do the grown-up thing: I cry and beg them to give me a chance, they politely refuse and bundle me out of the building.

It's also a 'no' from Rose Bruford, even though my sister's flatmate, who works on the beauty pages of *Woman* magazine, does my make-up and I am wearing a trendy burgundy lipstick, which, on reflection, makes my mouth look like a dog's bum hole.

Swings and Roundabouts

I have a place to study drama in Manchester, but I have lost G. He goes to stay with his successful actor brother in London and doesn't come back. He makes friends with Joanna Lumley – apparently there is nothing going on, apart from vague plans to record a single together – and starts going out with an actress who is with the RSC. It gets worse: at some showbiz event he meets Kate Bush, and they are pictured together sitting side by side. Kate, who is only a year older than me, spends four weeks in 1978 at the top of the charts with the iconic hit 'Wuthering Heights'. Meanwhile, I am stuck in Lytham St Annes, wearing a brown Crimplene pinafore dress, supposedly revising for my A levels.

Thank God this all happens before the internet: I would have been the biggest Twitter/Insta stalker in the land.

As it is, I am sickened. I take a swig from every bottle in my parents' drinks cabinet and attempt to throw myself downstairs, pre-dating Princess Diana's stair stunt by a number of years. I cannot do myself any damage: the stairs are thickly carpeted, and I have a fat arse.

But, God, I am miserable. I insist on seeing G when he visits his parents and he is very gentle, promising that he still wants me in his life.

When my cousin gets married in London, G meets me for lunch in a pizza place, where he is kind but firm, a bit like the LAMDA adjudicators, expertly moving his head so that I cannot get my tongue into his mouth. Not that I tried this with the LAMDA adjudicators. Our relationship is over and I need to come to terms with this.

Back in Lytham I develop some kind of malaise, which manifests itself in an inability to get out of my bed. I am tested for glandular fever, but the results are inconclusive. I barely go to school, my A levels loom and I have yet to finish Bleak House. I make an excuse to go round to G's house and cry all over his mother. She has two sons and isn't used to hysterical young women, but she is very kind.

My own mother would prefer me to snap out of it, preferably in time to pass my A levels. I try to read Bleak House the night before the exam: it's about seven hundred pages. I go into the exam hall not completely sure what the main characters are called. I am lucky to get a grade D, which counts as a pass.

Even more disappointingly, I get an E for my Art A level; again, it counts as a pass, but I could have done a lot better. In later life I will pick up my paint brushes again. Sadly, I seem to be artistically arrested at a grade E A level, but I persevere and pretend not to be livid with my own crapness. 'I paint for my mental health,' I lie. In reality, I want to sell my crappy efforts for thousands of pounds.

I fail my General Studies A level. I am eighteen years old, I'm supposed to be 'bright', but I am an underachiever. Fortunately, my parents are too relieved to be furious: with two A levels I will get a grant and they can get rid of me in September. Good riddance: right now I'm a bit of a miserable cow.

Obviously, I leave it too late to apply for halls of residence and end up bagsying one of the last available student rooms for rent in Manchester. This turns out to be the top floor of a suburban terrace and not what I had in mind at all. It comprises a bed-room, a kitchen (which used to be a bedroom) and a bathroom.

I will be sharing this chintzy flatlet with a complete stranger. My parents are beyond caring; I'm just going to have to get on with it. They drive me to Manchester in a white Maxi, and, with a massive sigh of relief, drop me off with one of my mother's Gobi fruit cakes, a suitcase of clothes and some bedding. Incidentally, one day my future husband will purchase this white Maxi off my father. He doesn't actually want it, but my father can be quite persuasive.

It's the autumn of 1978, a time when parents didn't escort their uni teens to John Lewis to purchase a bumper fresher's kit, com-plete with snazzy duvet covers and matching pillowcases. They packed you off with a burnt pan and those sheets 'your father put his big toe through'.

I strike gold with my unknown roommate. Julie is from Sheffield and the first thing she takes out of her bag is a bottle of Cinzano.

Her father is a butcher, and regularly sends parcels of meat to the little thirties terrace that we share with our disapproving landlady. Mrs Knight loathes our guts. She is a tightly buttoned-up Christian woman and has been conned into allowing two loud-mouthed, heavy-drinking, chain-smoking heathen tarts into her house.

Sometimes the meat parcels Julie's dad sends us get lost in the post and arrive 'on the turn', in which case we curry the contents and Mrs Knight goes berserk. I can't say I've had a sausage vin-daloo since.

We arrive early in September; by Bonfire Night Mrs Knight gives us four weeks' notice to leave. Honestly, what a cow!

Julie is studying fashion at the Toast Rack, which is part of the poly much closer to town than the drama school.

The Toast Rack, so named because it looks like a toast rack, is one part of the domestic science colleges, designed in 1959; the other building is built in the shape of a fried egg, haha (true); both buildings have now been decommissioned and the site is up for sale, with planning permission for two hundred flats. This feels sad: who wouldn't want to study in a fried egg or a toast rack?

The Horniman Building, aka the Capitol Theatre, which the drama students occupy, is geographically independent from the rest of the poly, situated in Didsbury (nice then, very posh now). Five miles out of town, it's an attractive art deco thirties design, opened originally in 1931 as a cinema. It was then converted in the fifties into a TV studio, where it became home to the infamous *Armchair Theatre* plays.

It even has its own resident ghost: one of the *Armchair Theatre* actors passed away during a live recording; hopefully he was sitting in an armchair at the time and went comfortably.

The building changes hands again in 1968 when it's purchased by Manchester Polytechnic and it's this incarnation that I will be attending for the next three years. Not quite three years as it turns out: I flake out at the final hurdle, but – hold your horses – let's start at the beginning. Oh, by the way, the building (which should have been listed) is demolished in 1997 and replaced by ... wait for it ... flats (yawn).

'The World is Full of Actors Pretending to be Human' (J. D. Salinger)

On my first day at Manchester Poly School of Theatre I wear a tan-coloured pair of dungarees, pulled in tight at my waist by one of my dad's brown leather belts, an old army shirt with wings on the epaulettes and a second-hand little tweed hacking jacket with leather buttons. My handbag is a wicker basket normally purchased for carrying kittens. This is all very well, but, because it opens at one end, every time I unclip the lid everything falls out.

I am not trying as hard as a girl I know in St Annes who made a name for herself by eating raw green peppers and keeping all her worldly goods in a kettle, but I am trying quite hard. I am also wearing all the make-up, with at least three shades of green eyeshadow on my eyelids.

Two other girls are wearing dungarees, one navy, one in a ticking fabric which reminds me of Andy Pandy; there are only eight of us: so much for sartorial originality.

We are a motley bunch and I realise with a withering clitoris that very few of the men in my year have been chosen for their looks.

Among the chaps we have an ex-jockey (short), a man in his fifties who is mortified by his own toenails when we wear footless tights for movement, another who looks like he's been dressed by his nana and does impressions of bus doors opening and closing, and a moody dark-haired boy who reads graphic novels and never, ever puts his shoulders back. Two of the boys wear ties, but not in a punk kind of way.

By contrast most of the girls are good-looking, at least one is divorced with kids, one is older than she looks and will get sick of people saying 'Bloody hell, I didn't know you were that old.' There is also an extremely pretty posh girl, with a posh name and a posh voice, who will be forced to do any accent other than her own for the duration of her time at the poly, a slightly aggressive Doc Martens wearer, who will not last the first month, a Gloucester milkmaid and a black girl with pigtails and glasses. She is the one who will undergo the most radical transformation over the next three years. B will finally emerge as a stunning shaven-haired beauty, who has an affair with a tutor who wears a kilt and keeps a knife down his sock. It's all a bit confusing, and I'm not sure who will be my pal.

But no matter, I'm not here to make friends with girls. That can wait. After all, I have Julie keeping me in a constant supply of chops and mince at home. No, I'm on another mission.

I am class of '78 at the poly. Class of '77, the year above me, contains a 'person of great interest', a bona fide pop star no less. Second-year drama student Graham Fellows, he of the thick pudding-bowl haircut and lanky leg, has just scored a top-ten hit with the novelty record 'Jilted John'.

Jilted John is Graham's alter ego, a nerdy nice boy whose only way of getting back at the lad who steals his girlfriend, Julie, is to compose the chorus 'Gordon is a moron'. On Top of the Pops, Gordon the Moron is played by Bernard Kelly, another fanciable hunk on the Manchester scene.

My mission is to snog Graham Fellows. I should be concentrating on training to be a really good actress, but when I think about these early days of the first term all I can remember is lolling about in the school canteen, a small windowless dining room/common room.

There is actually very little space in the building to hang out, and no outdoor space, apart from a car park. This isn't really a problem: Manchester is rarely dry or sunny enough to sit outside, and anyway back then you could smoke indoors. And that's what everyone does: everyone smokes and eats pies and chips and sponge and custard served by a delightful one-handed dinner lady called Margaret, and then we drink endless cups of tea and smoke some more, until, at the end of the day, we all cross the road and start drinking and smoking in the pub opposite.

The Parswood is a big, solid thirties red-brick job where the locals and the students do not mix. It becomes my refuge, especially when I discover that I suffer from claustrophobia in a fencing mask, which necessitates wagging off early on Friday afternoons and getting pissed instead.

It takes me about a week to get off with Jilted John. It is the night of the freshers' ball. Back then I have enormous stamina and spend the afternoon buying old men's pinstripe waistcoats at a jumble sale before getting ready for the big night out.

The band booked for the gig are called Jab Jab, from Huddersfield. I recall nothing about the music, I'm not dancing, I'm too busy cruising like a snog-hungry shark for fresh snog blood. I kiss a boy called Richard, who looks like he is auditioning to be the Artful Dodger in an am dram version of Oliver!, and then head out to a party for drama students only.

Here I ensnare the second-year pop star, shoving aside any competition with the wiles that only a one-track-minded eighteen-year-old possesses. Bingo: he takes me back to his flat on the back of his scooter. I'm slightly let down by the Vespa. Back in Lytham, I tend to ride pillion on Harleys. Nevertheless, it's a tender and romantic night, and we make love while he plays me every single track from his upcoming album.

At 4.30 a.m. I refuse his gentlemanly offer to stay the night and make my exit. I have no idea where I am, so I hitch a lift home.

About a week later, Graham sidles up to me and presses something into my hand. I can't imagine what it is, but I play it cool. He's been friendly but distant since freshers' night and I have been determined not to be a bore. I go to the girls' toilets and uncurl my fist: it's a little plastic bag containing all the hairgrips that fell out of my hair while we were in bed. From then on, he is just a mate and I sadly watch him eyeing up my Gloucester milkmaid classmate.

Our paths cross post-drama school, first on a 1981 musical called *Visiting Day*, in which I have a non-singing role, and later we become good friends when he plays a part opposite Caroline Aherne in a Radio 4 series called *On Baby Street*, which I write with my dear friend Julie Balloo (not the butcher's daughter).

To this day I still think he's great.

Coming Off the Rails

After Julie and I are chucked out of Mrs Knight's we find a nice big double bedsit in a huge Victorian pile of a house in Didsbury's Moorfield Road.

The best thing about this house is that our landlord is mostly absent, and downstairs there are four *boys*, all students and all very different, like a variety tin of biscuits. One is very tall and can light his own farts, one is Maltese and I have a crush on him forever, which he refuses to reciprocate, one doesn't like us/me and the other is a desperately good-looking Italian who we occasionally have to hide from sobbing girls in our wardrobe.

Julie and I live on the first floor, the two Sues live opposite, and next to the bathroom is a single bedsit accommodating a quiet, angry man who will eventually have a nervous breakdown and leave, but only after playing Elvis Costello's 'Oliver's Army' on repeat for three days.

Eventually, when the two-bedroom top-floor flat becomes available, the two Sues and Julie and I move up there. The bedrooms are smaller, but we gain a sitting room.

We are cheerful in this flat. Julie wears her knickers on her head to hold her hair back when she washes her face in the kitchen sink, we have a massive fat-backed black and white telly complete with the cliché coat-hanger aerial and we are forever trying to stuff foreign coins that won't fit into the electricity meter under the sink.

I drink a lot of cider and eat a lot of sausage rolls, and, despite cycling to school, I am getting rather plump.

During the summer holidays, between my first and second year at drama school, my sister gets married and my cousin Elizabeth and I make massive-bottomed bridesmaids.

My sister, in white, looks like a tiny Jemima Puddle-Duck. Liz and I, trailing behind her in pale blue, fill the aisle with our bums. We can barely walk side by side, we are in danger of getting wedged.

I am still, however, very pretty, and boys don't seem to care.

The original G still writes to me, on beautiful paper and in different coloured ink, but is leading a very adult life in London, living with his brother in a flat in Chiswick, which is painted all the colours of a cassata ice cream. (I will visit at some point and inevitably sleep with him.)

Julie and I occasionally entertain gentlemen guests at the same time, but it's getting harder, and more sordid. At some point I shag a lad who she ends up dating. The lad in question is very short but a very good dancer. They get serious and I can't believe it.

I shag someone else who then tells me by post he has venereal disease and I have to march myself off to a sexual health clinic in town, where I am given a clean bill of health and a lecture.

No one seems to use condoms; we are all on the pill. I am playing with fire: AIDS is on the horizon and herpes is a very real threat. Blithely/stupidly I carry on. Sometimes I sleep with blokes because their flat is close to the club/pub and I can't be bothered to go home, sometimes I shag blokes because I'm scared of what they will do if I don't. I have so many lucky escapes.

I hitch everywhere and get in anyone's car. The Yorkshire

Ripper has been doing his worst and yet I'd still rather hitch than take the bus. I'm too idle to learn the bus routes – far easier to stick my thumb out and persuade the driver (middle-aged men mostly) to go out of their way for me.

I'm not alone in my behaviour, but I think I'm possibly more relentless than most. I'm not even that fussed about sex. I like the flirting and kissing best, but I always feel like once I've got the ball rolling it's my duty to see it through to the end. I mostly fake my orgasms; being drama-school trained, most blokes don't suspect a thing.

Not that I'm paying much attention to my training right now. I'm skating on the surface, getting by doing as little as I possibly can. I'm wasting my opportunities and what little talent I have, but I'm too vain to realise it.

At some point in the second year, our movement teacher hurls a comment at me which sticks: he tells me that I am 'too big, too big in every way'. I am in my leotard at this point, bulging around the tummy and thigh with sausage rolls and pie-based lunches. 'You're like a big bottle of lemonade, you just go off, it's too much, you're just too much.'

I probably wouldn't have been so hurt had he not been the only fanciable tutor in the building.

I resolve to lose weight. Fashion has been on my side for a while and I've been hiding my new borderline size 14 figure under sixties-style stirrup slacks and big baggy mohair jumpers. Thank you, New Romantics, it was a good time to chunk up.

The second bombshell of the second year is that Julie no longer wants to live with me; she wants to live with the pocket-sized boyfriend. I'm heartbroken, possibly because she has found the thing that seems to elude me: a person she is content to keep going back to.

I can't recall how badly I behave about this, but after she leaves the flat I don't really see her again. Forty and more years later, I can picture her with her pants on her head smiling and dancing, but I do not see her in real life again. Not ever.

Every time I play Sheffield I wonder if she went back there and if she'll turn up, but she never has and I cannot find her anywhere online. Julie, if I owe you an apology, I'm sorry.

At the end of the second year I go home for the summer holidays. My mother is in hospital having a kidney or a cyst removed, maybe both; typically, all I think about is how this is going to affect me. I basically have to look after my father and my little brother, because my sister is off being a smug married, having moved into a desperately cute little flat in Gypsy Hill.

I covet this flat very badly indeed and cannot help feeling that she is beating me hands down. She is going to be successful and I'm not sure I can bear it, because I might not be.

I have embarked on a diet and for once I am taking it seriously. I've been 'cutting down' ever since the movement teacher's comments and waistbands are already getting looser by the time I get back to Lytham.

A slimming tip in a magazine suggests replacing rice and pasta with crunchy raw white cabbage. I play my conjuring trick in the kitchen, cabbage for me, pasta or rice for Ben and Pa. Neither of them notice. Gradually, I cut out all carbs and start experimenting with low-calorie soups. I find that if I boil up a load of veg and mix it with a tin of low-cal Heinz veg soup, it might look like a massive hearty broth, but it actually contains very few calories. I start stewing apples, adding Sweetex and cinnamon and mixing it with plain yoghurt. At this stage I am still eating the occasional boiled egg, maybe some roast chicken, only I leave the potatoes off my plate. My brother and my father are oblivious. They are eating like kings. I heap their plates with all my forbidden chips and extra slices of bread and butter.

I think my father is pleased to see me 'shift a bit of timber'.

Like many fathers of his generation he is vain on my behalf. In 1980, there is no such thing as body positivity.

As for my mother, she is coping with having a vital organ removed and in no fit state to realise that her greedy second daughter, who has never shied away from a second helping, could unknowingly be developing an eating disorder.

Sometimes I smoke out of my bedroom window to keep the cake cravings at bay. In any case, with my mother having been out of action for so long, the tins in the pantry are empty, save for some stale burnt flapjack and a few fruitcake crumbs. Occasionally I take the lids off the tins and inhale hard. I've started taking speed in Manchester and vow, when I get back, to take some more. It takes the edge off your appetite and makes you dance all night. Win-win, what's not to like?

Heading for Disaster

I go back to Manchester for the third year and there is an audible and extremely satisfying gasp as I make my entrance into the smelly canteen. It sounds like the reaction to a conjurer's trick, and in some respects it is: I've magicked away at least a stone.

I am wearing a yellow sweatshirt, faded jumble sale drainpipe Levi's and yellow Anello & Davide leather Mary Janes, the most delicious pair of shoes I have ever owned. Thinking about those shoes, I can still feel the little leather button fastener between my fingers.

People don't half bang on about my dramatic weight loss. I revel in the attention and wait for a compliment from my movement tutor . . . and wait.

I am totally happy with my new look. I'm probably eight and a half stone and a size ten, which is pretty normal for a five-foot four-inch twenty-year-old. I feel light, I feel supple, I am gorgeous, I'm wearing my end of perm hair in Heidi plaits which I cross over the top of my head. Sometimes I tie ribbons to the end of each pigtail; it's a cute look and I know it.

Not only do I have a new figure, I have a new home: 2A Old Lansdowne Road is a notorious drama school address, one of

those word-of-mouth places where only those in the inner sanctum get to stake their claim on a room.

Vacancies usually come up when previous drama school occu-
pants make the brave move to London or move in with a partner.
There are no civilians in the building.

I move in with the Gloucester milkmaid. Frances is in my year,
and it has taken me a while to realise how very beautiful she is.
Fran is from the countryside, she is full-fat cream, green fields
and hay bales. She has a proper bosom and hips and thighs, but
she also has a waist, long brown hair and the ability to pirouette
across a room. She is a trained dancer with bones deemed too big
for the ballet. She does everything with an odd grace. I've never
seen anyone roll a cigarette so beautifully.

The flat is incredible. Fran and I have the run of the first
floor, although we share a communal bathroom with downstairs,
where a big homosexual American actor rules the roost like a
massive shagging rooster.

Fran has painted her room white; the mattress is on the floor
and her sheets and duvet are also white. Everything is cloud-
white and calm; even her nightie is white.

On Sundays, Fran goes out in her slippers and buys the *Sunday
Times* and a packet of chocolate digestives, comes home, makes
herself a cafetière of proper coffee and retires back to bed to read,
drink coffee, smoke and eat chocolate biscuits. She is the closest
thing to a fictional character in a book that I have ever met. She
could be written by Jilly Cooper, Edna O'Brien, Fay Weldon or
Virginia Woolf; she could be from any time.

She is less frantic than I am; she doesn't need to go out as
much, she prefers pints and roll-ups with college mates in a tiny
pub round the corner called the Railway Tavern. Meanwhile I
continue to go cruising and partying. One night I pick up some
bloke, drag him home and realise, too late, he looks like a ferret.
In bed, he starts to piss on my face. I'm not into this and flee the

room and get into bed with Frances, who wedges a chair under her doorknob and together we sleep under her fresh white duvet, my piss-soaked hair on her fresh white pillows.

By contrast my room is a mess. It's very big and painted a depressing navy blue. I sleep on a mattress on the floor in sheets that can easily go an entire term without being washed.

I am still losing weight. I now have my food routine set in stone. Breakfast is an orange and a handful of sunflower seeds (soon to be ditched), lunch is a small pot of cottage cheese and equal half-measures of stewed apple (artificially sweetened) and natural yoghurt, and supper is a low-cal soup with a ton of extra boiled veg added to the pan. For snacks, I eat carrots dipped in Marmite. I don't particularly want to lose more weight, but I am terrified of putting it back on again. I decide I need a safety margin: if I can just get down to eight stone three then I will have a four-pound safety margin. It's the only thing that makes sense.

Only when I get to eight stone three pounds, I figure that's my optimum weight, so if I get down to eight stone, I can afford to maybe have a proper meal one weekend, only I don't.

Fran worries. One weekend she cooks a massive lasagne. We are going to have lunch with friends. I agree to join in until I see her using butter to cook the veg in. Butter is a complete no-no for me. I seize it from her and throw it out of the window, at which point she starts screaming about how expensive butter is, so obviously I climb out of the window and start scrabbling around on the roof for the butter. I do not turn up for lunch.

Instead, I head into town and when I get back Fran is tight-lipped and it's pretty obvious our guests have been talking about me. There is nothing more I would like to do than sit down with our friends, have a glass of wine and scrape out that delicious-looking lasagne pan, all tomato-red and cheesy golden pasta. Instead, I go to my room and count out some sunflower seeds like a fucking parrot.

I love our kitchen. Unlike my bedroom, with its vicious navy walls, the kitchen is a milky pale blue. We have a beautiful old farmhouse table along one wall, and a glorious battered leather club armchair, where Frances sits in her white nightie, smoking roll-ups, refusing to come out with me.

She is getting fed up and I know she has started eating choc-olate in the privacy of the locked bathroom. I find the wrappers and feel triumphant. Baths are becoming uncomfortable for me now. I am so thin that one day, when I slip down into the tub, I actually graze my spine.

Frances goes to the head of school and blows the whistle. The head speaks to my mother, whose immediate response is to rally the troops (her sister Aileen) and come up to meet me for lunch.

I can see them both now, two big noses bearing down on me in their pleated skirts and good woollen jumpers. It's nudging winter and consequently I can hide my tiny frame under many, many layers. Weirdly, however much body fat I lose, my face re-mains resolutely roundish. I put some pink cheeks on and take them to a wine bar: after all, it is 1980 and there are a lot to choose from. We all have a ploughman's; my mother and my aunt have the pâté and the cheese combos. I stick to plain boiled ham, making sure I only eat the lean bits. I take forever to demolish the salad garnish, cutting my pickled onion into tiny bits, leaving the coleslaw (mayonnaise) and the ridiculous cottage loaf.

We discuss the food issue and I manage to con them into thinking that everyone is panicking over nothing and that I've actually stopped dieting. I explain that because my stomach has shrunk so has my appetite and I'm struggling to feel really hungry. This is a massive lie; I am constantly ravenous.

June and Aileen have pudding while I smoke and distract them with college tales about how I've been given a lead role in an upcoming third-year Greek tragedy, blah, blah.

They leave around four, seemingly convinced that I am

determined to get back on track, and I return home to skip supper – I mean . . . all that ham!

At this point I still think I am going to be an actress but every time I pretend to be someone else on stage, I am less and less convinced.

Case in point: the Greek tragedy that I told June and Aileen about is an adaptation of *Oedipus*, complete with eyeball gouging.

I am Jocasta; we are all wearing ancient Greek robes. I know my lines but am fairly clueless about what the entire play is all about. I can't be bothered to research it. Who cares?

When I am onstage saying my lines, something odd happens: I can hear another voice in my head. The other voice is mine and I'm taking the piss out of myself. Fortunately, the voice doesn't come out of my mouth, but it's audible to me. It says, 'Well, look at you being an ancient times Greek lady in your pretend gold Greek lace-up shoes which you actually bought in a sale when you lived with Julie. They cost £1, do you remember? Oh, so you're going to walk over there now, are you? Go on then, do it all Greek style.'

Oh Christ. Not only have I got an eating disorder, I've got my own internal heckler.

Cathy la Crème
and the Rumbabas

L ife in the third year at drama school isn't entirely about
denying myself food; it's also about getting myself an
Equity card.

In the eighties you can't perform unless you are a member of
Equity (the actors' union) but you need to perform to get your
Equity card.

The rules are complicated and tedious. Basically, in order to
get this card you have to do so many paid gigs and have a certain
number of gigs booked for the future. It's mental and unfair, and
some girls end up stripping.

In 1980 there is a lot of stripping work: tits are everywhere,
on Page 3, peeping out from behind displays of roasted peanuts,
on beer mats, tits, tits, tits. You can strip at lunchtime in pubs
where men drink pints, watch you strip and then go back to the
office. I don't have the tits for stripping, and neither can I sing.
However, because I look like I might be able to sing, I am asked
to join a band.

Cathy la Crème and the Rumbabas is masterminded by a
pushy ex-drama school student called Mark. Cathy is a girl who

missed a great deal of college for personal reasons and is now in our year. Her best friend is a girl called Debbie Sticky, who takes me to bed one afternoon for a pissed exploration of what it might be like to be bisexual. Her breasts are the softest, whitest things I have ever touched, but then I have never baked bread.

Cathy writes punk poetry; she knows John Cooper Clarke, who is one of the few people who performs at the poly that makes me stop snogging random strangers in order to watch.

John is mighty – he is still mighty – he is a massive influence on my career, and I adore him.

The band is a strange mishmash of music, mime and spoken word. Two of the members are proper musicians. Their stage names are Ossie Mandias and Kelvin Rockola; Mark (Marco Alpha Romeo Casanova) is a jack of all trades and Cathy is a poet. I become Jenny Eclair in keeping with the cream cake theme. This is a very common trend on the punk poetry scene: loads of people have a performance alter ego, it makes signing on easier.

I don't realise it at the time, but I am creating the comedy bones of a character that will entirely consume me and at times be quite damaging. Right now, it's just a laugh. I coin the name from a memory of pretending to be French in a Blackpool nightclub. I have no idea why I used to do that; I don't speak any French, I don't look French. I'd have been much more convincing pretending to be Deutsch, but people only find the Germans sexy if they're wearing thigh-length boots and stomping around with whips. So, I'm seventeen, pretending to be French in the Adam and Eve and this twenty-something starts chatting me up. 'What's your name?'

'Jenny-Clare,' I rasp sexily in an 'Allo 'Allo! French accent, hitching my middle name onto my Christian name.

Him (in broad Lancashire): 'What, Jenny éclair, like in the cake?'

And for some reason I squirrel this name away.

Cathy is incredibly generous and at first she lets me perform her poems, but then I start writing my own. It's fairer, even though I completely rip off her style. I just make mine filthier.

And so it begins. I have a full-blown eating disorder but I am also on my way to getting my Equity card. Sometimes I sleep with Mark, but then he gets a proper girlfriend who is older and more glamorous and still is.

I sort of have a boyfriend for a while; he is younger than me and worryingly prettier. I think he might be another Mark. He peroxides his hair and wears a great deal of eyeliner, so that's something we have in common. There's a lot of staring at each other and stroking faces, but I've gone off sex. I've suppressed my appetite for food for so long it's affected my libido. I don't really have the energy. Also, I have screwed around a lot: maybe I am running out of fucks?

He is a plaything and a toy, and I admire how he wears silk shirts and big balloon trousers, but I don't really have room in my head for anything more than counting calories and not eating. Being anorexic is a full-time job. I also have drama school, which I attend less frequently, and gigs, which I always turn up for.

We play anywhere, but I particularly remember being the warm-up act for Divine, the seventies gay icon and drag queen extraordinaire. Divine is famous for eating dog shit in John Waters's notorious film *Pink Flamingos*. She is literally larger than life and electrifying, but, having been born with a congenital heart condition, she is dead by the age of forty-two.

The gay clubs are an eye-opener, but I pretend not to be shocked and gradually get used to the smell of poppers.

Equally jaw-dropping are the scenes in Manchester's notorious Press Club, an after-hours drinking den for the gentlemen of the press, opening hours 11 p.m. to 6 a.m.

We normally start performing at about 3 a.m., by which point everyone in the place is blind drunk and no one, including us, has any real clue about what is going on. Quite often our audience is crawling around on their hands and knees.

Cathy and I wear black sixties crêpe cocktail dresses and black kitten heels. Sometimes we add a splash of diamanté.

We sing some old songs, 'Tequila' and 'Perfidia' and Elvis Presley's 'Wooden Heart' in German (at last it's come in useful). We mime an operation and an underwater ballet, and I wish I had kept the scripts but I'm not sure there ever were any. One of the poems I wrote survives and, I'm really sorry, but this is how it goes:

> Oh dear Agony Aunty,
> I've a discharge in my panties,
> It's not VD
> I'm sure of that
> I've never had trouble before with my twat
> [there is more]

I'm twenty, and that's the only excuse I have.

Mark is ambitious. His next step is to create a theatre company, which he names the Pan Communication Theatre Company (after the flute-playing god), and he persuades the Gallery Wine Bar on Peter Street that what they really need to be doing is lunchtime theatre.

Conveniently, Mark's sister is the playwright Bryony Lavery, who will go on to have an extremely successful career. But I think in 1981 she is just 'practising'.

We perform one of Bryony's early pieces. *Helen and Her Friends* is about two girls visiting their dying friend in hospital. I play Helen, the dying one. Apparently I look the part, and don't even have to audition.

To be honest, physically this play is right up my strasse. All I have to do is lie there in a real hospital bed (cheers, Manchester Royal Infirmary) looking tragic. This is quite easy. I don't know it at the time, but anorexia has one of the highest rates of mortality of any mental health condition. It's also one of the hardest to treat.

I found a flyer for the show recently and it says 'the performance will last 40 mins and the bar will remain open throughout'.

The idea is that people will pop in on their lunch break for a pint and a play. The wine bar is close to Granada Studios, where they film *Coronation Street*, and Pat Phoenix, aka Elsie Tanner, comes in wearing what looks like six fur coats with her boyfriend, the actor and father of Cherie Blair, Tony Booth.

My mother travels from Lytham to see the show. Poor June is subjected to watching her mentally and physically sick daughter pretending to be on the verge of death. I can't imagine how triggering this must be. But my mother is made of stern stuff and sits through it wearing her 'theatre face'.

The menu at the wine bar at the time is offering baked potatoes with a variety of delicious fillings for 90p, including kidneys in port wine. Maybe June cheered herself up with one of those, though I think she may have stopped eating kidneys, having recently lost one of her own.

Anorexia

I have a joke in my stand-up about how people react when I tell them I used to be anorexic:

'They look at me as if to say, "Well, I didn't know you could recover *that* well."'

Being a hefty girl in my sixties, it seems unlikely now, but food and my weight have been a struggle for so many years of my life and I still have some latent control issues.

I am very strict about mealtimes: lunch can never be before 1 p.m., and I still won't eat pudding, cake, biscuits, chocolate or butter.

However, I don't keep scales in the house, refuse to enter into conversations about diets (dull) and accept, with only the slightest resistance, that I'm nudging a 16, especially around the arse, and that most doctors would advise me to lose at least a stone, possibly three.

Slimming is a huge deal when I am growing up. Everyone's mother is on a diet, Ryvita is the crispbread of choice, shakes are available at the chemist and there is a great deal of celery-chomping going on.

Calorie-counting has just been invented and there are little pocket-sized books you can buy in the newsagents, usually featuring a tape measure on the cover, detailing how many units are in most everyday foods. This becomes my bible.

I grow up during a time when women who are considered fat and ugly are called 'ugly and fat' to their faces, when Miss World wannabes parade in oddly shaped, slightly sexless seventies bikinis and their vital statistics are broadcast without anyone batting a false eyelash. Look at the pretty slim girls, numbers on their wrists, smiling, smiling, smiling, 36–24–36, always in inches and never in centimetres, which would have made it at least funnier.

I have experimented with losing weight from around the age of fourteen, when it becomes fashionable at school to push away 'starch'.

But I am naturally greedy and occasionally, when I am left alone in the house, I am capable of eating one fry-up directly after another. Three is my record and I only stop because I've run out of clean frying pans.

I am a different build from my sister, who is still stick-thin, mostly because she genuinely likes exercise. Sara cycles everywhere on one of those punishing fold-up bikes and is the kind of woman who owns her own kayak.

My sister goes on activity holidays which include swimming around Greek islands or walking Hadrian's Wall with the book club (the one that only reads impenetrable books); meanwhile, I go on painting holidays and lift nothing heavier than a wine glass or a paint brush.

As a teenager, my sister's thinness is a constant source of fury. I cannot borrow her clothes (I am too fat) and once I get a roll of tummy flesh trapped in the zip of her purple velvet loons. My brother, always a weedy kid, has, I'm glad to say, grown into a massive six-foot four-inch slab of a bloke. Ben is fit but heavy. Once, when attending a pilates class, he sits on a glass table in the reception area and breaks it, hahaha.

Ben and I share the same prescription for high blood pressure meds: we are like our father, who insisted on getting served first at the golf club bar on account of the fact he'd had a quadruple bypass.

'Those with single bypasses,' he argued, 'could get to the back of the queue.'

Anorexia is very hard to explain to anyone who has never had an eating disorder; it is a strange self-inflicted masochism. It's not the same as bulimia. Anorexics secretly think the bulimics are cheats; in reality, anyone with any kind of eating disorder is doing themselves terrible harm and we all have bad breath.

When I see anorexics now, mostly teens, in school uniforms which are hanging off them, I always feel the urge to speak to them. I want to tell them that I know, and I also want to tell them to their faces that actually they look shit (but in a nice way).

Anorexia is virtually unheard of when I am at school. Lots of girls are on a diet, but no one manages to take it to extremes. This might be because it's a pre-internet all-girls school and the pressure is less, or maybe it's because the chocolate sponge pudding with the bright green mint custard, mostly served on Fridays, is irresistible.

Maybe girls are puking up in the toilets, but I never hear them and I don't know anyone who personally indulges in the 'fingers down the throat' routine.

By the time I get to drama school, however, anorexia is catching on, and these days kids under ten are being diagnosed, which makes me weep.

It is so hard to have a genuinely healthy relationship with food. Even now, when body positivity is a 'thing', we are not entirely convinced, and the media is equally confused. Some foods are still labelled 'naughty' – oh, I'm so naughty, I'm eating two squares of chocolate. In fact, one of the reasons why I don't eat chocolate is because I hate the way it's pushed at women – all those crappy slabs of cheap shit chocolate on offer at the till, all those underhand 'cheer yourself up with chocolate, you miserable old cow' messages. 'Lonely, rejected, haven't got a boyfriend? Never mind, eat chocolate.' Nothing is used as an emotional battering ram in the same way as chocolate, so fuck you, the chocolate industry, I'm not buying into your nonsense.

I used to love chocolate: Lion bars, they were great. If I'm honest, of course, I think the real reason why I don't eat chocolate is that I'm afraid once I get the taste for it again I might never stop.

There is a monster inside me (as well as under the bed and inside the wardrobe).

I have a slightly addictive personality. I say 'slightly' because I usually manage to pull myself back from the brink, but I have to have rules and I have to obey those rules.

I also think I have always been auto-competitive, so when I started dieting I inevitably became really good at it; so good that it takes me years to function normally around food.

The one thing nobody tells you about anorexia is how boring it is – it's boring for me, it's boring for my friends and it is boring and frightening for my family. I make my mother cry; my mother never cries, but when I come home from Manchester for Xmas early, because I am unwell, I throw an egg at her face and refuse to eat Xmas dinner. I accept some turkey breast and some carrots, but the idea of gravy, Xmas pudding or a mince pie is out of the question. I make everyone tense and smoke at the table while everyone is still eating.

I smoke all the time, Silk Cut constantly between my scrawny fingers. When I go out wearing a pair of yellow tights, a bloke shouts, 'Last time I saw a pair of legs like that they were in a butcher's window.'

I buy clothes from children's departments, my knickers droop and there's no point wearing a bra. In winter I am suddenly covered in a fine down of soft hair, like an animal pelt. My body is trying to keep me warm. I am always very cold.

I am referred to a mental health unit at the nearby Withington Hospital in Manchester. My therapist is a young Asian man who is allergic to cigarette smoke. I refuse to talk if I can't smoke. We reach a compromise: I can smoke as long as I sit on the window-sill with the window wide open. We are on the top floor of the psychiatric block; someone in the car park sees me balanced on the windowsill, presumes I'm going to jump and raises the alarm. So that goes well.

Over several more sessions, I am grilled over my home life and when my relationship with my parents is called into question I feel very angry. My parents are nothing to do with this.

Only, of course, they are; they are part of the bigger picture, but they certainly aren't to blame. I have collided with a disease that pretends to be my friend.

Anorexia is never your friend: it doesn't want to see you slim, healthy and happy, it wants to beat you, it locks you in a box and even though you know exactly where the key is, and how to use it, you refuse to help yourself.

And nobody talks about how mind-numbingly tedious it is to wake up and immediately think about not eating. But for a number of years not eating food is all I think about – don't eat this, don't touch that, don't even lick it. Don't, don't, don't, don't, don't.

Opportunity Lost

I go back to Old Lansdowne Road at the beginning of 1981. I'm in the final stretch of my drama school training and I have wasted so much of it.

At this point I don't have periods; this is a common side-effect of anorexia. The body simply goes into shutdown mode and refuses to allow you to fertilise an egg and develop a foetus when you're not eating enough to nurture yourself, never mind another human being. I am twenty and the last thing I think about is having babies, so I'm not fussed; it saves all that monthly hassle of buying tampons and when I see Frances's discarded wrappers in the bathroom bin, I smirk.

So here I am, emaciated and hairy. I have a strange relationship with a boy in the first year, who has bad skin but a sweet face. A lets me sleep on a camp bed in his flat and doesn't touch me; he is just really kind. Years later I catch sight of him in an episode of *Midsomer Murders*. I Google him and am glad to see that's he's doing OK.

I am still with the band, and I have recently scored my Equity card. Fran is at home when it comes through the post and sweetly she brings it along to the Gallery Wine Bar, where I am having a wee in one of the ladies' cubicles. She slips it under the door, and I feel weak with relief (and probably hunger, but I'm used to that). I celebrate by getting pissed and not having anything to eat, because I've spent all my calories on lager.

Prince Charles is going to marry Lady Diana Spencer in July 1981; she is younger than me and a virgin. The previous year, clocking that picture of her in the papers in a see-through dress, I think she has fat legs. Obviously she comes a cropper with an eating disorder, too, but not yet. First there is the wedding and the babies, then the madness and the sadness.

Cathy la Crème and the Rumbabas are rehearsing on the day of the wedding, but we stop and watch some of the ceremony on a small black and white telly in a hot attic flat. Diana's dress is ridiculous, and I can hear my mother saying it could do with a 'good iron', but I cannot find it in me to despise the royal family like everyone else seems to. I keep quiet about my family trip to the Palace. My political sensibilities are about as dormant as my reproductive organs.

Fran is seeing an older man; he's a historian (later to be a TV historian), he takes her out for dinner and who can blame her. Without me hanging around nibbling my tragic carrots, she can order what she likes and stuff her face until she has to unbutton her jeans.

We start to spend a lot of time avoiding each other.

The course at the poly isn't a degree course, so there are no third-year finals to fret about and I continue to make as little effort as usual. In any case, I've got my Equity card, so job done really.

Fact is, there is very little academia involved at the poly whatsoever. If you want a degree you need to do the drama course at the university down the road.

This is where Rik Mayall, Ade Edmondson and Ben Elton

met up some years previously. I don't know them, they are always 'before me'; in fact, the only one I ever really meet is Ade, who is delightful.

By 1982 the Comedy Store is already up and running in London, but I am safe in my Manchester bubble. No one is really doing that much better than me, apart from Victoria Wood, of course. I will be jealous of Victoria for my entire career and cannot believe it when she dies far too young.

I wish I had managed to crack her armadillo shell, but she kept her friendship circle close, and I don't think she thought much would become of me. She once commented in an article that most people on a bus wouldn't know who I was. She was right, just as she would be today, but it rankled. In the years since her death I have come to the conclusion that she was a genius and if you're going to be obscenely jealous of someone, then they might as well be worth it.

Victoria is doing a sketch show for Granada with Julie Walters. It's called *Wood and Walters*. I am at the peak of my anorexia, and I audition to play a role in a Miss World sketch, featuring loads of weird-looking women. Sensibly, Victoria doesn't see the joke in casting an obviously sick girl in a comedy sketch and I don't get the gig.

However, the band are offered a slot, and we troop down to Granada Studios, where we spend the day titting about before the recording in front of a studio audience. Victoria is too busy/shy to come and say hello, but Julie pops her head into the dressing room. She is a Manchester Poly alumna and jolly with it.

The other guest is an older woman in her seventies with mauve hair who plays a character called Phyllis Pearce in *Coronation Street*.

Jill Summers is fascinating; her father was a trapeze artist, and her half-brother is the father of the prime minister John Major. The British government are never far removed from comedy.

She sings a song about being a bus conductor and goes down a storm.

Cathy la Crème and the Rumbabas, on the other hand, die on our collective arses; the batteries run out on the drum machine and there are no spares to be found. We quickly rejig our set and perform something unrehearsed.

Part of the reason why Victoria is so brilliant is that she will not let her standards slip. We just aren't good enough. Snip: we are edited out of the programme.

It won't be the last time this happens to me, but it's gutting at the time.

To this day I still don't have a degree. I think I got a diploma from Manchester and, considering how little effort I made, I'm lucky to have that. However, I do have an honorary doctorate from Middlesex University, hahaha! Cue some stand-up!

Not as many perks as I thought – thought I'd be able to pop into my local chemist and order myself a load of drugs I've been wanting for ages, thought I'd be able to ask complete strangers to strip down to their underwear for me, but no, and apparently I'm not allowed to give mouth-to-mouth resuscitation to young men who basically don't need it. To be honest with you, I've been struck off.

Doors Opening /
Doors Closing

A s I approach the end of my three years at drama school, I need a headshot to send out to casting agents. A photographer comes to the school and takes a black and white photo of me looking suspicious against a tree.

I can remember exactly what I am wearing for this shoot. Under my denim jacket, my jumper is burgundy and hand-knitted. I have a pair of light purple enamel elephants in my ears (I've still got them) and out of shot I am wearing a baggy pair of children's camouflage trousers and a pair of plum-coloured ankle boots with a turn-down cuff.

I buy a lot of stamps, for this is the olden days way, and wait for the offers to come flooding in.

The first proposal is from a company that wants young people to be extras in a Pink Floyd video to accompany a new release called *The Wall*. I'm outraged: extra work! Who do they think I am? Well, judging by the finished video they obviously think I'm about twelve. All the kids who end up on screen are ten years younger than me. Ridiculous.

I get called in to meet the *Coronation Street* people and get

offered a part playing the girlfriend of a baddie who robs Brian
Tilsley's garage. This is a big deal. It's a location shoot, just one
last question: 'Can you drive?'

'No.'

'Oh, sorry, then you can't play this role.'

Fuck, shit and wank.

My father's attempts to teach me to drive from the age of
seventeen grind to a halt when he turns to me and says, 'Jenny,
I've taught brain-dead squaddies to drive armoured vehicles all
over the world, but there is no way you are ever going to learn
how to drive your mother's Mini. Now, please excuse me, I have
a migraine.'

As a consolation prize, the channel gives me a strange part in
a shit science fiction drama. I play Timmis, a time-traveller who
is entirely sprayed gold. I have to walk across a field in a big hat,
talking about protons and neutrons before getting shot. They
'shoot' me by tying a rope around my waist, instructing me to
walk across the field and then, without warning, pulling at the
rope and yanking me off my feet.

It goes on the CV.

More up my street is a character that I don't recall having an
actual name but is possibly referred to as 'Cackling Slag 1', in the
ITV musical *Visiting Day*, a Graham Fellows (Jilted John) vehicle.

I have a Polaroid of me sitting next to 'Cackling Slag 2', who,
on close inspection, turns out to be a very young Mrs Patmore
from *Downton Abbey* (aka the wonderful Lesley Nicol).

As per every drama school, before the end of our final term
we have our third-year 'showcase', a custom that continues to
this day. It's a kind of cattle market for wannabe actors to show
off their wares to the industry, by performing specially chosen
pieces for theatrical agents and casting directors. Ours is held in
London on an actual West End stage, which is a bit of a thrill.

All I remember of the monologue I perform is that it contains the line 'Oh, look behind the bushes, isn't that the postman fucking Princess Margaret?' I recall nothing else. I don't get an agent, but I do manage to nip into Top Shop, so all is not lost.

Drama school is over. I miss the last few weeks due to not being able to get out of bed. I don't turn up for any of the end-of-term celebrations. I don't think I am very well. Everything is coming undone.

2A Old Lansdowne Road is being sold. This is gutting news. Gradually the rooms empty out, until only Fran is left, determined to sit tight. 'They'll have to carry me out,' she insists, rolling a cigarette in our lovely kitchen. Her mother has recently been to visit: she is beautiful, too, and drinks gin out of an egg cup.

I move five minutes around the corner into a bland little self-contained bedsit with ensuite kitchenette and shared bathroom down the hall.

I want to live by myself, I want to give me and my anorexia more privacy. I will be able to manage it better by myself, without being watched like a hawk by people who actually care. Bye, Fran.

My eating disorder is like a lover. I prepare special meals to please them; my latest thing is to make a salad dressing out of low-calorie lime cordial. I no longer drink real milk; milk powder contains fewer calories. Sometimes, as a treat, I will spoon a mouthful of the dried stuff into my mouth. It's sort of a bit like ice cream.

A man sees me at a party. I am jumping on a bed very near an open window: it's the summer, the party is on the top floor, and as I begin to sail through the window he grabs at my petticoat. Fortunately I am wearing something a bit Victorian. He starts writing me poetry, inviting me to the ballet and buying me orchids. I'm overwhelmed. I can't tell if he is good-looking or satanic.

Lots of things are overwhelming right now. The price of

carrots has gone through the roof, and although I am still gigging with the band, I am increasingly on my own, literally. There is a New Year's Eve gig somewhere miles from anywhere and I am the only one to turn up in the snow. For the first time in my life, I perform my poems solo. The boys have fallen out and I don't know where Cath is. My course is over and the band is done for. Shit.

Possibly the highlight of our career was performing in the middle of Kendal Milne department store, in ladies' fashions just before Xmas, where we spent several hours being trampled by desperate late-night shoppers and being told off for swearing in front of children.

Occasionally I take myself off on an adventure. One night I sleep with a man whose marriage is unhappy, largely because his wife keeps a pickled onion under her pillow to suck on when she gets the urge. Everyone has their own story.

To earn extra money I clean a wealthy alcoholic's house. He could be in his sixties but is probably younger; his face is very dry and red, and I have to clean very quietly because he is always hungover. My job is to find the booze he has hidden around the house and pour it down the sink, and to throw away the meals he has left to burn in the oven. I take a plastic bag and squirrel some of the bottles home with me, clanking as I leave.

The unlikeliest thing to happen next is also the reason why I will vacate Manchester.

At the beginning of the eighties there is a new and short-lived non-mainstream newspaper in Manchester called *The Flash* and its owners have their fingers in pies.

Considering I never have my fingers in a pie, I need these people, because these are the kind of people who have projects on the go.

One of these projects is to manufacture a young female pop star – think Toyah (punk) crossed with Kate Bush (theatrical big-eyed whimsy) with a bit of Nico (um, you know, just Nico) thrown in.

This is the problem: they don't really know what they want, but they want me to be it.

I am twenty-one, I can't feed myself, but I want to be famous. I go along with it.

They pay for a recording studio and technicians, and there is talk of stylists and being dressed like a Pierrot doll, even though Leo Sayer has already been there, done that.

The idea is that I will go into the recording studio, pop on a pair of headphones and record a brand-new eighties version of the Kinks' 'Tired of Waiting', while on the other side of the glass partition the moneymen and studio bosses clap each other on the back, drink beer and light each other's fags.

There is only one question they have forgotten to ask: 'Can you sing?'

The answer becomes apparent when I fail to be able to count myself in. I don't understand what they mean by 'four bars'. No worry, I can come in on a physical cue. The music starts again, it could be 'My Old Man's a Dustman' for all I know. There is white noise in my head, as if I am standing under Niagara Falls. A man waves his arm, I start, and as I sing I watch as the faces on the other side of the glass begin to laugh and then stop laughing when they realise how very badly wrong this has gone.

I am bundled out of the building and unceremoniously dropped home.

I mentally start packing that night. I cannot stay in this city.

Caaaaamberwell

I arrive in south London in the spring of 1982, around the time the Falklands War kicks off. I can't say it bothers me; my head is so tightly wedged up my own arse that I might as well be in a coma when it comes to global and political events.

Meanwhile, back in Manchester, things are about to get interesting with the opening of the Hacienda. Trust me to miss that.

I go and stay with my school friend Jane, who lives in a council flat on the Tulse Hill Estate and goes to Camberwell Art School. Apparently, there are always rooms to rent advertised on the school noticeboard. I jot down a few numbers and simultaneously take down a card asking for life models. I've done a bit of life modelling in Manchester, both for the art college and for a few evening 'gentlemen's photography clubs', held in church halls and Scout huts, where men with shaky hands would ask me to pose with an inflatable beach ball. Being a very thin girl, I think I was a source of disappointment to some of these photographers, none of whom seemed to be able to breathe easily down their noses. But art schools love a bit of bone and Camberwell is more than happy to employ me. And so I regularly pitch up, ditch my kit and loll about. Sometimes I'm asked to stand but I tell them my circulation is poor and, ideally, I need to be sitting or preferably lying down with an electric bar fire in close proximity. They are very accommodating. Occasionally nowadays I think about all these paintings: surely some must survive in the attics of Camberwell, pictures of a twentysomething me, like Dorian Gray in reverse.

I make friends with the girl who runs the bar. Liza is dark and beautiful with an unpronounceable surname; she is also a shit-hot painter and still is today. Check her out at @lizaadamczewski on Twitter and Instagram.

For a while I have a room in a dismal flat on Lyndhurst Grove. The couple who own it are South African and both are mean-spirited and unattractive. They have a living room which I'm not allowed to use, but just in case I should stray out of bounds they put a lock on the phone.

What they don't put a lock on is the bathroom door and the ugly man is forever walking in on me. I cannot imagine this being about sexual titillation – I have the breasts of an eleven-year-old – it's about power and being weird. I am already really struggling with a bad eating lapse, i.e. barely eating anything, and when I realise he has been in my underwear drawer I lose my appetite completely.

My sister lives fifteen minutes away, in Herne Hill. She has a three-bedroom Edwardian house with the name 'Ebeneezer' spelt out in stained glass above the front door. I desperately want her to ask if I'd like to come and stay, just until I find my feet. She even has a cleaning woman. But she doesn't, and I refuse to beg. To be honest, I don't blame her. I wouldn't want me either. I'm a fucking nightmare, I don't eat and I smoke constantly.

Things perk up when I get a job in the wine bar down the road. Bartholomew's has recently been refurbished and it's all reclaimed church pews and vintage tables. Apparently Cliff Richard has already been in for supper and at some point I serve Princess Margaret's daughter, whatsername, Lady Sarah

Chatto (extremely polite), who is studying at the art school, and the local MP Harriet Harman (delightful) also drops in now and then.

For a moment it feels like Camberwell is on the up, a trick she will attempt to pull off many, many times in the forty-odd years I've lived here.

Let me try and explain Camberwell and my stupid loyalty to a place that is in the middle of London and yet doesn't have a tube station.

Camberwell is in the south London borough of Southwark and is the less well-known sister to Brixton and Peckham. In the old days you'd hail a cab in the West End and they would refuse to come south of the river, because according to cabbies (back then) no one in south London had any money and they'd never get a fare going back into town. Hmmm, tish tosh.

Camberwell is home to one of the finest roads in London: Camberwell Grove is a plane-tree-lined Georgian beauty and in its eighties heyday the Grove pub was where everyone who was anyone/wanted to be someone/to sleep with someone/to sleep with someone who wanted to be someone hung out.

In fact, there are pockets of loveliness all over Camberwell, and as for Peckham, far from being a high-rise hellhole, it's home to some spectacular houses overlooking the Rye, where, of course, William Blake saw his angel, which doesn't surprise me: he'd probably had a few pints in the Grove.

Camberwell has been my home since 1982. I'm allowed to slag her off (she is very much a she), but, much like my sister, if anyone else dares criticise her I won't stand for it.

Camberwell has a library, a swimming pool, an art school, the South London Gallery, King's College Hospital complete with helipad, a park with a massive paddling pool, tennis courts, a summer aerial school and a tree trunk carved into a massive whale. It also has Denmark Hill railway station (Victoria in eight mins) and one of the leading psychiatric institutions in the whole wide world, the Maudsley, thank you very much.

It may not have a tube station, but Camberwell is on some of the best bus routes in the world. Dear readers/listeners, I give you the 176, from Tottenham Court Road to Penge. Sit on the top deck, obviously.

SE5 is where Boris Johnson and Carrie thing attempted to bed down for a while in 2019, and the neighbours reported them for a domestic. Once upon a time I lived around the corner; the local Brunswick Park had a resident albino squirrel and two of my all-time favourite pieces of graffiti were nearby: 'Sex? Shag my mum!' (complete with correct grammar) and, in massive capitals painted on a wall, 'LIZA MINELLI EATS TOO MUCH TAGLIATELLE'.

Beat that, Hampstead.

More than forty years later I still live in the same postcode.

Finding My Feet

I sort of hate London, which is a massive disappointment, because I expect to love it. In some respects, moving to London is a bit like having a baby: the first few weeks are terrifying, it's demanding and expensive and so tiring and you don't know what you're doing, and you don't know why you ever bothered, but you can't just pack it in because what would everyone say?

But gradually it gets better and one day you're on a bus crossing the Thames, you're sitting on the top deck and the sun is shining, the river sparkles and suddenly the skyline makes sense. There's St Paul's and the National Theatre, and that's the back of the Savoy and this is my stop for getting off to go to work and this is where I live now.

Things really start to improve for me in south London when, while waitressing in Bartholomew's Wine Bar, I meet Ruth. Ruth is a tall, very beautiful Black girl with bad posture. She really needs to put her shoulders back, but won't. Ruth doesn't walk, she lopes, she is very tall, shaves her head and is married to the singer Joe Jackson. The marriage doesn't last, and later Jackson will refer to it as 'a disaster', which is rude if you ask me.

Joe is an unlikely pop star. He has two massive chart hits under his belt, 'It's Different for Girls' and 'Is She Really Going

Out With Him?', which is, coincidentally, something people might have said about him and Ruth. Let's just say, looks-wise Joe is punching way above his weight.

It's the summer of 1982 and Joe is touring the States. Ruth lives with a fat resident cat called Rip Torn in a two-bedroom flat littered with dope roaches on Camberwell's premier street, Camberwell Grove. The flat is on the third floor and is decorated in slightly depressing dark sand colours; there are gold discs on the wall and the place is a tip.

I adore Ruth, but she is chaotic and at times her unhappiness and messy family background make her hard to deal with. I am used to being the nutty, needy one. There can't be two of us.

My parents come to visit, and Ruth gets nervous. She decides to relax in the bath, only to emerge an hour later, with a hand towel around her waist and a joint hanging from her bottom lip. I think I hear my father mutter 'Crikey Moses'.

Ruth is an incredible singer herself. She gets a band together, knocks everyone off their feet, features on the front cover of *Time Out* and seems poised to rival Joe. But it all falls apart and we lose touch.

I wish I'd been a better friend, but I was out of my depth, I had my own career to fight for.

Ruth lives in Melbourne now. I bumped into her once while I was doing the Comedy Festival. These days she is a brilliant and beautiful jazz singer, who also performs a Nina Simone tribute show. She is still a raving beauty, but I'm not sure if she has ever learned to put her shoulders back.

I live in Joe and Ruth's spare room. It used to be Joe's dressing room; he may have done some cross-dressing, as there are some huge size 11 stilettoes in the wardrobe. I couldn't care less: I'm out of the real weirdos' house, it's the eighties, everyone is interesting and everyone is experimenting, and a lot of young people on the street look like they could be on their way to a fancy-dress party.

I hang out with 'Liza unspellable surname' from Camberwell School of Art and her friends in the Grove. The place is heaving most nights. One of my casual Grove pick-ups, who I spend a night innocently snogging, is a very young Tim Roth, later to become Mr Orange in Tarantino's *Reservoir Dogs*.

My eating is still very erratic, and I don't seem to be getting any acting work, even though I keep sending out those CVs, so I get another bar job. It's summer and there is a basement wine bar in Covent Garden's piazza called the Crusting Pipe, which, should you ever choose to visit, still exists!

In '82, they open an upstairs section, with seating outdoors under the stone colonnades. We serve a limited menu: a cream tea, scones, jam and clotted cream; a ham or cheese ploughman's with individual cottage loaf; or a pint of prawns, with mayonnaise and a lemon-wedge finger bowl on the side. Oh, and we also do cheesecake, which I remember being huge in the eighties. Literally, they arrive in boxes, uncut and as big as bicycle wheels.

I find the trays very heavy because I weigh the same as a pint of prawns. I am also very disapproving of customers who have pudding on top of their ploughman's. Such uncontrollable piggy greed, I think, wishing I could somehow land face down in the black cherry cheesecake.

In the early eighties Covent Garden as a tourist attraction is in its infancy. There is still a fruit and veg market, tucked to one side, boys bouncing wooden barrows off the cobbles, gutters full of cabbage leaves and split tomatoes.

But the place is gradually being taken over by trendy hair salons, bars and clubs. Down on Long Acre there is an American vintage clothing store called Flip where I buy most of my tiny clothes. Fashion is a moveable feast in the eighties. It's hard to pin down any one look: there are influences from all sorts of eras, fifties quiffs, Teddy Boys and prom dresses, Hawaiian surf dudes, and the new City boys with red braces. As the decade marches on, there will be the Sloane Rangers, girls in pie-crust collars and Laura Ashley skirts, versus the sharp-suited shoulder-pad brigade.

I just want to wear whatever Keren, Siobhan and Sara in Bananarama are wearing. I do my best on my waitress's wages and in homage to the girls start wearing a big red bow in my hair. Occasionally I pop into the newly opened Whistles, which is a neighbour of the Crusting Pipe, but I can't afford anything. Sometimes I really worry about my future. This isn't how it's meant to be. What if nothing ever happens?

One summer morning I am walking down Camberwell Grove to catch a bus into Covent Garden when a pair of ankles and a car catch my eye. The ankles are narrow and tanned, the owner is wearing deck shoes and the car, as I later find out, is a vintage racing Porsche, the exact same model as the one James Dean was driving when he was killed.

The ankles poking out from under the car belong to a thin man; you have to be thin to be able to slide under an old Porsche. He wriggles out and our eyes meet. I shoot him my best flirty come-hither look and sashay down to the bus stop.

Over the next week or so, I keep bumping into him. He seems to live in a white house with a blue front door and rather grand pillars further down the road. He will need a hell of a lot of persuading to eventually let me move in.

This is Geof

The man pitches up at the Covent Garden wine bar one lunchtime. Philippa, a friend from Manchester, has joined me as a fellow Crusting Pipe waitress and, as she moves off to serve him, I physically hold her back. 'Table six is mine,' I hiss. 'I love him, and I'm going to marry him and have his babies.'

I have always been part witch.

Later, he tells me that he followed me. Ha!

He asks me what I'm doing there, and I reply, 'Waitressing, for my sins.' He probably ordered the ham ploughman's; he certainly wouldn't have had the prawns. By the time I've given him his bill we have arranged to meet that night. I'm waitressing again, but at Bartholomew's; he offers to come in around ten, wait for me to finish up and walk me home, so that's nice.

Somewhere, in the lock-up of shame where all our shit is stored, is a bill in my handwriting for that night. He pays for 'a gl of hse red, one fr bread and ch and a bottle of Soave to take out'. Hahaha, got him.

We go back to his place.

He is older, divorced from his wife, with no children, but he has this flat which he bought as a complete wreck just a couple of years ago. Apparently the previous owners kept Alsatians, and when these dogs covered the carpet in shit, the owners just put another carpet on top. When eventually all the layers of carpet made it impossible to open and shut the doors, they took down the doors and cut several inches off the bottoms.

The flat has been restored to its beautiful Georgian bones, the shit sandwich carpets are gone, the floorboards are bare, in fact the whole flat is very bare; there is a small kitchen and bathroom, a huge sitting room, an entrance hall big enough for a dining table and two bedrooms.

I am twenty-two, he is thirty-three, and I know instinctively that this is the man I need.

He is less sure.

I will just have to work on him.

There is bad news further up the road. Joe is coming back from tour and it's time I moved on. I can't move in with Geof, it's too soon, even though I'd bite his hand off if he offered.

For a while I live on a shelf in a room with no natural light; it's essentially a large cupboard in a flat down the road. I share with a builder/musician called Drew, who I would probably throw my hat at, if not for the fact that he has a girlfriend commonly known as 'luscious thing', and because of my relationship with Geof, of course. If I'm going to risk fucking that up, I'm not going to do it with someone who lives literally ten doors down.

Drew is friends with Paul Young. I think he occasionally plays/writes music with him, and we have a fabulous long garden which is great for parties, but I can't live on a shelf forever.

Come on, Geof.

Geof refuses to cave in. His ex-wife swiped all his money and nabbed an Edward Wadsworth painting while she was at it, so if she's reading this, can we have it back, please? It's worth a lot of money and you didn't pay for it.

Fortunately, I've made a new friend at the wine bar. Claire is a six-foot part-time catwalk model. She doesn't do editorial because her teeth aren't great on account of the speed, but she does the international live shows. She has a sexy photographer boyfriend with motorbike and biker boots, and she persuades Southwark Council to give her/us a two-bedroom council flat. OK, so she may have told them she was in an abusive relationship and she may have gone to a meeting with a faked black eye, but this is the eighties: it's dog eat dog, we're twenty-two, the girl is resourceful and I really like her.

We're on the thirteenth floor of the Castlemead Estate on Camberwell Road – from our kitchen and bedrooms you can see St Paul's. The flat is a maisonette with the bedrooms and bathroom on one floor and the kitchen and living room above. It's a great flat and it would be almost perfect if the lift wasn't forever out of order and if we had enough money to buy any furniture. I sleep in a sleeping bag on a camp bed and I have three other pieces of furniture in my bedroom, a clothes rail, a pink aluminium hostess trolley and a Perspex display unit designed for cakes, which would once have sat on a counter in a café. I put my pants and socks in the cake dispenser and Geof comes round to help me paint the room a soft grey. This is when I think he may take pity on me and invite me back to his to stay forever. He doesn't.

I basically move in with Geof by stealth. It's like *The Great Escape* in reverse: a spare toothbrush in his bathroom one week, low-calorie mayo in the fridge the next. Gradually I smuggle in some underwear and a few changes of clothing. He barely notices it. Ha.

One day there is a massive old mahogany chest of drawers for sale outside the Grove pub. I bagsy it and buy some blokes a pint each to carry it over the road and round the difficult staircase into Geof's flat. It was a bargain, I insist. I'm like a dog marking my territory. The chest is soon full.

Geof has a job like a grown-up. He is the art director of the *TV Times*, he has a sizeable income, the Porsche and a collection of expensive shoes. He buys his suits from Kenzo, Paul Smith and a shop in Covent Garden called Two Zebras. He is possibly the most civilised person I have ever met. He wears white shirts and wide fifties ties, he went to art school and had a meteoric but sadly briefly successful career as a sculptor in the seventies, with an exhibition at the Hayward, among other galleries. But when a show in America goes horribly wrong, his confidence crumbles and, with a wife to support, he decides to get a proper job with the *TV Times* as a graphic designer.

There are perks: he gets a fistful of luncheon vouchers every week and we spend them on cocktails in Rumours cocktail bar and rotisserie chickens from Europa on the King's Road, the only supermarket to open on a Sunday in the early eighties.

At some point the Porsche is taken to a garage off the Walworth Road; it needs extensive repairs which will take weeks. During a manoeuvre of cars, so that more cars can be squeezed onto the lot, Geof's pride and joy is left out on the street for a couple of hours and a lorry reverses into it, smashing it to smithereens. It isn't insured and the tax disc is out of date. Geof gets a fine, the car is a write-off and it's the first time I ever see him cry.

I'm not sure if he'd cry now if I got backed over by a lorry, but I like to think he would squeeze the odd tear out!

I get to find out more about Geof once I inveigle my way into his flat. He loved his father very much, but he had a catastrophic stroke and died 'a vegetable' (as people genuinely used to say) at sixty-two, with a locked desk full of bills. He doesn't like his mother, who is manipulative, with a spiteful streak.

When I first meet Marge, I encounter a sweet little old lady complete with knitting bag and puzzle books, but I soon realise there is a deep current of fury and bitterness swirling around that innocuous little frame. But who can blame her? It takes Geof a long time to tell me that once upon a time he was one of three brothers but two died of diphtheria within weeks of each other.

I don't like Geof's mother, and I am relieved when she dies, but I can never blame her for her rage. Anyone who loses two children has every right to hate the world and everyone in it. Especially yet another woman who is threatening to take her only remaining son away again.

The boys' deaths are not spoken of when Geof is growing up. To this day he is vague about their names but thinks one of them was a Charles. But I don't think that's true, because his own middle name is Charles and parents just don't do that.

The polite thing to do back in the fifties is to sweep such tragedies under the carpet. Women miscarry, lose babies and their sons and daughters to disease and accidents and are expected to button their lips and get on with it. It's just as bad for the men, for the daddies, but olden-days men have to do their screaming silently.

About fifteen years ago I found a black and white photograph of Geof and his brothers. They are on a beach, Geof is the youngest, still in bib and braces, his brothers are in shorts, they are all grinning, one has sticky-out ears and looks extra cheeky.

We put it in a frame. It's the saddest photo, but it's important to remember those children and to understand how grief can poison you, especially when no one has ever allowed you to let that poison out.

Alternative Comedy in the Eighties – A Quick Guide

Before I start banging on about how I finally begin to elbow my way into performing, I need to explain what was going on with live comedy in the early eighties. You can skip this chapter if this kind of detail bores you, but for the comedy nerd it might be interesting.

Basically, the early eighties comedy scene in London is in a state of flux. Alternative cabaret has been invented, although some would prefer the tag 'New Variety', but no one really knows what it means.

The one thing for certain is that the old-fashioned comic (99 per cent of them male), the kind of guy who tells generic gags, which he may or may not have written, is being squeezed out by a new wave of comics, who tend not to wear a dinner jacket and frilly shirt while cracking one-liners about 'Pa*is' (disclaimer: not every seventies club comic).

Weirdly, I feel strangely guilty now about the sneery dismissal of the old-school club comic by my generation. Many were highly skilled working-class blokes, just trying to make a living. We are all products of our time, and there are social and political reasons for all those naff mother-in-law jokes (post-war veterans with no jobs being forced to live with the wife's family, with inevitable results), while a great deal of the racist crap was a reflection of a vile racist society and based on utter ignorance.

I have no doubt that many of these blokes weren't complete arseholes, but things had to change. I just wish we hadn't been quite so smug about it.

The Comedy Store, with its iconic laughing logo, opens in a Soho strip joint in 1979 and is monopolised by Alexei Sayle and the *Comic Strip* mob for a couple of years, until it moves premises, at which point the *Comic Strip* gang slip seamlessly into telly, launching the careers of (among others) French and Saunders, Ade Edmondson, Rik Mayall and Ben Elton.

Ex-Cambridge Footlights member Sandi Toksvig, although not part of *The Comic Strip*, also performed on the very first night of the Comedy Store; by 1982, she has been snatched up by the kids' telly show *No. 73*, which is massively popular and launches Sandi into a lifelong career of performing, writing and presenting.

Meanwhile, over in a basement in Leicester Square, the new Comedy Store opens its doors to anyone who has the guts to get onstage and battle it out with the audience, the resident 'very shouty' compère (Alexei Sayle) and a gong. The gong is used to 'gong' people off.

I steer clear of the club for a while. I am twenty-two and a bit chicken. I think maybe I'm a performance poet rather than a straight stand-up. I'm not sure I have the stomach for a gong show-style venue. In any case, once French and Saunders have exited the club scene into telly land, the number of women performing on the London comedy circuit in 1982 is literally in single figures, which begs the question, are we actually welcome?

Fortunately, the Store isn't the only venue in town, but, whatever the club, audiences genuinely aren't used to seeing women onstage and yet Victoria Wood has made it onto telly, despite never touching the London circuit. Victoria is massively popular from the off; how weird, then, that there is this massive mistrust of other female comics. This will continue for years.

The women most likely to turn up on a bill in those early London club days are Helen Lederer (specialising in tortured middle-class anxiety), Jenny Lecoat (usually described as 'feminist with a guitar') and me, 'the Camberwell Cupcake' (according to *Time Out*).

Helen and Jenny are the two faces I encounter most regularly on the circuit, not that we ever play the same bill. In those early days, having two female performers on the same night just isn't done. I think the assumption is that everyone, including the audience, would suddenly start menstruating.

What often gets forgotten is that there are a number of other women making a name for themselves in the eighties, not necessarily as stand-ups. There is a healthy spoken word/poetry circuit, which I crash and meet the current queen, pink-haired, tattooed Joolz Denby (known simply as Joolz), who I'm a teeny bit scared of, even though she is always very sweet to me.

Meanwhile, the posh end of the cabaret circuit, i.e. the more esoteric venues, small theatres, private parties, etc., is ruled over, quite rightly, by the ubiquitous Fascinating Aïda, masterminded by the invincible Dillie Keane.

Many years later I will work with Dillie on two *Grumpy Old Women* shows and adore watching her perform every night. She is not only a great musical turn, she is also a fabulous physical clown. During one of the shows, we perform a sketch about getting drunk at a party, which Dillie beautifully embroiders by miming a dropped sausage roll getting lost down the cavity of her cleavage and trying to get it out, and it's a nightly masterclass.

These days, when articles are written about eighties pioneers of female comedy, Dillie and Fascinating Aïda are frequently *not* mentioned, which is outrageous.

Other names are forgotten, too. Some fall by the wayside
(neglected into oblivion), others choose to opt out. You can only
bang your head against a brick wall for so long. It's hard to look
back and correctly assess exactly what was going on. All I know
is that it was tough, but no one stopped you from trying. At
twenty-two, I am both very lazy and very driven. Deep down, I
believe I belong onstage.

Leaving aside the gender imbalance, what the eighties circuit
does provide for the punter is an extraordinary smorgasbord of
cheap entertainment.

There is a healthy crossover of street acts wanting to come
indoors, a bit of juggling, some spoken word and lots of clever
female musical acts such as the Flatlettes and the Fabulous
Singlettes, glammed-up girls putting a comedy twist on old classics, and groups like Denise Black and the Kray Sisters, including
Josie Lawrence, who is still ripping up the Store on Sunday
nights with the improv group the Comedy Store Players almost
forty years on.

Also knocking around are the brilliantly named a cappella
close harmony singing group Sensible Footwear. Three women
in Doc Martens stomping their own political comedy furrow,
before buggering off to Canada in the nineties. I'm really sorry if
I've missed anyone out: obviously more comedy chicks arrive as
the decade moves on but these are the early eighties faces that
spring to mind when I think back to those days.

OK, now that I've got that out of my system, let's get back
to me.

Will You Please Welcome...

J ust as I can't live on a shelf forever, I cannot be a waitress forever.

In 1982, rather than risk the bear-baiting pit of the Store, I answer an ad in the back of the *Stage* asking for 'novelty acts' for a pub gig in Wimbledon. I am booked, unseen, by phone.

These are the pre-internet days and being new to London and its complex transport system, I set off just after lunch. The first thing that strikes me is how posh Wimbledon is. It's a bit like going on a very short holiday to another land.

Geof agrees to come and pick me up; he doesn't want to come in and watch, he is too nervous. I'm relieved. I don't think my material is his cup of tea. To be honest he's still not entirely convinced.

I am beside myself with nerves, but at the same time I feel a weird sense of bravado because I have nothing to lose. I will become more anxious in later years, when the stakes get higher and the failures hurt more.

I wear one of my vintage black cocktail dresses and read a handful of poems out of a large notebook.

Most venues at this time don't have mics and I am forced

to yell my material into the crowd, gurning and using my very northern performance poetry voice. In my fifteen-minute repertoire is the classic 'Tits', which goes like this:

Tits

I've got this problem,
With my figure,
My tits will not get any bigger.
A 36 D cup is my dream.
I've done the exercises, bought the cream,
Whatever I do, they won't expand,
I reckon I've got a retarded gland . . .

There is another verse, but I'll spare you.

I share a stage with a mime act called The Great Smell of Brut, and Gertrude Shilling, a posh woman in her seventies, whose son is the milliner David Shilling. David is famous for making his mother the most extraordinary hats which she wears to Ascot. Gertrude comes on stage with a selection of her hats, chats and sings some songs.

It's what you might call an eclectic evening.

I do OK, and luckily for me a chap who has recently opened a new performance space in a room above a pub is in the audience. Colin Watkeys runs the Finborough Arms with his then girlfriend Nica Burns. The venue is used both for theatre and comedy. Nica is an actress, but in the future she will ditch those dreams and concentrate on directing and producing.

Today she co-owns six West End theatres and is the powerhouse behind the Edinburgh Festival Comedy Awards. Over the decades that follow, our paths will cross many times.

The Finborough Arms still operates as a fifty-seat fringe theatre. Every time I drive past, I can visualise myself climbing the stairs at the back of the pub, into the venue and round to the kitchen, where I would get changed into my gig frock next to a deep-fat fryer. I seem to spend a lot of time getting changed next to reeking deep-fat fryers and being terrorised by manky big-balled pub dogs which are the wrong side of 'protective'.

During these early days of alternative comedy, the spirit of the music hall is very apparent on most bills and it's rare to see five stand-ups one after another. Forty years ago, the shows are very mixed; alongside the straight comic, an audience might see some poetry, a bit of magic and a novelty act.

I love a good novelty act and some of my favourites over the decades include Hugh Jelly, who would lie down naked except for his pants over a washing-up bowl full of water, before standing up with the bowl somehow suctioned onto his big pink tummy and making an extravagant bow, while wearing a big ladies' shower cap.

Later on, I work a lot with Woody Bop Muddy, an ex-art student who performs an act called 'Record Graveyard', which goes down a storm at university gigs. Basically, Woody would buy a load of naff LPs at car boot fairs and jumble sales and play a track on a portable record player while the crowd bayed 'Save it' or 'Nail it'.

If more people shouted 'Nail it', the record would be smashed up and nailed to a wooden stake. Maybe you had to be there.

I don't manage to cross paths with Julian Clary while he is performing as Gillian Pie-Face but I work a lot with him when he morphs onto the circuit as The Joan Collins Fanclub, a double act with his Jack Russell sidekick Fanny the Wonder Dog. Julian is stunning, sweet and hilarious. He wears a great deal of primary coloured latex with bondage trimmings. Soon after we meet, he gives me a copy of Armistead Maupin's *Tales of the City* and I still have a rubber Fanny the Wonder Dog brooch. I think Julian is the first to get into 'merchandise'!

There don't seem to be as many novelty acts around as there

once were; maybe this has something to do with the dwindling number of street performers? I'm not sure; all I know is that it's a long time since I've seen anyone shove a firework up their bum, light it and proceed to sing 'There's No Business Like Show Business' à la Chris 'The Piss' Lynam.

I dunno, health and safety have got a lot to answer for.

That said, I don't want to be the kind of old fart who says comedy isn't what it used to be – it's better. More people have a voice, the audiences are more comedy savvy and there is space again for all the weirdos and oddballs. I think it just went through a phase in the nineties when it became very corporate, very booted and suited and a lot of people who didn't have comedy in their bones came into the industry to make a great deal of money out of it.

But let's not race ahead. It's the early eighties, I'm getting my gigs by writing to and calling clubs direct, but word of mouth has always been the original social media and, considering the circuit is pretty small at this time, it's quite easy to become a regular face.

My early material is rude: I am probably one of the rudest performers doing the rounds. I genuinely don't set out to shock; being potty-mouthed isn't a conscious decision, it's just what comes naturally.

I perform poems about my tits, having an itchy fanny (the classics) and, of course, sex:

Soiled

Did the earth move for you,
He asked
As they lay
Post coitally curled together,
In the digger
Of a JCB.

The Party's Over

(I used to perform this staggering about the stage,
pretending to be very pissed indeed)

The party's over
And I don't give a toss,
If nobody fancied me, that's their loss.
I didn't come here just to pull a bloke,
It's not really worth it, for a one-off poke.
Anyway, with a bellyful of ale, their efforts are a joke,
All that grunting and a groanin', you think they're
      gonna croak.
Celibacy, it's a new way of life,
One easy way of ending all that strife, of will he or
      won't he and can he stand the pace,
And he remembers your name but not your face.
So I'll go home now, throw up in the sink,
Put my pyjamas on and have a hot milky drink,
Jump into bed, all on my tod and think,
Oh God, isn't life a sod.

Later on, I write a very long poem, called 'Neville and the
Breville', about a man who bites into a cheese toastie and burns
his mouth so badly he has to have a skin graft from his arse, resulting in him being the only man I knew to have authentic 'bum
fluff' on his chin.
      Me: 'I'll see if I can find it.'
      Book editor: 'Don't bother.'
      Me: 'Oh, OK.'

One of my biggest challenges is fathoming out the magic formula
of venue address, the A–Z map of London and public transport.
I'm not sure which is tougher, writing new material or arriving

at the gig in one piece, on time and not in tears. To this day I am still hideously early for shows. I can't stand being late and I'm forever grateful for the invention of the mobile phone and satnav.

One night I am mugged on Clapham Pavement by two men, who each put an arm through mine and sort of carry me down a back alley, where they punch me in the head and steal not only my handbag but my gig bag, too, the one containing my lucky dress, lucky shoes and lucky (unwashed since Manchester) fishnet tights. Hmm, maybe they weren't so lucky after all.

This is one of the very few acts of violence that I encounter in over forty years of performing,

Sex on the Circuit and How it Changed

I happen to write this chapter the week following the Russell Brand revelations on Channel 4's *Dispatches* and in *The Times*. Am I shocked or surprised? No: the name and accusations have been circulating for years.

However, during the rumour years, before the story actually breaks, I'm not entirely convinced. Maybe like my mother I'm prone to giving people the benefit of the doubt. There is a slight element of fabrication surrounding the gossip, a little bit like the old rumour that Prince Harry is James Hewitt's son (spoiler: he isn't).

But when Brand disappears almost entirely from our screens (both large and small) about five years ago, I am more suspicious.

Because that's not how careers work, not for men, especially not for men under fifty who still look OK, if a bit ridiculous and eternally fossilised in some Jack Sparrow/land of Johnny Depp aftershave ad.

The Brand rumours echo the pattern of allegations that circulated around Phillip Schofield for years: the whispered tittle-tattle about dressing-room 'shenanigans' (as my grandmother would have put it). These went hand in hand with other rumours, including the one about the household name who quite possibly doesn't write his extensive range of very lucrative books.

Maybe between writing this and being published, more famous dominoes will fall?

Certainly, younger women in my industry have stories to tell, and I believe them.

There is currently a list of predatory men on the comedy circuit whose names are shared among performers who might be at risk, plus a WhatsApp group originally created in 2018, called the 'Home Safe Collective'. Originally set up to help women get home safely from the Edinburgh Fringe, HSC has gone on to share information about sleazeball promoters, dodgy performers and anyone else you might need to watch out for while attempting to make a living.

I am not included in this WhatsApp group. There are perks to being a ferocious sixty-four-year-old woman; as I currently joke onstage, 'men don't want to get in my knickers any more, but they'll have a crack at my bank account'. I'm more likely to be scammed these days than touched up.

Creeps don't fancy me, and therefore I don't get hassled: not that I ever did really, not even when I was really young and a great deal more vulnerable.

In hindsight, this seems odd, and I've racked my brains to try and understand why. Here's what I've come up with.

When I first start gigging in the early eighties, all my jobs are live gigs in pubs and clubs. I am a small blonde woman in my early twenties, I am cute and there are photos to prove this. And yet there is no one that I work with in those early days who makes me feel sexually uncomfortable.

I am often uncomfortable in dressing rooms for different reasons, mostly because I feel self-conscious about whether I'm funny enough to be there, among all these blokes who are casually telling jokes and being witty, seemingly without effort. My tongue seems thick in my mouth, and I feel like I'm choking on my own unfunniness. To relax, I smoke my head off, drink lager, laugh along and make the occasional quip (pre-rehearsed in my head), basking in pleasure when anyone listens and laughs. 'I can keep my head above water,' I tell myself. 'I can, I can.'

The great thing about being new to an industry that in itself is very new is that there is yet to be a hierarchy. For a while I rarely encounter anyone who seems to be pulling ahead of the pack. None of us are famous . . . yet.

In the future, some of us will be, some of us won't (so much talent crumbles to dust) and some of us will almost get there but be constantly mistaken for Su Pollard (me). It's when the big bucks flood the business that some people start abusing their power and position, but in the early eighties the world of live 'alternative comedy' is an amateur's game. It's run by enthusiasts; the world of promoters and agents has yet to crowd in. We compete, but it's just for whoever is sitting in the audience on the night.

Most of the male stand-ups are very ordinary-looking: Paul Merton performs in his pyjamas, Mark Steel wears a shirt and a crewneck jumper and looks like his mum got him ready for the gig. Comedy is a refuge for misfits and the unemployable, everyone is skint and travels by bus and tube. I write a joke about how getting off with a male comic would probably involve going back to his flat and changing the newspaper in a budgie cage.

The idea of it being sexy is a joke in itself, but, over time, this changes and comics start looking sulky and having cheekbones and interesting hair and, before you know it, comedy is the new rock and roll.

This is a phrase coined when David Baddiel and Rob Newman play Wembley in 1993. Incidentally, I have a ringside seat at this gig and wear a massive pink fake-fur jacket and watch, appalled, as the massive audience decides to turn against the support act, who is Sean Lock. Sean has a horrible time and I feel pissed off on his behalf. It's a myth that there is no such thing as a bad audience: this lot are a bunch of twats, until the headliners appear.

But all that is almost a decade down the line; for now, it's the early eighties and all is cosy. It's a world of lager and fags, the coke and ego combo which will be so prevalent in the nineties has yet to kick off and stand-up gigs are still listed under the theatre section of *Time Out*.

Very soon we will have our own cabaret and comedy corner and our heads will start swelling and telly will come sniffing and then things will get a little meaner, but for most of the eighties I can hand on heart say that no one propositioned me, backed me into a corner or tried so much as even to snog me, certainly not against my wishes.

There is definitely a new breed of sexy stand-up, who might be in it for the fame and the shags, but I still believe that comedy attracts the oddballs and freaks. Case in point: the number of comics who have recently been diagnosed with ADHD or autism is huge. I think it always was.

I tried to do an online quiz to check my own neurodiversity but got bored and distracted halfway through and never finished it. In all seriousness, I am not on the spectrum, I just hate filling in forms.

What has to be admitted when talking about comedy and sex is the appeal of the funny man: funny men are sexy, we all know that funny men can laugh your knickers off and I've watched men live on stage who I wouldn't give a second look to in a pub and felt my loins stir. Even now, when, to be honest with you, I'm chalk from the waist down, or 'half woman, half Rennie' as I say onstage.

But I'm not sure women comics have the same magnetic pull.

What I do know is that I haven't heard of any female comics abusing their status in the same way that Russell Brand has been accused of doing. Maybe that's because women are barely ever given enough status to become monsters.

The Trouble with Women

By the mid-eighties there are more female comedy playmates on the circuit, which should be great, but isn't. I'm going to be honest here: rather than see these new faces as potential allies, I see each and every one as a terrible menace. This is because I am paranoid and insecure.

In my defence, the world of comedy c. 1985 isn't exactly embracing the idea of women getting 50 per cent of the laughs, 50 per cent of the line-up, 50 per cent of the airtime and certainly not 50 per cent of the money. Other women feel like a threat; there is so little work for us it's hard to share, especially when the odds are already so stacked against you.

Looking back, what's incredible about the eighties is how much sexism we actually put up with without burning anything down. We just accepted it, it was normal.

Change has been iceberg-slow, but it's happened.

Watch an old comedy panel show now and it will instantly strike you as peculiar. It might take you a minute to understand why. It's because there are no women on it. Today, an all-male line-up looks quaint, absurd even: why are all these blokes sniggering together and why are they all white?

Things have definitely shifted for the better. That said, I still haven't been on *Live at the Apollo*, *8 Out of 10 Cats* or *Have I Got News For You*. Good: I don't really ever want to work with Paul Merton again.

I can no longer blame my sex, so possibly ageism is the last 'ism' to fall, or maybe I'm a bit shit (I'm not). OK, rant over.

Just because I'm sixty-four doesn't mean that certain things don't hurt.

The two names that make the biggest impact on the comedy circuit in the mid-eighties are Jo Brand, aka the Sea Monster, and Hattie Hayridge, who will later appear as Holly the computer in *Red Dwarf*.

I watch Jo one night at the Tunnel Club and marvel at her stance, her Doc Martens sure-footed confidence, her refusal to take any shit. I feel like a fake. *She's a proper stand-up*, I fret to myself.

Hattie, too, feels more assured than I am. She is the first deadpan female comic on the circuit and, rather than behaving like a maniac on stage (guilty), she stands stock-still and has the courage to explore a quietly surreal Hattie world of her own. Both Jo and Hattie make it onto *Saturday Night Live*. I don't, so I don't watch it.

I'm blind with jealousy, but it's also good for me. This new influx of talent is the kick up the arse that I need. I have to start working harder.

So, aged twenty-five, and gradually growing out of the anorexia (literally), but still without periods, I begin morphing from poet into stand-up. The transformation period is clumsy and difficult; my poems feel safe, I can read them from my notebook. What if I forget the stand-up bits? I'm far too frightened to improvise.

Throughout my career, and until very recently, I have been a very scripted stand-up. I write shows, I learn shows and I perform shows. Only in my sixties can I relax enough to let go.

Improv comes over from the States around the mid-eighties and quickly gains popularity. London learns the ropes from the American stand-up Kit Hollerbach (who will go on to marry and divorce Jeremy Hardy) and Mike Myers, a goofy Canadian who will later go on to be globally famous. I regularly bump into Mike on the circuit when he performs a double act with Neil Mullarkey, aka Mullarkey and Myers, who perform sketches based on their shared love of cartoons, B-movies and bad TV.

They're ace, but would I have put money on Myers becoming a massive film star? I don't think so!

While I learn to pepper the gaps between poems with jokes, I keep up the poetry side by writing a poem once a month for *Company* magazine.

Company is the closest UK contender to *Cosmopolitan*; it's a bit less high glamour, more user-friendly and essentially it has a sense of humour. Almost half a century later, humour is still rare in women's magazines, which are still very timid about celebrating funny women. It's as if they presume comedy and fashion can't mix. Well, that's bollocks. Comedy goes with everything.

Company's mid-eighties editor is Gill Hudson, who is very generous and doesn't mind what I write, as long as it fits into a small box at the bottom of a certain page. I write poems for *Company* every month for a couple of years. Here's one from 1987:

The Tarot Man

The tarot man says,
'Choose a card, any card.'
This is hard, there are a lot to choose from,
I hesitate,
The tarot man says,
'You are indecisive.'
Quickly, I choose a card, any old card.

'And rash,'
He adds.
And I think, Blimey, he's good.

I think this poem sums up how I'm feeling. I genuinely haven't a clue what I'm doing.

The Double Act Experiment

I'm not sure whose idea it is to get together and do a double act, but for a while in the mid-eighties Helen Lederer and I have a bash at this most elusive of comedy relationships. To this day, I am very fond of Helen, who in recent years has done a brilliant and brave thing in creating Comedy Women in Print, which has an annual writing prize for funny female novelists.

In the eighties she is rather more established than I am, and I think maybe if we pool our resources then something unique might emerge, only neither of us has a clue as to what that might be. All we know is that we cannot be anything like French and Saunders, which makes things very tricky.

Helen lives in north London, I live in south London, but I like going to her flat, even though I can't yet drive and it's quite complicated by public transport. Six years older than me, she seems to live an incredibly civilised life and her Czechoslovakian/Welsh heritage, incredible blue eyes and mass of yellow hair fascinate me.

Helen seems to be suspended in aspic. She has barely changed since we first met; some of it is genetic, some of it is thanks to 'work', which she happily admits to. She also has an enviable collection of beautifully cut black jackets and a style that is forever Helen.

I am twenty-five and I think Helen is both posher and cleverer than I am. She is certainly better educated: she has a university degree and went to a superior drama school (London's Central School of Speech and Drama, which easily trumps my Manchester Poly). She also makes me laugh. One day she makes me laugh so much on the phone that I shit my pyjamas and Geof comes home to find them soaking in the bath. 'What happened?' he asks. I tell him, he rolls his eyes.

While Helen makes me laugh and I make Helen laugh, what we can't do together is make an audience laugh. I can only remember doing two gigs, one in Shepherd's Bush and one at the King's Head in Islington. Both are a disaster. After the King's Head show, Helen climbs out of a rear window and exits the pub via a fire escape over the roof rather than face the silent disappointment of the audience out front.

But it's after the Shepherd's Bush gig that we call it a day. My diary entry for 12 April reads, 'Helen and I have decided not to embarrass our audiences anymore.' I wish I knew where the scripts were; all I can remember of our onstage humiliation is Helen becoming quieter and quieter, while I compensate by shouting everything very loudly.

A great double act is a wonderful thing to watch; sadly, we are excruciating.

Apart from French and Saunders, the female double act is a weirdly rare beast. When racking my brains and remembering the eighties, the only girl duos I can recall are The Flaming Hamsters, Sara Crowe and Ann Bryson, two gorgeous, funny young actresses who write sketches together and later star in a series of Philadelphia cream cheese ads, which hopefully bought them both houses. There's also Rabbit & Doon, Anne Rabbitt and Doon Mackichan (later of *Smack the Pony* and a great deal more) and ... well, as I say, I'm racking my brains.

Post-French and Saunders, the next female comedy pairing to make any real impact are Mel and Sue, who emerge like comedy butterflies on the scene at the Edinburgh Festival in 1993.

Why is that so?

Why do so few women team up and become successful on the circuit? Even now the number of female double acts currently gigging is relatively small. Favourites on the pod/live circuit are the brilliant Scummy Mummies, the musical real-life sisters Flo & Joan, and Ruby Wax's daughters, Siblings.

Podcasts have given the female double act a bit more scope, and this is where you will find a growing number of lady twosomes, who, free from the practical constraints of gigging, have found a platform on which they can comfortably perform together, without leaving the house (e.g. me and Judith on *Older and Wider*).

In many respects other women comics have formed the backbone of my career. Even the failed Lederer and Eclair experiment is instrumental in teaching me something, mostly about the importance of finding somewhere private to cry after a traumatic gig.

I return to solo gigging, and by 1986/87 there are even more really good women working in comedy venues up and down the country. The London scene in particular is booming and it seems I have new competition every week.

I try to swallow my entrenched jealousy by holding a 'girls in comedy' drinks party in the flat I share with Geof in Camberwell.

I tell Geof he must absent himself and invite anyone who's available, including two new Aussie girls on the block, namely Julie Balloo and Dreenagh Darrell. Dreenagh is a force of nature and has a great gag about sucking off a pig. As we all know, pigs have corkscrew-shaped penises, so the joke goes, 'I went down on a pig [mime corkscrew penis] – dizzy for weeks!' Julie is set to become a dear friend and longtime writing partner, but neither of us knows this yet and when we first meet I am taken aback by her friendliness and suspect for a while that she must fancy me.

The flat is full of shrieking women comics and smashed-up mince pies. Linda Smith stays the night and in the morning when Geof catches sight of her asleep on the sitting-room floor with her flowing long blonde hair, he comes back into the bedroom and tells me 'an angel is sleeping in the next room'. Linda dies of ovarian cancer in 2006. She is forty-eight years old. I am still angry on her behalf.

Tough Crowds

In one of the two diaries that I still possess from the eighties there is an entry dated Tuesday 18 June 1985: 'Let us draw a veil over this evening, suffice to say, the students at Reading are worse than animals.'

I've started doing a few university gigs: the September/October bookings are for the freshers, while the June dates celebrate the end of term/leaving. Both can very easily get out of hand. Forty years ago, young people like to get pissed. Really, really, obnoxiously pissed. Getting pissed and behaving like a pillock is seen as some kind of badge of honour; boys seem to think girls will be impressed by their arseholery. There is a lot of arseholery around. Most of the uni gigs are really badly managed. One night I knock on the office door of a student ents officer to get my gig cheque, only to be met by a girl (possibly a fresher) pulling her pants up and an older boy throwing a knotted condom into the bin. Inevitably it misses and proceeds to leak all over the floor.

On another occasion the ents manager is so pissed he mistakes me and Mark Steel for the headlining band and gives us their envelope of cash. The gig has been so horrific we sit outside on the fire escape, divvy up the £600 between us and run off into the night.

I am heckled mostly for my lack of tits and jokes: student gigs are interrupted with cries of 'Tell us a joke, show us your tits,' followed by 'Don't bother, she hasn't got any.' Obviously it is tedious.

It's not just on the student circuit that heckling is becoming increasingly common; it's crept into the London clubs and pubs, too.

Some venues are more notorious for heckling than others, and for some reason I don't believe I can be a fully-fledged stand-up if I don't perform in these places. The worst culprits are Jongleurs in Clapham (yuppie heckling), the Comedy Store (pissed after-office heckling) and the infamous Tunnel Club (insane local heckling).

Let me explain the Tunnel Club to you. It opens in '84 at the back of a pub called the Mitre Arms, which squats in a derelict no man's land somewhere between Greenwich and hell. The location, then and now, immediately conjures up drug deals in car parks and bottle fights; it's gritty cops and robbers stuff, bodies in boots of old Jags but with a hysterical canned laughter track on top. Imagine if Guy Ritchie wrote a film set around an eighties comedy venue.

I love it and I hate it.

Getting there is complicated, so Geof drives me (looking like a coke dealer himself in the massive gold Jaguar Mark 10 that is ours for a while), dropping me at the bottom of a footbridge near the mouth of the Blackwall Tunnel. Sometimes when I walk across the footbridge to the club I consider throwing myself into the traffic below. I don't want to die, but I don't want to do the gig either.

It's not just me that's scared of the Tunnel Club. One night, pre-show, I hear Harry Enfield puke up in the toilet. He's scared, too. At the time Harry is in a double act called Dusty and Dick, who do spoof Pathé News-style crime caper sketches. They're great. Harry is a brilliant character actor, soon to star on *Saturday*

Night Live, with Stavros, the Greek kebab shop owner, and Loadsamoney, the fictional monster 80s builder, while Bryan Elsley will leave the live circuit and go on to create *Skins*. Both are very nice men. Many years later Brian will ask me to do a tiny cameo on *Skins*, which gives me some much-needed street cred for five minutes.

Only the truly maddest acts have no fear of the Tunnel, and there are a few. Acts like the iceman who basically just chips away at a big block of ice in order to release a rubber duck, and Chris Luby, a slightly unhinged chap who dresses in full Air Force regalia and does impressions of military aircraft and the Edinburgh Tattoo. Basically, if Luby gets heckled, he just drowns them out with artillery fire. Other regulars are the Greatest Show on Legs, which stars originator Martin Soan, Malcolm Hardee, plus a rolling third member, their signature showpiece being the naked balloon dance, which basically does what it says on the can.

Malcolm Hardee is the brains behind the Tunnel Club. In some respects, he is a terrible, terrible man. He joins the Greatest Show on Legs after a stint in prison and is both the dearest and most dangerous company you can keep. I am part in awe, part terrified of him, but over the years we forge a funny little friendship, which I think is built on some kind of mutual respect. Although one night this respect wears thin when we end up sharing a B&B. There is only one bedroom left; fortunately it's a twin and I agree to sharing it, as long as Malcolm doesn't try anything on. Ten minutes after lights out, he requests a handjob. When I refuse, he sighs and asks permission to 'have a wank'. I sigh, mutter 'If you must,' then roll over and fall asleep.

Malcolm compères at the Tunnel Club on Sunday nights and mayhem usually ensues. There is even a documentary about the venue, which is available on YouTube. It couldn't exist now in the way it did then. It is both the best of comedy and the worst and it's the audience who decides how things will go. Ah, the Tunnel Club audience: unlike any other, they are comedy savvy and smarter than most with their heckling. One night when the evening is threatening to be over by nine o'clock due to so many acts being booed offstage, Malcolm decrees a heckling ban. I'm the next act up; the audience 'hum' me offstage.

They aren't always so cute. Hattie Hayridge one night wears a knee-length dress onstage and, mid-act, a bloke gets out of the audience, walks up to the stage and lifts her skirt above her head. Everyone can see her pants. This is not a primary school playground prank, this is assault, but everyone laughs.

Malcolm is a 'character'. He is known to have the biggest testicles in show business and will regularly get his knob out for an uncannily acute impression of the French president Charles de Gaulle. He is most likely an alcoholic, a great shambling physical wreck, and yet the women in his life are bright and beautiful, ditto his kids.

Things happen to Malcolm, seemingly without intention. He accidentally steals Freddie Mercury's fortieth birthday cake and in an effort to get rid of the evidence donates it to an old folks' home in south London. Apparently, hot on his trail, the police find only 'crumbs'.

He lives on a barge on the Thames, called the *Wibbly Wobbly*, which is an accident waiting to happen. On 31 January 2005 Malcolm drowns in the river. He is pissed in a dinghy, trying to get to his floating home. Legend has it he is still clutching a bottle of beer when his body is found.

His funeral is huge, and both desperately sad and simultaneously hilarious. After the service, his coffin is carried out to Elvis singing 'Return to Sender'. Malcolm is Malcolm even in death.

Desperately Dabbling

Throughout most of my twenties, which coincide entirely with the eighties, I am in a quandary over my career. I gig a lot all over London and beyond, but it doesn't seem to amount to much. Occasionally *Time Out* say nice things about me ('riotously witty', 'deliciously melt-in-the-mouth') but I don't seem to be making the same sort of progress as other comics. Deep down, I'm not sure whether I'm just 'acting' at being a stand-up. After all, I'm theatre-trained: surely by now I should have a West End play or a telly soap under my belt, but I haven't. It's getting embarrassing, and I feel sorry for my parents. Neither of them actually says anything to my face, and, to give them their credit, they never once have a 'quiet word'.

It must be hard for them, meeting up with friends whose kids are fast-tracking up their career ladders. Maybe they just talk about my brother and sister and tactfully leave me out? Or maybe they are brutally honest: 'Oh, Jenny, yes, living in sin with her older divorcee boyfriend, and when she's not serving food that she wouldn't eat in a million years to people who look straight through her, she's telling filthy jokes for a living, hahahaha, yes, very proud.'

Happily, in 1983 I get a part as a German-speaking maid in the hugely popular comedy drama *Auf Wiedersehen, Pet*. I think I get it because I have 'fluent German' on my CV. I also have horse-riding and ice-skating.

I receive the script in English, such is their faith that I will be able to translate into Deutsch, ha. I get a real linguist who lives down the road to do it for me and am word perfect for the table read. This job is followed by something very similar. Shit, I'm in danger of being typecast in a language that I can't really speak. Fortunately, the German-speaking maids dry up and instead I get a lead role in an RCA student film.

I play a girl with a massive birthmark on her face, who wets herself in a phone box. I go very Stanislavski on the weeing but need a tear stick for the crying scenes! Deep down, I sort of know that I haven't got what it takes to be a really good actress. I mean, how many parts are there for women who can't really do anything apart from urinate on cue?

I waitress part-time for many years on and off, and the worst-behaved punters by far are the regulars in a basement wine bar in Holborn, where purple-faced barristers drink red wine at lunch-time, spill oxtail soup down their fronts and slide their hands over waitresses' bottoms. They are a disgraceful bunch, and I am vaguely embarrassed that this is the world that both my brother and sister have chosen to inhabit.

My sister is living in London. She is successful and married (although this turns out to be disastrous) and she and P (or the shit, as my mother later calls him) not only have the three-bedroom Edwardian house in Herne Hill but a three-bedroom thatched weekend cottage in Wiltshire. That's six bedrooms altogether, and she is not yet thirty.

Incidentally, by the end of the decade she will have moved to a five-storey Georgian number on Kennington Road, which I will use as Edwina's house in *Moving* many years later.

Meanwhile, Ben is studying law at Aberystwyth, where he will meet Penny, his one true love, future wife and mother of his kids, Gabriel and Daisy, before embarking on his own career as a criminal barrister. In fact, while I am writing this he has been defending a case at the Old Bailey, which I presume for a barrister is a bit like doing a season at the RSC. If I ever end up in a Crown court, I couldn't think of anyone I'd like to defend me more. At least if I went down, I'd go down laughing.

Let's be honest: the reason that I am able to tit about and fail for so long is mostly due to Geof putting up with me. He never once mentions bills, I pay what I can when I can, which is hardly ever.

I know that I'm lucky to be out of the renting game and that Geof is a lifeline, the flat is glorious and the years we spend there, from 1982 to 1990, are very happy.

87 Camberwell Grove is on the first floor of a white stuccoed Georgian house with pillars on either side of the blue front door. We have no garden, but we do have a tiny balcony and we live opposite Lorraine Chase, the model and star of the Campari telly ads. I am fascinated by Lorraine: she seems to live the most glamorous of lives. Black shiny cars pick her up and drop her off, she plays tennis in tiny tennis whites and is always immaculately dressed. She is a real live celebrity and has the lifestyle, shoes and jewellery to match. She still lives in Camberwell. I bump into her sometimes: she is an utter joy, a proper south Londoner, and still drop-dead gorgeous with a fabulous wardrobe.

Fame has always fascinated me, and I always wanted it very badly, but it just isn't happening fast enough. Everything is so bitty.

Geof is still working for *TV Times* and earning a decent wage, enough to keep him in Joseph suits and Paul Smith ties. He has always been better dressed than me, he believes in buying quality stuff that's made to last. These days I wear an Italian raincoat he originally bought in the late seventies; it cost £200, a fortune back then, but it's still immaculate. I can safely say he is the first and only man I've ever slept with who keeps his shoes on wooden shoe trees.

Geof is incredibly generous. For birthdays and Xmases he takes me to Butler & Wilson on the Fulham Road, which is a trove of costume jewellery, and festoons my ears, neck, wrists and fingers with massive fake pearls and oodles of diamanté.

I still have some of it, but because I don't look after anything properly most of it is broken and missing half its precious gems; turns out some of the pearls aren't fake.

I'm not sure what contribution I make to our Georgian love nest; I am a very heavy drinker and, according to my diary, hungover most of the time. I'm frustrated, waiting for success but far too distracted by the Grove pub over the road. This is also where Vic Reeves and Bob Mortimer hang out, but our friendship groups don't really overlap. I do a couple of their comedy nights in various venues in south London during the eighties but feel left out of the joke. They are paving a new comedy path and their fans are besotted, I feel old hat, and one of my diary entries reads:

Very cross tonight, did a stupid gig in Streatham playing second fiddle to Vic Reeves who was compèring his Rub-a-Dub Club. I was out of my depth, his fan club were in and they were only interested in Vic and his sidekick [sorry, Bob]. I didn't think the acts were getting a fair crack of the whip and I told Vic how I felt, then drove home in a temper.

I still admire them. These days I love Vic's artwork and I think Bob's recent autobiography is a wonderful thing. But I am jealous, jealous that when they do have telly success and invite a woman onto their show it's not a funny woman, it's Ulrika Jonsson, who will go on to be appallingly treated by the media and the industry that she is part of.

Many years later I'm at a radio award ceremony sharing a table with Marianne Faithfull, who nods towards an empty place setting with the name 'Bryan Ferry' written on a card, rolls her eyes and says, 'Poor Bryan, crippled with shyness.' He seems fine when he eventually turns up. Anyway, Ulrika is at this do, and suddenly all the male guest hosts start joking about how many children she's had by however many men. One after the other they start their speeches with the words 'I am not the father of Ulrika's latest baby', in a Spartacus piss-take.

FFS.

Extra-Curricular Activities

To take my mind off the fact that my life is a shambles and, even more frightening, that I am literally growing out of my anorexia and putting on weight, I swim every morning in the old Victorian pool which still exists in Artichoke Place.

I still swim in the same pool, but only with the over-sixties brigade so that I don't have to compete with my sister, who is an early morning 'fast lane' type. Sara is one of those annoying swimmers who takes her sessions really seriously and uses professional swimming aids.

The last time I did share the pool with her I swam a really fast length of crawl just to piss her off. 'Since when have you been able to do the crawl?' she demanded. I couldn't reply. I didn't have enough breath in me.

Back in the eighties, when I'm not swimming or attempting to write, I try and think up little side hustles. The time is ripe for new enterprises: for instance, my mate Janet has her own sandwich round in west London, mixing up her speciality coronation chicken filling in the bathtub, which goes down a treat round Hammersmith.

I decide to make some greetings cards and attempt to sell them into a nicky-nacky-noo shop in Clapham. I experiment with mosaic fish shapes and march along to the shop, where they gently point out that, although they like them, they need envelopes and cellophane wrappers. Each one takes me about three days to make. There is no way they can ever be cost-effective. Another moneymaking scheme bites the dust.

For a while I work for London's premier lookalike agency, not as a lookalike (keep your Su Pollard jokes to yourself, thanks) but as their Girl Friday. Lookalikes are big in the eighties and we have Jeannette Charles on our books, who is more like the Queen than the Queen, plus a Prince Charles doppelganger who is done for cottaging and dropped like a stone covered in frog shit.

I spend most of my time opening letters from grandmothers insisting that their granddaughter (photo included) is the spitting image of Princess Diana. None of them are.

The agency is housed in the basement of a massive house in Clapham. It's so vast it has a lift and a ballroom and a huge attic bathroom where one of the Cadbury's Flake adverts is filmed. The house belongs to a photographer called Michael Joseph, who made a name for himself in the sixties by creating the cover of the Rolling Stones' album *Beggars Banquet*. It's a fabulous photo and for a number of years after the album is released Joseph is in high demand in the fashion and music industry, hence the house.

Michael's wife runs the lookalike business with her sidekick Susan, while I perch at a third desk, mostly fetching sandwiches from the (to me) impossibly exotic deli in Clapham Old Town.

At one point the office branches out into casting pop videos, which is how I get to dance on Culture Club's 'Karma Chameleon'.

Sadly, I am lumbered with one of the peasant outfits and end up, totally unseen, gyrating on the banks of the Thames in sackcloth, while the chosen few are dressed up in Edwardian splendour and invited to dance on a steamboat with the band.

I watch the video on YouTube while writing this, and even I can't spot me. Damn the editing.

However, on the day of the video shoot, Boy George helps himself to my crisps and such is our instant bond that to this day we follow each other on Twitter! I am a huge fan of his work and if you've never heard the soundtrack to his fabulous musical *Taboo*, do yourself a favour and download it now.

Another time I completely disappear from the screen is in '82, the year before 'Karma', when I am invited on London Weekend Television's women-only chat show headed by Janet Street-Porter (title long forgotten), to read a poem. At the recording, rather than appear onstage the producer thinks it will be funnier if I just stand up in the audience and perform my chosen piece from the stalls. This is a fucking awful idea and when I stand up and start performing the audience members on either side of me are so horrified by my 'interruption' that they start tugging on my sleeves in order to get me to sit back down. Despite receiving a thank-you letter signed by Janet herself, in which she spells my name wrong (Jennie), I am cut from the show.

I receive this news by telephone two hours before the programme is due to air. I think I am both relieved and furious.

Janet S-P and I will go on to work together on *Loose Women* many years in the future, when the two of us will get into terrible tabloid trouble and make the front page of the *Daily Mail*, haha.

I dance on a few more pop videos, but nothing of any note. I'm a useful background groover, though I cannot follow choreography to save my life. That said, I have always been able to show off on the dancefloor, a combination of natural flexibility and not giving a shit.

In 1983, Channel 4 start airing a new sketch show entitled *Who Dares Wins* and I am chosen to do some background and 'featured extra' roles, which means I might get the occasional line. It is filmed out in Limehouse, where delicious free cast lunches are eaten on a barge moored in the Limehouse Basin.

I quickly gain a reputation for doing anything I'm asked, which results in me taking part in a sketch that requires holding a live chicken under a restaurant table, the joke being that it's so raw it's actually alive. I am so nervous of the chicken pre-empting its cue and escaping that I hold it extremely tightly, then worry I may have killed it.

Another time I play a plague victim in a pit, which involves being covered in various prosthetic weeping sores and boils made out of Rice Krispies. Which is fine, apart from the fact that I have a gig at Jongleurs directly after the recording and it takes forever to peel my scabs off.

Apart from writing poems for Company magazine, I have a bash at writing some short stories and send them off to Woman's Weekly! They return the manuscripts with a very nice rejection letter, stating that, despite the stories showing a great deal of promise, my writing is too derivative of the novelist Fay Weldon. They are completely correct. I am a huge Fay Weldon fan and, without meaning to, I've absorbed her style and been found out.

I try not to despair, but when I think about my future I imagine myself living in a skip eating tinned cat food.

Fortunately, as the eighties scroll past, I start getting casting calls for commercials. Most of these experiences are humiliating, but I do score a financially rewarding Electrolux vacuum cleaner ad.

In the ad I play many different women from all around the world, all of whom are having huge fun with their Electrolux apparatus. Thanks to this ad, I also feature on a huge billboard in Vauxhall; the tagline in large letters under the ad says 'Nothing sucks like an Electrolux'. Inevitably someone scrawls, 'I do – phone Sonia on 701 . . . ' across the billboard.

All the Fun of the Festival!

I first perform at the Edinburgh Festival in 1983 when I am given a slot performing poetry in a bar called Buster Browns next to the Waverley railway station. Punters wobble in off the trains and see a young blonde woman wearing a black cocktail dress holding a notebook and presume I am a waitress. I never once get through the act without being asked for a whisky.

The venue is shambolic: the fringe festival is still finding its comedy feet and it certainly isn't the stamping ground for TV executives looking for the next new thing. Not yet.

I stay with a friend of my aunt's out in Portobello, which is great for fresh air and sea views but impractically too far out of town. I spend more money than I'm earning getting cabs back to my digs, apart from the time I get a lift back with a New Zealand comic who, pissed off his head, steals a car from a petrol station and we laugh all the way to the seaside. I will retain this reckless and potentially dangerous streak for much of my adult life, possibly until my forties when suddenly it all gets too tiring.

Nica Burns, the nowadays theatre impresario, is instrumental in me playing the festival, and the following year her boyfriend Colin Watkeys, who runs the comedy night at the Finborough

Arms, decides to take three comics up to Edinburgh to perform at the Masonic Lodge on Hill Street.

Dubious Entertainment consists of myself, Rory Bremner and Mark Steel, two stand-ups and a very wet-behind-the-ears newbie impressionist. Rory is fresh out of uni; he has family in Edinburgh. One night he says he has someone in to see the show who he thinks will find me hilarious. 'Who's that?' I ask. 'My mother's cleaning woman,' he responds.

Mark and I stick Rory on first. I go on in the middle and Mark tops the show. To access the stage we have to walk through a fully operational pub kitchen. Mark falls out with the chef and every night he has to run through the kitchen dodging blows from this furious bloke, which makes me laugh more than anything.

It's a mistake to stick Rory on first. This year there are TV scouts in town and after seeing Rory they make a beeline for the bar downstairs so they can be the first to greet him with a pint when he comes offstage. Rory's career takes off much more quickly than either mine or Mark's, but the great thing about writing this forty years on is knowing that we all get there in the end, we all get some recognition. I occasionally bump into Mark, who still makes me laugh out loud; he is not only hilarious, but the nicest man, and although I haven't seen Rory for ages I feel a great fondness for him.

Neither Rory nor Mark ever question my ability to do the job. We are equal but different.

Geof designs the artwork for *Dubious Entertainment*, which mostly comprises fliers and stickers which we stick on lamp posts all over town.

The first time I do Edinburgh on my own is in the mid-eighties, when for some reason I decide to call my debut solo show *The Perry Como Hour*.

This is insane. I am not well enough known to get away with this kind of prank. Geof designs me a poster, which I insist must feature Perry Como's face. All there is to suggest I might appear is a strapline across the poster reading 'Guest Starring Jenny Eclair!'

I cannot think why I ever thought it was funny.

For those who are too young/groovy to know, Perry Como was an American middle-of-the road, cardi-wearing crooner, a bit like Andy Williams or Val Doonican. Mmmm, no, I don't suppose you know who they are either. OK, I suggest you either skip this para or do some Googling. Suffice to say it is a ridiculous thing to do and backfires massively.

The show is further hampered by the fact that I am performing in a church. To give you a geographical clue, the venue is St Columba's by the Castle, which that year is being run by an all-female collective called Women at Work. The idea is to have lots of jolly bonding barbecues for audiences and acts alike, but all I can remember is a great deal of infighting, and lots of crying. Rhona Cameron, the Scottish soon-to-be stand-up, is hired as my technician. She operates from a crouching position in the pulpit, and, because she can't see me, I have to prod her with the end of a long-handled broom to let her know when I'm ready to start. Thus cued, she presses a button and Perry starts singing 'Magic Moments'. Christ.

I struggle with finding an audience for this show. A lot of old ladies turn up expecting a singalong and then can't understand why a hysterical blonde woman is swearing in the house of God.

However, one night Dawn French and Lenny Henry pop in, word gets around and I sell out for the rest of the week. Thanks, guys.

A couple of decades later, Rhona joins me and Annette Badland (who will later record one of my *Little Lifetimes* for Radio 4) on a tour of the first *Grumpy Old Women* live show. It's the third time around the block for this show, which originally toured the country with the lovely Linda Robson (who will go on to nab my *Loose Women* slot after I get fired) and the inspirational Dillie Keane.

But all that is a long time off. Right now I have lost quite a lot of money and learned quite a big lesson, which, in a nutshell, is not to put the name of an ageing American crooner on your festival poster.

Edinburgh becomes a regular feature in my summer diary, but I often forget to write that diary, and the venues and details are vague, although I know I did a terrible cabaret/theatre/magic show in '85. This plays at the newly opened Pleasance Theatre with its famous cobbled courtyard. To be honest, the show is equally cobbled, with one critic writing, 'If only the show, like Jenny Eclair, had been sawn in half.' I spend the weeks performing that unnamed show feeling embarrassed to be living in my own skin. Another lesson learned: I need to be in full control of what I do onstage; accidents happen when I lose that control, do stuff that other people tell me to do and end up looking like an arsehole.

Things improve in 1988, when I do an hour-long split-bill show with my Aussie friend Julie Balloo.

We call the show *Originally Brunette*, have a classy black and white photo taken by my French photographer pal Joelle and Geof designs us a really smart poster.

For once, I feel ready for the festival. I also feel something else, which is pregnant.

Carrying a Bun Onstage

Due to being underweight for so long, I only start to menstruate again in 1987. I recall wearing green tartan trousers and having to throw them away. It's a shock, and I feel weirdly both upset and relieved. I get myself a Dutch cap in a little plastic box, but like the mouthguard I am equipped with in my sixties, due to 'grinding and clenching' issues, I mostly forget to put it in.

In June 1988, Geof takes me on holiday to the Greek island of Halki. We are staying in a lovely traditional apartment overlooking the marina (albeit with no flushing loo) and we should be having a lovely time.

Only we aren't.

I feel awful, all the time. It's a two-week break on Halki and all I want to do is go home.

I am reading the uber-fashionable Patrick Süskind's *Perfume*, which is a mistake as my own olfactory system has gone into complete overdrive and I can smell the fishermen tenderising octopuses on the harbour wall below our bedroom: smack, thrash, smack.

I feel worse than those octopuses. I lie down whenever I can; I feel like I've been on a very long coach trip; I'm tired and nauseous.

Geof thinks I'm malingering and silently eats tubs of chocolate chip ice cream on the balcony while I burp into the pillows.

Towards the end of the holiday I start to suspect I might be
pregnant when my bosoms swell and for the first time in my life
I have what looks suspiciously like a cleavage in my bikini top.
Also, I've gone off wine, so if I'm not pregnant there is something
much more serious going on.

On 7 July, safely back in London, Geof gets up early and waits
for a chemist to open. Meanwhile, I store my first wee of the
morning until my bladder feels as though it might burst, like a
balloon full of hot piss.

Geof returns with the necessary kit and I wee all over the
stick; steam rises off the thing, and I'm slightly surprised that it
doesn't melt. Ten minutes later, a very definite pink line appears.

I am pregnant. This is entirely unplanned and yet instinctively
I know that this is what I want.

I show Geof the stick and we giggle for a while. Both of us are
slightly embarrassed: we have done a rude thing and now another human being is coming into the world, maybe. Hopefully,
if nothing goes wrong? The first thing we do, once we pull ourselves together, is tip our coke supplies down the lavatory. Once
I flush it all away, I will never take the stuff ever again (oh, apart
from once in Edinburgh about four years later and the guilt
nearly kills me).

I'm so lucky to have stopped taking cocaine when I did. Over
the next few years it becomes a drug that far too many comics
waste their talent on.

Cocaine makes you brave onstage for twenty minutes, but it
makes you lazy offstage; you don't bother writing new stuff, you
stop trying so hard, your career stalls and you are trapped forever
on the club circuit, never quite making it to the top of the bill.

We tell people our mad news far too soon. Friends are happy
but taken aback. My sister is a bit hacked off, because she too

is pregnant and it's very typical of me, as a younger sister, to 'copy'.

My mother is prissy about us not being married, so I put the phone down on her. My father rings me back, tells me he is absolutely delighted and that 'your mother is just being silly'. She is: we get over it, although over the years I will occasionally throw it back in her face!

I am tired and I puke up a lot, including at Heathrow airport on my way to perform at the Edinburgh Festival.

Julie and I and a number of other performers, including Julie's boyfriend Paul Merton and the legendary Arthur Smith, are sharing Number 13 North Park Terrace, which makes me instantly neurotic. Number 13: what if my baby has two heads?

I have an attic room, which obviously belongs to a twelve-year-old girl. I find her diaries and read them to lull me asleep now that I can't booze.

Julie and I are gigging nightly with the *Originally Brunette* show. The premise is that we are pen pals and at the start of the show we read out fictional letters to each other, before performing our individual acts.

We take it in turn to go on first. Julie has always been a dream to work with; the only thing we fall out about is her taste in terrible Mexican restaurants, which, considering I'm in the first trimester of my pregnancy, give me appalling heartburn. All I really want to eat are bacon-flavoured crisps, and prawn cocktails, preferably made with very sweet Marie Rose sauce.

The show goes well, so well that I get a Perrier special commendation, which will in later years hatch into the best newcomer award. The main prize is won by the late Jeremy Hardy, who is very young, very talented and does a very funny routine about buying a lemon squeezer from a jumble sale. The Perrier Award is a big deal in the world of comedy that I inhabit and, even though my special commendation goes more or less unnoticed, it means a lot to me. Once upon a time I'd have celebrated myself shit-faced, but I go home early, feeling smug and sober.

Even better than the commendation is that the little pen pal idea that we base the show on gets picked up by Radio 4, who commission us a year later to write a sitcom based on this premise.

Dear Jenny, Dear Julie will be broadcast in the autumn of 1990 featuring Julie and me, Paul Merton, Helen Lederer and my *Just a Minute* pal Nicholas Parsons. It is the beginning of a long relationship with the station, culminating most recently in seven series of the fifteen-minute monologues *Little Lifetimes* – but right now I am twenty-eight, pregnant and clueless about my future.

I genuinely have no idea if my career will amount to anything and, secretly, I think the baby will be a great excuse to opt out if it all gets too much.

After all, Geof can always look after me/us. From the moment I met him I have always viewed him as the man who would save me, mostly from myself. Well, now there is a baby to save, too.

Looking back, I see this festival as a turning point in my career. I work better because I'm not drinking. I also like the attention being pregnant gives me and I make sure everyone, including (especially) the press, is made aware of my condition.

In 1989, there are so few women gigging that being a pregnant lady comic is a noteworthy novelty and I go around cradling my non-existent bump. I have yet to have a scan.

Back in London, I am monitored by my GP because, instead of putting on weight, I have lost five pounds. I am controlling my eating because I still have a little bit of leftover anorexia brain and, quite correctly, they suss this immediately. Pregnant ex-anorexics have a high rate of slipping back into old ways.

Fortunately, hunger, greed and a bit of common sense win the battle of the food dilemma and I start to bulge all over. I am slightly shocked but manage to get over myself.

My sister's baby is born in October, two and a half weeks early. Sara spends the day in court, pops out for supper, goes into labour and has the baby thirty minutes after arriving at St Thomas' Hospital.

This is typically efficient of my sister.

The tiny 'cousin in waiting' is pink and fair and his name is Zachary, an ideal playmate for the boy or girl that I'm due to deliver in just under five months' time.

Later in October, I have a second scan to check the baby's spine, which hadn't been properly visible during the first scan. Apparently it's nothing to worry about and we aren't expecting anything horrible as they move the transducer over my gelled-up belly. Only there is an atmosphere around the examination bed and eventually a nurse tells us the baby's head is small for gestation. There is a chance they may have a condition called microcephaly, which is Latin for tiny head, and could mean developmental problems. But, then again, my dates might be skewed!

We have three weeks to wait until they can be sure. This seems like an eternity and I cry a great deal. I also go out that night and do a twenty-five-minute gig at the Town & Country Club.

My GP is wonderful. He manages to get the next scan brought forward and it's third time lucky. We still don't know if we're having a boy or a girl, but whatever they are, their head is now measuring just fine.

What the scan won't tell us is that this baby will be as bald as an egg until he/she/it is about three.

I keep on gigging, the baby gets bigger, we start thinking about names and suddenly impending motherhood becomes very real. It's too late to back out now. I sit in the bath and the baby bump rises above the water like an island made of solid pink blancmange and I wonder if my thighs will ever return to their vaguely normal circumference.

I gig until I am eight months pregnant. By this stage I am enormous and it's the only time I don't get heckled at student union gigs. It seems even the most pissed-up students don't like the idea of telling a heavily pregnant woman to fuck off. It's great.

Motherhood

My daughter is born in the early hours of 24 February 1989, a Pisces, like her mummy.

The moon is shining through the window, I am kneeling on all fours, bellowing like an ox. I think I may have pushed so hard before she emerged that I slightly shat myself, but the midwives are like conjurors and a clean paper sheet is magically repositioned beneath me as I bellow on.

It isn't a long labour. I'd only gone into King's because my vision became blurred while watching a classic episode of *EastEnders* the previous evening. Dirty Den had just been shot, and all of a sudden I was seeing two of everything on screen: two Dens, two guns, two bunches of daffodils. Double vision can be a warning sign of pre-eclampsia. I know this, despite the fact that, due to my gigging schedule, I have attended only one antenatal class.

Around 9 p.m. Geof drives me round the corner to King's in our dark green Mercedes Fintail, a beautiful car and the inspiration behind the baby's middle name (Mercedes, not Fintail). We enter via A&E which looks like a war zone, Geof gets me into a wheelchair, which has the steering capacity of a fucked-up supermarket trolley, and we keep crashing into the wall.

It turns out that I do not have pre-eclampsia. However, despite my waters not yet breaking, I am in labour, and by the time they examine me I am five centimetres dilated. They offer to pierce the membrane of the amniotic sac with what looks like a crochet hook, and I think, *Might as well, now that I'm here.* There is an immediate gush of warm liquid.

My labour is rapid and pretty intense; we don't have whale music or fairy lights, there is no time for an epidural. I try a little gas and air, but it makes me feel nauseous and insane so I make do with swearing and biting Geof's hand.

They keep encouraging me to lie on my back, to put my feet in stirrups, which seems mad when my body is instinctively telling me to turn over and kneel with my bum in the air. I do what my body tells me to do.

Once the baby's head pops out, like a tricky cork from a bottle of champagne, the rest of her, her body and limbs, follow like a slither of purple eels.

She is one of the most hideous sights I have ever seen.

Geof does not see the goblin; he is instantly smitten. I find myself talking out loud, saying all the things I'm meant to say: 'Oh, my baby, my precious love, blah, blah.' Inside I'm thinking, *Christ, what have I done?*

I want nothing more than to be at my parents' house in a single bed, alone, without this nightmarish responsibility. I want tomato soup and Jacob's Cream Crackers. I want my mummy.

I cannot deliver the afterbirth, I can't muster up the energy, I've lost interest in the whole enterprise. They start talking about 'going down to theatre' and just before I'm given an anaesthetic, I summon one final mighty push and hideous thing number two plops out of my vagina. It is a never-ending horror story: all I want is a bath and sleep, but they won't let me. I have to feed this purple-faced creature.

Geof is released to tell friends and family, to celebrate, drink beer and sleep.

I am trapped.

I am still trapped. It takes me several weeks to fall in love with my child, but from then on I am besotted. I still am. Phoebe Mercedes is the light of my life, she is my pride and my joy, my one and only.

Before she was born I fancied having lots of children, preferably five girls, all with names beginning with P – Phoebe, Pandora, Persephone, Pearl and Pony (OK, I ran out of P names that I liked). With any luck they would all be able to sing close harmony and I'd make a fortune out of them.

Once I give birth I immediately change my mind: one is enough. Baby number two is off the menu. I have never regretted this, not for a second.

I don't think my fragile career would have withstood a second baby. Childcare is much cheaper in the late eighties/early nineties but I'm a freelance stand-up, I'm not yet properly established. Let's face it, if I can't get onto *Saturday Night Live*, I can't afford another kid.

Fortunately, Geof isn't fussed: Phoebe has always been his be-all and end-all; another baby would never match up. Job done.

While I am still in hospital recovering from the birth (this is back in the day, when a five-night stay isn't unusual), the baby and I are visited by a host of lady comics, who squawk into the ward like exotic parrots, waving Barbie Dolls at my newborn.

In time, some of these women will go on to have their own babies, some won't. To this day I refuse to believe in the cult of motherhood, and I firmly believe that many women (and men) are better off without kids.

I'm very lucky not to regret having Phoebe.

That said, there is a particularly low moment, which haunts me to this day. The baby is still brand new and immobile, and I am consumed by resentment, so I lie her in the middle of the bed, surround her with pillows and punch the pillows until I have no strength left. Obviously Geof is not at home; he would have locked me out of the house.

It takes me a while to acclimatise to motherhood, and I feel better once friends start producing, too. There's safety in numbers and I can relax once I know that I'm not the only one to have potentially fucked everything up.

Don't Give Up
the Night Job

I play Mummy for a few months until I realise I am bored out of my skull. I am also getting fatter and fatter; breastfeeding makes me ravenous and I can eat a block of cheddar standing by the sink. Looking back, I think I am in a state of panic. My adoration of this baby is without question, despite the fact that she is very bald, prone to blotchiness and has a twisted foot. This eventually rights itself, although she will always have weak ankles and be the last in her class to ride a bike or skip! I love my baby, but I'm not sure I'm really cut out for motherhood. I feel a bit mad, but also very frightened about getting back on-stage. Who am I?

Geof realises I am losing my nerve and makes me gig again after about six weeks. He drives me to the venue, which is a weird posh nightclub somewhere in Chelsea. I feed the baby in the back of the car, do the gig, come out, feed the baby and go home. This will be how we manage until I stop breastfeeding. I must remember to thank Geof one day. Many of my female circuit companions never manage to revive their careers after having children; they have the talent, they have the desire, some of them just don't have the support.

It is the tail end of the eighties; things have moved on since my mother's day – working mums aren't expected to do all the domestic crap on top of everything else.

That said, June goes to her cremation not understanding why I didn't fill the freezer with nice little dinners for G while I was on tour. Ha! But even in the late eighties/early nineties there are plenty of men who don't want to come home from a hard day at work and pick up the baby reins. Fortunately Geof just gets on with it.

While he sits in the car, I walk onstage and make jokes about having post-birth labia 'like spaniel's ears'.

Having a baby makes my material stand out for a while. In 1989 the pool of women on the circuit is small and the number of mothers even smaller. Only my Australian mate Dreenagh has two, including Odyssey, who is severely disabled. Dreenagh is a single mother. I don't know how she does it. Possibly because she *is* a single mother and there is no one telling her she needs to stay home!

Five months after Phoebe is born, I run away to Vienna to play a 'housewife' in a TV coffee commercial. I leave my daughter in the capable hands of my sister's live-in nanny, Rhona, who is Scottish and Norland-trained no less. While I spend the flight hand-pumping breast milk down the sink in order to stop my tits exploding at 35,000 feet, Rhona gets Phoebe onto a bottle and by the time I return home she is happily guzzling formula. I am free.

In return for my boobs being mine again, my child refuses to look at me for three days. I have betrayed her, and she is punishing me; she drinks from her bottle and will not meet my eye. Oh, great! And I bought her a wooden Pinocchio at Vienna airport.

I put a card up on the noticeboard of the local Safeway supermarket: 'Non-smoking nice girl wanted to look after six-month-old baby.'

I do not care about qualifications, I don't ask for references, I decide to trust my instincts.

Dominique comes into our life, aged nineteen. She is down from Wakefield and has the accent to match. She is a pretty girl, sunbed-gold with dyed auburn hair, who lies about not smoking and we all adore her.

Dommie works for us for three years. For a while she and a mate live with us after getting chucked out of their accommodation (the friend got into trouble for catalogue debt). Geof loves it because they pop to the garage down the road every night for booze and fags and bring him back chocolate.

Once I have childcare I need to make a certain amount of money to pay for said childcare. For several years I have been treading water, giving myself the option to give up if it all gets too hard. I don't have that option any more. I need to work harder.

My career is given a surprise boost in July by winning the *Time Out* Best Newcomer Award for comedy, which means I get more club bookings, which means more money to pay Dominique. Occasionally, I find the freedom of being released to go out to work so intoxicating that I stay out later than I need, lying about being last on the bill, anything to sit in a pub for another half an hour with half a lager.

While writing this book I find a poem I wrote about my daughter in October 1989 which I perform on the circuit:

My Baby

My baby is 8 months old,
She is tall and bald,
Like Jerry Hall without the hair.
She has four teeth and a crease in her cheek.
People say,
'What's his name?'
And I reply,
'Phoebe Mercedes Eclair Powell,
She is the most fantastic baby in the history of the universe.'
She can chew a tissue,
And bang a wooden spoon,
She likes a good laugh,
And she likes a good cry,
She weighs 20 pounds in her nappy,
But 26 pounds sometimes.

Suddenly I have a career, a partner, a baby and a nanny (of sorts), and soon we will move from our very comfortable two-bedroom first-floor flat down London's prestigious Camberwell Grove (estate agent-speak) to a four-storey Georgian wreck of a place with a garden on the borders of Peckham just five minutes away.

I am thirty when we move into Brunswick Villas: no wonder my daughter's generation hate our guts. But, although I look back with complete bewilderment, how did we have so much, so young? I still resent the casual use of the word 'boomer'. It's so fucking dismissive. Neither of us inherited a penny to buy this place, and we certainly didn't get any handouts. Even so, what we had then would be an impossible dream today. And yes, of course I think the housing situation is shit, but it's not just shit for young people, it's shit for older people who are increasingly never getting rid of their kids.

In our day, it was 'eighteen and out'; that just isn't possible any more. It's all wrong, but I promise we never foresaw our good fortune backfiring in our children's faces.

It's not all plain sailing, combining work and parenting. In the summer of 1989, before we move, I attempt to direct a friend's play in Edinburgh. I have never directed anything before or since, I have no idea what I'm doing and I'm eternally grateful to the brilliant cast member Doon Mackichan who kindly takes over and tries to salvage the thing.

Later Doon will star in *Smack the Pony*, and a few years ago she very brilliantly performed one of my Radio 4 *Little Lifetimes* monologues, playing a dead wife who comes back to haunt her ex-husband and his new girlfriend. She is a complete knockout.

On a more positive note, by the end of this first year of motherhood I have recorded the Radio 4 pilot of *Dear Jenny, Dear Julie* with Julie Balloo, been commissioned to write the series and got a new agent. I shan't name him because he dumps me a few years later, before dying of a cocaine-induced heart attack.

Showbiz, eh?

The Georgian Wreck

Number 2 Brunswick Villas is a fabulous shell of a house. The water runs into a bath via a hosepipe from a tap on another floor and it's basically uninhabitable, but we move in regardless.

The baby plays in rubble and cement, but beneath the chaos are the fine bones of Georgian loveliness. I still miss the staircase and the way its mahogany rail curled all the way up to the top floor.

There are original wooden shutters and we open up the basement with a JCB so that our kitchen can be enormous. Not that we have a cooker; we have a microwave and a hob. Neither of us cook and one day Phoebe comes home from playing with a friend and informs me that 'you can make cakes in your own house'. 'Not in this house, sweetheart,' I reply. I microwave her some My Little Pony buns from a packet mix and she looks sad.

We eat mostly sandwiches and the child exists on pasta and other people's baking. But we have space and our own front and back doors and a garden, even if it's full of broken glass and nettles. Geof designs everything and works his arse off. Within a few years the garden is a south London mini Versailles and he has silver-leafed the downstairs toilet.

The Edinburgh after my excruciating directorial debut, I am back at the festival with a play co-written with Julie Balloo and Maria McErlane, aka Maria Callous from the stand-up circuit.

I don't know what possesses me to trail up to Edinburgh with a toddler (and Dominique) in tow, but the festival has become a compulsion. I don't think my career will progress unless I keep proving myself every year with something new.

Thirty Somehow is a title we came up with for the festival brochure deadline. We have no idea what the piece is actually going to be about, but eventually it transpires it's about teenage cannibalism, and based on the 'Four Marys', a continuing saga about four school chums called Mary, which appeared weekly in *Bunty*.

Yeah, it's pretty niche. *Bunty* was a popular gals' comic (1958–2001), and the Four Marys – Fieldy, Cotty, Simpy and Raddy – the schoolgirl stars of one of its most popular weekly stories.

In our play, the Four Marys win an essay-writing trip to Norway and after a plane crash over the Andes (or is it the Alps?) only three come home. Nicknamed the Bodo Babies after the Norwegian mountain they are rescued from, the trio find instant teenage celebrity, cue a *Top of the Pops* number-one hit.

The play catches up with the survivors in their thirties when an avalanche reveals fresh evidence as to the whereabouts of the missing Mary.

Whatever happened to that lost girl on the mountain? Dear reader, we ate her.

I know, it sounds insane, and it is, but it is 1990 and we are pre-empting pop culture and reality TV by a number of years. The play is a cult hit of the festival and we sell out for the entire run.

Maria and Julie share a flat just yards away from the theatre, where they get up to all kinds of antics. But because I am a working mother, I have to trek in from Morningside, where I'm renting a big baby-friendly flat, which doesn't stop me from occasionally staggering in at midnight, pissed out of my head.

Luckily, Dommie is very understanding and I train Phoebe to find her own shoes when 'Mummy has a headache'. I also start smoking again, because my character does in the show. Having co-written the piece, I could have avoided this, but I didn't and within weeks I'm back up to twenty a day.

Back in London we are part of the Perrier season at the Palace Theatre, even though we aren't nominated for the prize (too theatrical) and the play is filmed by Channel 4, and slagged off by most of the papers when it's broadcast on the telly. Hey ho: no one said it was going to be easy.

Despite the TV adaptation being dismissed by the reviewers, Julie, Maria and I are commissioned by Channel 4 to write a sketch show. We come up with *The Girls from Quimley Lodge*, some of which is filmed in Brunswick Villas.

The premise is inspired by *Thirty Somehow*, only this time we take the idea of a magazine for young ladies and the sketches are based on stories within the magazine. The comedian Nick Hancock plays the female editor of the magazine, who is bed-bound on the top floor of a yet to be decorated Brunswick Villas. Meanwhile, down in the basement, me, Julie and Maria pretend to be the Brontë sisters, playing Twister despite one of the sisters having consumption and coughing up a lung. Another sketch sees Julie and me running up many flights of stairs in order to train for a job we have applied for as 'lighthouse keepers'. Sadly we've read the ad wrong and the job advertised is actually for some 'light housekeeping'. Then there's the one about the girl who is at drama school, but dreams of doing a secretarial course and practises shorthand under the bedclothes at night.

We laugh and laugh and laugh, the cameramen laugh and the sound men laugh: we feel success in our bones. An all-female sketch show is new, it's cutting edge. We don't get a series.

You can still find the pilot episode on YouTube apparently. I haven't dared look.

So it's back to the circuit, but other jobs creep in. I occasionally get asked onto Radio 4's *Just a Minute* with my *Dear Jenny, Dear Julie* pal Nicholas Parsons. Unbeknownst to me at the time, JAM will become part of my comedy career from the mid-eighties until we lose Nicholas in 2020.

I do my first guest slot before Phoebe is born and am made to feel terribly self-conscious by Clement Freud, who is a complete shit. Freud dies in 2009 and is posthumously accused of sexually abusing children. When I hear this, I'm not surprised; he was vile. The last time I guest on *Just a Minute* with him, he is an elderly and frail man, accompanied by a female nurse from an agency who is visibly upset by his predatory behaviour backstage. Freud was rude and bombastic and a terrible bully; he was also ghastly to Nicholas Parsons throughout their entire working life.

Good riddance.

Nicholas, on the other hand, I adore. He is never anything but kind to me, and when he dies I cry and cry.

The Texas-Sized Turkey

The offer to do a sitcom comes out of the blue. I audition for the part of 'Box Office Girl' for a new Channel 4 show called *Packet of Three*.

From what I can remember, it's a toss-up between me and Josie Lawrence for the part.

I nab it, which is surprising considering Josie is a much better actress.

When we make the pilot, I am carrying a great deal of post-baby weight, but when it comes to making the series I have lost so much of this weight the director thinks I have AIDS.

I need to quickly explain something right now. In my teens I am chubby, cute and very available; in my early twenties I am anorexic and odd-looking but sort of pretty; in my mid- to late twenties I dabble once more with plumpness, and shift from being pretty to quite plain (almost on purpose). But in my thirties I blossom into being really quite beautiful. I can say this now because, despite it being a long time ago, I can remember very well the power that looking fabulous gives me.

For a number of years I am simply gorgeous, not entirely naturally, but I have always been good with make-up. Even now, give me ten minutes with a make-up bag and I can transform myself from hideous old boiler to attractive older woman. All I need is foundation, blusher, lipstick and a black eyeliner for my false mole which is a real mole but one that I darken for effect.

Sadly, I can't wear eye make-up any more, because I have chronic dry eye, but in the nineties I am the mistress of the smoky eye! I also start doing a fuck ton of yoga.

OK, let's get back to *Packet of Three*. This is a weird one, a show that should work but kind of doesn't. It's set in the fictional Crumpsall Palladium, but in reality we film in Wakefield Opera House and the premise is that Frank Skinner and I work backstage, while Henry Normal is the MC for the real acts that appear on the real stage in front of a real audience.

So, it's a hybrid, part fictional backstage sitcom, part genuine variety show. It's original and innovative and written by the three of us, with extra material from the comic Donna McPhail, who is appointed to help me.

Poor Donna: she's a great stand-up, but we have zero writing chemistry and, compared to working with Julie, I don't really enjoy the process. I think Donna finds me annoying.

Once the series has been commissioned, Phoebe, Dommie and I move up to Holmfirth, famous for being the location of the rural sitcom *Last of the Summer Wine* (and don't they know it), and set up home for the duration of the filming, with Geof driving up at weekends.

Henry is a poppet, still is, but Frank and I have a more complicated relationship. We both have killer comedy instincts but his are sharper than mine. I feel he always gets to the joke before me. I'm sort of in awe, but I also feel that sometimes he talks over me. The bottom line is that Frank is a brilliant stand-up and I am in his shadow.

People still come up to me and chat about *Packet of Three*. It's mostly blokes who remember how absolutely filthy it was; the conversation usually begins with 'I wasn't allowed to watch it, because my parents wouldn't let me, but ... ' Sadly the reviews aren't written by pre-pubescent boys.

I remember idly flicking through *Time Out* while waiting for a train and accidentally reading a crit of the first episode. Under a photo of the cast is the line 'May God forgive all those involved in this Texas-sized turkey'.

Hahahahahahahahahahaaaaaaaaaaaargh.

Somehow, we manage to get a second series.

In the intervening year, Henry is unceremoniously dumped, which is mean, considering the idea was his in the first place. He is replaced by the very brilliant Kevin Eldon and someone called Roger Mann – neither of these bookings have anything to do with me, although I am a huge fan of Kevin's and will adore working with him on various jobs throughout the years.

In the break between series, Frank has also won the Perrier Comedy Award, the Edinburgh Festival's holy grail for stand-ups, which makes his management (later to be mine) very demanding about his billing. Frank is promoted and in series two he appears both backstage in the sitcom bits, and in front of the curtain as the MC.

His management buy him a PlayStation for his dressing room. 'What is he, a twelve-year-old boy?' I seethe!

During the final rehearsals in London before we all pack up and go north again, I have a row with Frank and lose my voice. We are days away from filming; the doctor cannot find any physical reason why I cannot speak. Apparently it's 'all in my mind'.

Oh, great.

I resort to seeing the hypnotherapist I once encountered on *The Jonathan Ross Show*, when I was booked some years previously to see if this fellow could increase the size of my tits – I know, right!!!!!!! God, we put up with so much shit.

Anyway, tits apart, this guy explains to me why my voice has decided not to work (I'm not being listened to, so why bother?)

and coaxes it back into action. By the time I leave his office in Hampstead, I can speak.

My favourite memory of filming this series, now called *Packing Them In*, is when Caroline Aherne comes to do a stand-up spot as her nun character and stays with me in my house. We spend the night gossiping, gossiping, gossiping. What a talent she was, what a bloody tragedy.

The other silver lining to the series is that I've been allowed to swap Donna for Julie and we laugh a lot writing a recurring two old biddies in a ladies' lavatory sketch, which no one else finds remotely funny.

During this second series Phoebe goes to a local nursery school and develops a lovely little northern accent, but Dommie does the one thing I ask her not to (not worth going into here, as it's both personal and complicated) and I have to let her go.

I might be overreacting, but we have one golden rule and she breaks it. There are lots of tears, but it's time to move on. I still remember her with huge affection and hope that she is very happy.

There is no series three and I think I'm relieved.

The Ginger and the Peroxide Blonde

Back in London we have a new nanny/life saver. I meet a curly red-haired Viking woman in a charity shop in Camberwell. She has a potato-faced toddler in a buggy, and I have Phoebe with me. I can't recall how this happens, but by the time we leave the shop Vanessa has agreed to help me out. Phoebe is only three, but I swear she looks relieved.

She is not trained and yet Vanessa is the wisest woman I will ever meet. She looks after a number of other local kids, and we are lucky that she can slot us in.

Eventually Phoebe becomes the oldest of three regulars, who also include Billy and Jacob. My daughter now has two ready-made pretend siblings, and Vanessa rotates the childcare around their three homes.

This works; sometimes I am tripping over other people's offspring, sometimes the house is empty and I can write in peace. It helps that the boys are adorable, and their mothers are brilliant, too. Phoebe is also at a Montessori nursery in the mornings; she wears a green checked pinny, paints terrible pictures and makes new friends.

I sort of neglect her quite a lot at this stage. One evening when she is about four and should probably have been in bed, we watch *EastEnders*, and suddenly she points at Barbara Windsor on the screen and says 'Mummy'.

I have taken to wearing a beehive on stage. Phoebe will also occasionally refer to me as 'the present lady'. Throughout her young life I buy her a lot of cheap tat from motorway service stations. Sorry, P.

The fact that my daughter is as nice as she is, is mostly due to Vanessa's influence. I am the badly behaved one in our house and occasionally Vanessa will put me on the naughty step.

Vanessa is still very much part of our lives; she is still our freckled red-haired Viking, and a ninja with knitting needle and crochet hook. She is part of my human safety net; both Phoebe and I can tell her anything and I think even now Phoebe sometimes tells her things she doesn't tell me. Children need to have more than just their parents to confide in.

In 1993 I take my first hour-long stand-up show since the Perry Como debacle up to the Edinburgh Festival. It's called *Peroxide Comedy*.

I am thirty-three and my telly career has already veered off the rails with the cancellation of *Packet of Three*. It's back to the stand-up, back to the festival and, once again, there is no summer holiday for the Eclair-Powell family.

Before I head north, I ask a girl I vaguely know to video and edit me getting my hair bleached, and once I arrive in Edinburgh I buy a second-hand telly so that I can play the video to the punters as they troop into the venue.

The video is accompanied by a soundtrack featuring only bleached blonde female singers, though I doubt anyone makes this connection! To this day hearing Transvision Vamp's 'Baby I Don't Care' sends me hurtling back to that show.

I'm possibly taking my stand-up seriously for the first time in my career. The previous year I'd performed a one-woman play called *Mummy's Little Girl*, about child stardom and pushy show-biz mums. It got pretty mixed reviews (the *Guardian* hated it) but sold really well. But the time has come to make a concerted effort to pursue a stand-up career.

Fact is, I am never going to make it as an actress. I'm just not good enough. Even I don't believe me when I'm playing someone else. I'm only convincing as me, or a hyped-up/more interesting version of me, and deep down I know this. Maybe it's time to play to my strengths, whatever they may be. I'm conflicted because, while I don't think I'm really an actress, I don't think I'm a natural-born stand-up either. I'm not like Frank, or any number of blokes on the circuit who seem to speak comedy as a second language. I have to work very hard at it. I need to write the jokes. I can't make them up on the spot and I need to learn them, all of them.

I do the full run and find by the end of it that it's perfectly possible to perform an hour of stand-up without coming off stage feeling like you're going to throw up and faint. The trick is to breathe.

Peroxide Comedy is intensely raunchy and sweary; it's very nineties.

I am very nineties. I start playing the ladette role to the hilt; my stage persona becomes a lot more swaggering. She is sexier. I start wearing skin-tight trousers and red leather spike-heeled ankle boots that match my scarlet lipstick, and the yoga sessions pay off. I am flat-bellied and my arms are toned.

I also have new management. I've finally joined Frank's team, Avalon Management, who have premises above a wine bar on Tin Pan Alley. Avalon are fast gaining a reputation for being the bad boys of comedy management. Their main rivals are Off The Kerb, run by the charismatic but quite bonkers Addison Cresswell, who will die far too young.

I sign up with Richard Allen-Turner, who, over thirty years later, is still my manager today.

Occasionally, over the decades, I will hate Avalon.

Belonging to a management group which represents lots of other comics can be difficult. There is always jealousy, someone else always seems to be doing better and they never buy me a PlayStation!

However, since the very beginning they have fought my corner and enabled so many things that would have been impossible without them. Avalon aren't just agents, they are also producers; they can juggle live tours with TV work, advertising deals with after-dinner speeches, book contracts with podcasts. It's never been a simple case of them just picking up the phone.

Once upon a time, Avalon consisted of just three members of staff, but the company is now vast with offices in the States and a massive HQ in Kensal Rise, with table football, a help-yourself drinks fridge and a glass fishbowl full of Werther's Originals in reception. Check out my pockets.

I don't often schlep out to Kensal Rise as it's a slog from south London, but if I do I always make sure it's worth my while. One day I'm going to get hold of the keys to the stationery cupboard.

I am disappointed not to get a Perrier nomination for *Peroxide Comedy*. I genuinely think I'm in with a chance, but when the list comes out I'm not on it. However, Donna McPhail is. I spend the day under my duvet, burning with shame and jealousy, but come the evening I have to get up and go and do my non-nominated show.

I am gutted. How long will I have to jump through these hoops? Why can't I just win something and get a nice telly job and earn pots of money? Why can't things be easier?

Because I am so riddled with jealousy, I dread Donna winning, but the Perrier Award that year goes to Lee Evans who, as we all know, is a superstar.

The Author and the Showgirl

In 1994 Richard manages to get me my first book deal: Virgin Publishing offer me 10K for writing *The Book of Bad Behaviour*. The deadline is short and when they ask if I have a computer, which will speed the process up, I panic and lie, 'Of course, hahaha.' What!!!!!!?

At the time, I am actually using a strange electric typewriter, with a built-in mini word processor screen which is capable of correcting one full line as you type . . . imagine!

Before that, it was Tippex or type it up again.

Geof comes home with our first Apple Mac computer. They've been using them at the *TV Times* for a while now and the art department no longer sit perched on stools at big wooden drawing boards. The past is beginning to disappear.

The plan is for me to write the book and then write a matching show which I can take up to Edinburgh and subsequently take out on tour. It's a plan. I just need to get on with it.

The computer is grey and very boxy with a fat back, like those tellies you still find in crap hotels. Apple is yet to get sexy, but I have never used anything else and PCs make me physically cringe.

A marriage made in Blackpool: June and Derek

Thrilled with myself, aged four

Drama school headshot –
aka the face of anorexia

JENNY ECLAIR

First stand-up headshot – 'very keen'

Jenny Eclair

Mother and child

Happy families

Bad Behaviour book and tour publicity shot

Prozac and Tantrums poster shot

Video cover shoot, *Top Bitch*

And the winner of this year's Perrier Award is ...

The original *Grumpy Live*
line-up: Dillie, Jenny and
Linda

Grumpy backstage in Oz

Fifty Shades of Beige with Susie and Kate

The controversial bra
and pants shot for *How to
Be a Middle-Aged Woman
(Without Going Insane)*

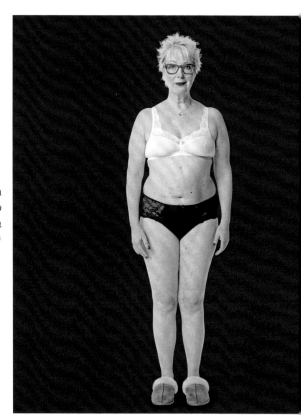

The Covid-delayed
60! (FFS!)

Taskmaster team,
series 15, with
Ivo, Frankie, Mae,
Kiell, Alex and
Greg

Arlo and Phoebe

Me and the old man

I am very proud of getting a book deal, even if the end result consists of pages and pages of illustrated smut, which retails at £6.99 and comes with a parental advisory warning.

The Book of Bad Behaviour is full of tips and hints as to how to behave badly at all times, anywhere and everywhere.

For example:

Children's Parties – what a nightmare!

These are best avoided. What I do is attempt to blow up a few balloons, but because I smoke so much my lungs collapse, so off I go to hospital, smiling and waving.

Here are some other ways you can spoil your child's birthday party:

1) Forget to hand out the invitations.

[And so it goes on. My solution for the party bag dilemma is to give them a disposable lighter each.]

It's very silly and I'm not sure I mean that as a compliment. It also contains material which would be far too offensive to publish now and, quite honestly, some of it makes me cringe. The nineties were a different world and sometimes that world wasn't very nice.

However, bits of it are vaguely funny: the idea of behaving badly in a toyshop and removing the microchip that makes a talking Barbie Doll say 'You're my best friend' for one that says, 'I am the antichrist, now give me back my nipples' still makes me snigger aged sixty-four.

Also, if I still had periods I might be tempted to use this gag, on childbirth:

Do you know, what really hurt was when the midwife referred to my vagina as the birth canal. CANAL! It's not that big, well it wasn't until this baby pushed her great fat head down it. Now it's gone like a badly washed jumper, all baggy around the neck. I don't use tampons any more, I just roll up the duvet.

Now that is a joke that I think still stands today.

I am pictured on the front cover with a blonde bob wearing a pair of devil's horns. I look like my thirty-five-year-old daughter.

The matching *Bad Behaviour Show*, which I write for Edinburgh and beyond, is introduced on voiceover by Kathy Burke. Kathy agrees to come to a mate's studio in south London and record an intro for twenty Silk Cut and a can of Red Stripe. We are both true to our word.

Kathy plays the Goddess of Bad Behaviour who is represented onstage by a female mannikin, which I have collaged in blood-red roses torn from magazines and seed catalogues! The Goddess of Bad Behaviour is the rebel in all of us, she is the hidden force that makes us stay out late, have that third 'last' drink and get up to all kinds of mischief.

I make my Edinburgh entrance by staging a fall down an entire set of stairs. Sadly, the stairs are positioned to the left-hand side of the raked audience seating and hardly anyone sees this choreographed tumble, apart from my flatmate Stewart Lee, who loves the entrance much more than any of the following content.

To cushion the fall, I wear a massive shaggy pink fake-fur jacket over a gold swimming costume and some snakeskin-patterned cling-on trousers. By the end of the run, my beautiful gold-heeled shoes are completely battered and I am covered in bruises.

It's a good show and some people love it. Yet again, I wonder if there's a tiny chance of a Perrier nomination. There isn't: not only do I fail to make the short list, neither does any other female comic.

The lack of female representation doesn't cause any fuss; we are used to it. In 1994 huge numbers of people still mistrust 'funny' women – this despite Victoria Wood and French and Saunders being adored by the nation. No one doubts their talent, but surely they are the exception, and anyway three funny women is enough. This is genuinely how it feels, as if once a woman crosses the threshold to success the door is firmly shut behind her.

When Jo Brand rather brilliantly starts barging her way into the premier league, I feel very third division. In fact, I'm so insecure that when no women are nominated for the award that year, instead of being incensed I am relieved. This is because my generation of comics, instead of feeling secure enough to support each other, see every other woman on a bill as a threat. You might really like them, you might be friends, but if there's a big gig going and they get it, it means they have won, and you have lost. It's unhealthy, and one of the biggest changes that I have seen in my forty-plus years of stand-up is that women comics these days actively want their mates to do well. They promote them; there is a culture of giving each other a leg-up. As a young female comic in the eighties and nineties I am far too desperate to behave generously, and I secretly want every other woman on the circuit to die on their arse every time they step onstage.

Like a Dog with a Bone

I am back in Edinburgh for the 1995 festival, sharing a top-floor flat on Dundas Street, one of those massive stone-stepped tenements with an entrance hall as big as an entire London flat.

Over the years I share various flats with various fellow performers, all of whom are male. Some are heavy drinkers, some are coke fiends, some are dirty stop-outs.

Others are like Chris Addison, who, on inspecting the facilities of the festival rental kitchen, marches off to John Lewis to equip the flat with a cafetière and some 'decent teaspoons'.

This year I am wearing black PVC trousers onstage which make me sweat so hard that my fake tan wears off around wherever they rub.

In my wardrobe I still have two pairs of glitter kitten-heeled ankle boots, in gold and black, which I believe date back to this era, and in my daughter's wardrobe, no doubt in a crumpled heap, is the sleeveless T-shirt I wore onstage. It's made from some kind of neoprene fabric and features a girl smiling on the front; once upon a time there were little glass beads on the tracks of her braces. These have since fallen off and the trousers rotted through at the gusset.

The show is called *Prozac and Tantrums* and the poster is a

Warhol-esque picture of me in purple, white and yellow, with my hair in electric rollers, false eyelashes *in situ* and a fag in hand.

I have been smoking since I was fifteen and, twenty years on, I have a twenty-a-day habit. I'm convinced that smoking helps me keep my weight down. I have been plump, I have been anorexic, I have been plump/bordering on fat again and officially fat post-Phoebe, and now I am probably in the best shape I will ever be. How healthy I am doesn't really come into it. I drink like a fish, wake up with an ashtray by the side of my bed and when I'm not boozing, which is basically from waking up to after the show (I'm not a complete pisshead), I'm knocking back the Diet Coke.

I am also not behaving particularly well. During my thirties I cannot believe how gorgeous I am, and I snog a lot of strangers. It becomes quite a habit. Geof is at home, Phoebe is tucked up in bed and Mummy is on the prowl. I go through a phase of regressing into my teenage slag persona and to this day I have no idea what really triggers it.

This is something which causes me huge shame almost thirty years on: I could have lost my family very easily, I could have lost the two people in the world who have always meant the most to me, who have tethered me to some semblance of sanity. Had Geof decided to give up on me, I have no doubt that I wouldn't be where I am today. He never said anything, and it was many years before I knew he knew; he just stood by and seethed. The fact is he loved Phoebe to the very roots of his being, and he knew she loved me. He played the long game and I'm eternally grateful.

At the time I have no real idea why I behave so badly. It feels like revenge, it feels like freedom, I do it because I can, I have the opportunities; I have alcohol in my bloodstream, but that's no excuse.

I am a young mother, insomuch as I'm really fucking immature. I crave excitement and I get that from fleeting snogs with strangers in bars.

Looking back, I'm really appalled. I have always been slightly scared of the things I can do; I have always had this streak of recklessness and this period of really awful behaviour will embarrass me forever. It's my only regret. All the other stupid things I have done in my life have taught me a lesson and I only really hurt myself, but this hurt Geof and I'm sure there is a tiny part of him that will never forgive me.

I can always try and blame the culture of the time, and I genuinely think the nineties are incredibly toxic; there is a huge amount of booze and gear going on. I don't do coke, I haven't done it since I got pregnant, but I drink too much *and* I'm also intoxicated by how much attention I can get.

There are photos of me taken around this time and you can almost smell trouble coming off me. *Prozac and Tantrums* is a highly charged show; my stage persona is the furthest away from the real me that she has ever been. I am a caricature of an ageing lads-mag babe, but it works.

The show fits the zeitgeist: the mid-nineties are decadent and I'm still just about young enough to get away with it and deal with the hangovers.

I spend a few weeks before the festival honing my material with a friend's husband, who just so happens to have incredible comedy chops. His name is Pete Richens and he is/was part of the infamous *Comic Strip* writing team and the lesser-known sidekick to Peter Richardson. Pete is married briefly to my old mate Liza Adamczewski, who I first met life modelling at Camberwell School of Art.

Pete is a tricky piece of work, an ex-junkie with a brain the size of the Elephant and Castle. My writing relationship with him is very tentative at this point; he has never written stand-up before, and I have never thought about structure. This is what he helps me with. He explains that a show can't just be a massive lump of material, that it has to have a shape. I take his notes onboard and rewrite and rewrite and rewrite, until I have a recognisable beginning, middle and end. There are some routines that I vaguely remember to this day.

There is one about a mood ring melting all over my hand when I realise that someone has put an empty Marmite jar back in the kitchen cupboard. This goes on to describe in terrible detail the revenge I wreak on Geof once he comes back from work. I think it involves a golf club round the back of his head.

There is quite a lot of cruel stuff in *Prozac and Tantrums* and when I say cruel, I mean vicious. E.g.: 'Men, you can't live with them ... and you can't just chop them into little pieces and boil the flesh off their bones 'cos that'd be cooking, and I don't do cooking.' I also have a routine about sending Phoebe out to fly-post the show for me, the only problem being that as she's so short my posters end up so low down that all over town dogs are pissing on my face. My poor innocent little six-year-old.

The audience loves it. For once I am completely in step with current comedy fashions. The press machine gears up a few notches and I am featured on the front of the *Sunday Times*, in a white ankle-length silk skirt and pink thirties-style blouse, marching across a grouse moor, beehive askew, with a gun crooked over my arm. 'Jenny Eclair hunts down festival publicity' reads the tagline. Obviously I have never shot anything in my life, but I have always liked a gangster movie and it's a good look.

I am so close to my prey that I can smell it.

Finally

I am in the now defunct Jenners department store buying myself some foundation when I miss a call from my agent (this is pre-mobile phones). He calls back: I'm on the list of Perrier nominees. The relief is overwhelming, and I spend the afternoon in bed, exhausted by a weird sense of vindication.

I realise now that many of you will have read or listened to autobiographies by proper celebrities and you may well be wondering why I'm so fixated on this bloody piddling prize that most of you have never heard of. I think it's because I don't know how else I'm going to break out of the middle; it's very crowded in the middle and I'm fed up with being an also-ran. Basically, I feel ready for some recognition and surely winning an award for the funniest show at the Edinburgh Festival Fringe will propel me into mainstream success, fame and fortune, hahahaha.

There are about five days before the award is announced and the pressure mounts, at least once the show slightly falls apart and I feel like I've blown it.

I'm the only female nominee, though I feel Rhona Cameron might have made the list had she not got into some late-night fracas and ended up punching a copper.

Happily, Boothby Graffoe (who, incidentally, is great) raises my chances by publicly stating that he 'needs the Perrier like a wart on his arse', thus knocking himself out of the running. The panel of judges don't take well to their endless traipse around every eligible show being so rudely dismissed. Good: it's just the American Scott Capurro, Simon Bligh and The Umbilical Brothers (an Aussie double act) to beat.

The award is announced at midnight on Saturday; the venue is a beautiful spiegeltent situated in Charlotte Square. I buy a black lace dress and take Sally Phillips (pre-*Smack the Pony*, etc.), who wears red lace as my date. We both look fabulous, and I figure at least if I lose I will look stunning in defeat.

Lee Evans is making the announcement.

I haven't seen him for so many years now, but he was always incredibly sweet, enthusiastic and genuinely nice. I was shocked when I heard he retired from stand-up almost ten years ago. Maybe he'll be back? I used to perform in tiny clubs with him back in the early nineties; he always had a towel on stage because he'd sweat buckets, I never saw anyone so physically dedicated to their craft. Once upon a time he'd been a very young boxer and it showed.

I am thirty-five, which would be considered old by today's standards. In fact, I wouldn't be eligible these days. I have been around the block many times; I have also been on the telly, albeit in a sitcom that most critics loathed.

But the rules are slightly different in 1995, and back then being a woman is still enough of a novelty to score points. I am also a mother and there aren't many female comics doing 'crap mum' gags either. My biggest rival is possibly the waspish, wise-cracking Scott Capurro, who is gay, hmm, but there has already been a gay winner in '89, while I would be the first female solo artist to win the bloody thing . . .

And I do!

It's a glorious moment. It's everything I went into show

business for. Flowers, champagne and the actual award (a small silver Perrier bottle on a wooden plinth) are thrust into my hands. There is also a cheque for five thousand pounds. Flashbulbs pop and my agent cries (possibly because he also manages Boothby and wanted him to win – haha).

I should have gone home after that moment; I should have taken a cab back to the flat, taken off the cheap black patent stilettoes I'd only bought that morning, had a bath, some toast and gone to bed.

Instead, I start jabbing at my self-destruct button and proceed to do a victory lap around all the bars in Edinburgh, before ending up, pissed out of my head, invading the stage at the Gilded Balloon and insisting on duetting with Leo Sayer. The rest of the night is a bit of a blur, but at 3 a.m. I finally admit defeat and hitch home by myself. My feet are bleeding so much that my tights are glued with blood to the insides of the terrible shoes.

My family are in Wales, staying at my sister's place. They are all there: Geof, Phoebe, my parents, sister and nephew. They stay up to hear the announcement on Radio 4. I forget to call them until I regain consciousness around midday the next day. I pretend to be delighted: 'I'm thrilled,' I trill, my voice hoarse from last night's screaming, but I'm not, I am in a terrible, terrible state.

The Albatross of Success

The day after my Perrier win, I am due to be interviewed by a female *Daily Mail* journalist over afternoon tea. Somehow, I make it to the Balmoral Hotel, where this woman expects a jubilant award-winner. Instead, she gets a hungover, shambling mess who can't stop crying. 'I can't cope,' I weep, 'I don't want it, it's too much.' The silver cake stand remains untouched.

To give this woman her credit she turns the recording device off, puts down her notepad and tells me to go home and rest. 'We won't be publishing this,' she assures me, and they don't – even though they are the *Daily Mail*.

I don't know why so many women find success so tricky, why we are almost happier playing the underdog, constantly on the defensive, ready for the next knock-back. This time, when the knock-back doesn't happen, I can't really deal with it; I feel an overwhelming responsibility, to myself and to women in comedy generally. I feel like a fraud.

In some respects I don't know how to not feel bitter; bitterness has kept me going for so long, and suddenly my modus operandi has been taken away from me and I feel panicked.

In the past, people's expectations were pretty low and I would often blow them out of the water. My worry now is that people will expect me to be brilliant and I don't feel very brilliant. I feel desperately homesick, I want Geof and I want Phoebe, but I still have a couple more gigs to do and I am not used to people clapping more at the introduction of my name than they do at the end of the show. I don't seem to be able to live up to the hype, I limp through to the end of the festival, I am emotionally and physically exhausted.

In the future, when I have a bunch of tours and a few West End runs (complete with matinees) under my belt, the idea of doing approximately twenty-one shows in just over three weeks will seem like chicken feed, but my paranoia is breaking me apart.

I need to go home. I am craving normality; I want to do a weekly shop and have a bath which hasn't previously been used by four hairy male comics and Phoebe needs to go back to school. There are new shoes to buy, chestnut-coloured Mary Janes, shiny as autumn conkers.

My daughter is six, her baby teeth are starting to fall out; she is a sweet-natured, sociable, imaginative kid who loves books, particularly *Babar*, dressing up, drawing and watching telly. I never feel I need to tell her what to do; I don't remember ever having to tell her off much. Maybe I leave all that to Vanessa?

She goes to a school where the motto is 'A child is a fire to be kindled, not a vessel to be filled', whose only promise in return for the school fees is that they will teach your child to read and swim. This is enough for me, and Phoebe is happy. She has friends from backgrounds insanely different from hers. One is rumoured to be a princess. Her mother is immaculate; when the child is chauffeur-driven to our house, Phoebe's rabbit sits on this child's lap and eats her frock. I offer to replace it, but the child's mother laughs almost hysterically. She thinks we are very poor.

Post the excitement of the Perrier win, my management flap about trying to exploit my new-found success. I'm mostly recovered but my confidence is actually eggshell thin. I act big in public and snivel in private. They are already talking about sending me back the following year: why would I want to return to the scene of the crime, I wonder. Deep down I feel as though I stole the bloody thing.

Not now; now it's just a tarnished silver object that sits on a bookcase in my study. I am no longer that woman, I'm three stone heavier and so much more experienced. Experience is eventually the thing that will give me confidence. Now that I'm in my sixties, no one can take forty-plus years of graft away from me. I have a back catalogue, I have done stuff people can't deny, I am not a fluke or a one-hit wonder.

I may not be as successful as I would have liked: no shiny-floor show, no prime-time telly series, no nice afternoon quiz show. Oh, to sit behind a desk and take the weight off my feet, like a load of middle-aged blokes do, but there is enough to be proud of . . . just.

Avalon keep me busy; post-Perrier there is a tour and a video and appearances on shows such as Des O'Connor's prime-time chat show.

This is quite the eye-opener. I am taken to a small cottage in the grounds of Elstree Studios, where two of Des's goons (I mean scriptwriters) go through my material, devising questions for Des that will trigger specially sanctioned gags from my stand-up set. It's long-winded and painstaking but, when it comes to the record, I get distracted by something that happens in the audience, veer off script and have a great time. I come offstage congratulating myself on being spontaneously funny. Go me. Unfortunately, Des disagrees. He hates what just happened and I am told backstage that if I want to appear on the show I will have to come back again and do it 'properly'.

Des's warm-up man, my mate Kate's brother, Ted Robbins, finds me weeping on a staircase and walks me across the car park to where a car is waiting to take me home. He is beyond kind: 'It's the business, not you,' he reminds me. I cry all the way home, but I go back some weeks later, do it Des's way and the interview makes it onto the telly. I watch a clip of this interview on YouTube while writing this book and I have to say I look fucking phenomenal. I am wearing a pair of black spangled skin-tight trousers with a matching jacket and I gasp when I see myself. Of course, it's before HD telly, but even so!

The *Prozac and Tantrums* show is repackaged as *Top Bitch* for the video recording. It's filmed at Her Majesty's Theatre (now His Majesty's), which is a whopping West End venue most commonly known for staging *The Phantom of the Opera*. I arrive in a stretch limo, complete with an unnecessary bodyguard, and perform the show twice to cover all the shots that are needed. It's intense and the end product doesn't sell very well.

That said, a copy in good condition on eBay today will cost you £30. I am almost tempted, but I've got better things to spend my money on!

Looking back, I know that even after all this, after getting what I wanted for so long, I'm not entirely satisfied.

Now that I'm in my sixties, I realise that success does not happen with the wave of a magic wand. It's a process, and for me that process has been one step forward, half a step back, for over forty years.

Trying to Do It All

I spend my Perrier Award prize money on a new washing machine and some other bits for the house. It's nice to be able to contribute a bit more financially at last. And, for a while over the next few years, the cash starts rolling in. I'm not talking silly money: I will never have a pool or a circular gravel drive, but it's more than I've ever earned before.

This is the start of the haymaking years, it's the nineties, and we are all trying to live the dream.

Phoebe both benefits and suffers from this and I have vague recollections of behaving in a ridiculously extravagant fashion over her birthdays and Xmases for a number of years.

For her seventh birthday I take her entire class to see *Grease* in the West End: twelve little girls in velvet party dresses stuffed into a limo, burgers at Fashion Café first and ice creams in the interval.

Then there's the Xmas when we buy her so many toys she begs for a rest halfway through the unwrapping. She is a massive Spice Girls fan and among the many gifts we shower on her head is a pink electric guitar that someone at Geof's office was selling cheap. Brilliant: she will *love* it.

Years later she admits to us the thing had terrified her. 'I felt

under this terrible pressure,' she confides. 'I thought, they want
me to be a pop star and I'm not sure I want to be a pop star.'
My little mite: somewhere there is a photograph of her looking
stricken with this guitar round her neck, an albatross by any
other name.

We also take her cousin Zack with us on a luxury holiday to
Antigua, which turns out to be really horrible. We stay in one of
those gated resorts where all the 'romantic touches' such as rose
petals on the bed are fake. In the distance a volcano rumbles an-
grily, the sky is dark, the glasses plastic, Zack falls off a golf buggy,
I have a row with a beach vendor, everything is ugly. Maybe I
should have started a pension plan instead, hahahaha.

I enjoy having treats.

I get my hair bleached in a salon in Chelsea, buy leather jeans,
a leather skirt, a pair of leather shorts with a matching waistcoat,
a big leather coat and a stockinette dress from Jean Paul Gaultier.
Some of these items still hang in my 'showbiz' wardrobe; most
have been nicked by Phoebe, who wears the leather shorts to
this day.

I think Geof enjoys me making money; he's carried the financial burden for the two of us for a long time. Things get fairer, but
we never, ever have a joint account.

We can afford takeaways and bottles of wine for friends
and there are family holidays in villas in Majorca with the
Thompsons and their two boys and I get black cabs everywhere.

Avalon really want me to be a very successful stand-up, but
I am already feeling slightly trapped by the persona I have created onstage. She is exhausting to live with. She is not me, not
the true me, she is highly exaggerated, a foul-mouthed drunken
sexpot, which is probably why I end up editing an edition of
Loaded magazine and doing a live gig for them in Northampton.
This ends with me and a number of Page 3 girls being heckled
off the stage under a shower of pint glasses (fortunately not glass)

and the real-life editor James Brown going AWOL and being discovered some days later in a ditch.

I am described as 'the most outrageous woman in Britain', when in reality I'm just a mum who is quite good at swearing.

Although I am very convincing at being this incarnation of Jenny Eclair onstage, I have a feeling she will come to a sticky end.

I am restless, I don't know at this point if I can be funny and completely authentic – I just know that stage Jenny is not something I want to be full-time; she isn't good for me.

However, like a dog returning to its own sick (a Stewart Lee phrase, I think) I go back to Edinburgh in '96 with a new show called *Wig On, Teeth In*, a title which basically sums up how I feel.

The reviews are good and I sell well, but I am relieved when it's over; my paranoia has been bad and I end up needing Valium for panic attacks. These attacks manifest themselves in the world tilting and me feeling like I'm falling off the edge. Geof and Phoebe are in Majorca with Zack; apparently people watch him on the beach with two small blond children who look like twins and presume he's a widower, and he plays up to it by mistily looking out to sea in a sad kind of way. Meanwhile, in Edinburgh I have to cling to the side of the bed during the night.

Hmmm, Valium: there's nothing better when you need it and I have needed some form of the stuff at various points in my life. Even now, I keep an emergency stash in my washbag.

The opportunities that arise post-Perrier are not life-changing, but they are what you might call diverse. They include a sex show on an obscure channel which I host rather cheerfully while wearing a great deal of latex. It basically involves me interviewing people with fetishes, including a couple who use a human-sized rabbit hutch for their elaborate sex games. The favoured scenario involves her being trussed up in the hutch eating carrots while he pops out to the shops.

Try as I might, I can't find any evidence of this show on the internet, but I know I didn't make it up. It was the first time I met Vanessa Feltz, who didn't have a fetish by the way, she was on as a relationship expert. I'm sure she will vouch for me!

Just texted her: she can't remember what it was called either.

I also make an hour-long documentary called *If I Were Prime Minister*, which is a queasy mix of politics and arsing around. I shouldn't have done it. I make up stupid policies which are meant to be funny, such as schools opening when the pubs open and closing when the pubs shut. Viewers are rightly annoyed and after that I steer clear of anything too political.

I am not a political comic; some of my friends are, but I'm achingly centrist, which, let's face it, leaves me open to abuse from all sides. These days I know not to stray into territory that needs more research than I have time for. I am not a stupid woman, but I am not well enough informed to do programmes such as *Question Time*, even though they've asked many times. No one needs half-baked opinions from so-called celebrities and, in any case, the money's shit.

Post-Perrier Award, I am not instantly famous. I don't get recognised on the streets, although I do occasionally get mistaken for a woman who runs a dry cleaner's in Streatham.

However, I am well known within the industry, an industry that doesn't really know what to do with me. After all, they already have their quota of funny women; having another might lead to confusion. People might start thinking women are equally as funny as men, they'd start expecting to see them on panel games and delivering the punchlines in sketch shows and sitcoms: where would that leave the men?

The nineties are far more difficult for women than we ever give them credit for. We are tit-deep in a culture that pretends women can behave like men, but this ladette nonsense doesn't actually do us any favours. Ultimately, it's damaging.

This is the era of 'celebrities' falling in and out of the Groucho Club, of powdery residue on the back of toilet cisterns everywhere, of Chris Evans asking Victoria Beckham if she's lost her baby weight, weeks after having Brooklyn, and weighing her live on *Don't Forget Your Toothbrush* – which, incidentally, has none of the charm of *The Tube*.

Unemployment is at an all-time low, money gets splashed around everywhere: the decade may have started with Thatcher, but Cool Britannia is on its way, and in 1997 New Labour will landslide their way to victory and Take That will split up.

It is a mashed-up decade; maybe every decade is? I am thirty-five when I win the Perrier and I still don't really know what I want to be: writer, actress, comic? I decide to have a bash at everything and sometimes my choices backfire.

The Pick 'N' Mix Years

A few years after my Radio 4 *Dear Jenny, Dear Julie* co-writer Julie Balloo has her first baby in 1993, we decide to try and harness our experiences of motherhood into a comedy drama and, thankfully, in 1997 Radio 4 take the bait.

The premise of *On Baby Street* is simple. I play Mother Nature, flitting in and out of the private lives and homes of three very different pregnant couples who live on the same street. There is a lot to be proud of: the writing is great, but the real magic comes with the casting.

Over three series we manage to book the likes of Kathy Burke, Keith Allen, Frances Barber, Caroline Aherne and my old drama school bedfellow Graham Fellows (aka Jilted John). Caroline is extraordinary. She has married the musician Peter Hook (of Joy Division and New Order fame) in a dress she swears was from Dorothy Perkins and a pair of shoes from Dolcis.

I cannot equate the prudish vest-wearing Caroline that stayed with me during *Packet of Three* with the role of rock star's wife. I wonder if Hookie ever gets a blowjob? It's the kind of thing rock stars expect and the kind of thing I can't imagine Caroline enjoying. She is as hilarious and unpredictable as ever; one day she tells us it's her birthday and we all sing 'Happy Birthday'. As soon as we're done, she says, 'It isn't really.'

Hookie comes with her to the recordings; he and Keith get on well and Keith goes into show-off mode whenever the rock star is around. On the occasions when this goes too far, Kathy Burke puts an end to proceedings by shouting, 'Oh fuck off, Keef', and he immediately stops being a prat.

On Baby Street can still be heard, often in the early hours of the morning on Radio 4 Extra; sadly the repeat fees amount to pennies. I cannot tell you how many times I have received cheques totalling £1.35.

In some respects, writing *On Baby Street* prepares the ground for some of my future writing; there is a voice and a language in the series that I will adopt later when tackling novels.

On Baby Street comes to an inevitable end when the babies are no longer babies. So Julie and I launch a new Radio 4 sitcom, *Just Juliette*, about a failed TV talk-show host who has disgraced herself by swearing on a live pre-watershed *Children in Need* TV show and has been cast aside by the industry. Guess who plays Juliette? Yup, bagsied the title role. No point writing it if I can't be in it, I reason.

Annabel Giles plays my agent. Here is a woman underestimated by the industry; she is beautiful, clever and hilarious, and she dies far too young in 2023 of a brain tumour at the age of sixty-four. She deserved so much more than she got from the business and it makes me angry.

Just Juliette is not the hit that *On Baby Street* was, and after two series we are done. Looks like we are going to have to go back to the drawing board, which is tricky because Julie is pregnant again. Turns out forty-one isn't too old after all.

Julie has severe morning sickness that lasts for days and puts her in hospital. I can't keep relying on her to help me with ideas. I'm going to have to work my future out for myself.

Avalon don't really want me wasting my time doing radio; telly is where true success lies, everyone knows this, and somehow we manage to twist Channel 5's arm into giving me my own late-night chat show.

Channel 5 is brand new. Initially they want me to be one of their 'faces', but later on they seem to change their mind and go for Mariella Frostrup instead!

The show is called *Jenny Eclair Squats* and when I watch excerpts on YouTube I'm not sure if it was before its time, a bit meta or quite shit. It's a mix of scripted and ad-lib chat with what you might call an eclectic mix of not quite showbiz folk. For example, the first episode, filmed in Brunswick Villas, features me, all breathy with a beehive and leopard-skin boots, trying to casually make conversation with Oz Clarke (wine expert), Sophie Dahl (supermodel) and Stewart Lee (Stewart Lee). I think it may have been the last chat show Stewart ever appeared on, and he is never without a cigarette onscreen. It's something I would do much better now, but in my thirties I'm so eager for the jokes to work that I forget to make the conversation flow, and I get impatient when people aren't funny. Nobody watches it and I don't know whether to be furious or relieved.

It's like there's still a massive hurdle out there and I can't quite clear it. I am beautiful, I am funny, but I can never jump high enough. Maybe I try too hard: I'm certainly an acquired taste – 'A bit like whelks,' I joke.

I am distracted from stand-up and telly by an offer that comes out of the blue. I'm offered the lead role in a West End play at the enormous Piccadilly Theatre. The play is *Steaming* by Nell Dunn, who also wrote *Poor Cow* and *Up the Junction*. Nell is an unlikely feminist heroine, a posh girl who has always understood how other people tick. *Steaming* had been a massive stage hit in the early eighties; maybe it was too soon for a revival?

Too late: the play is cast, and rehearsals begin. For those who don't know, *Steaming* is set in a Turkish bathhouse, where women of all types strip off and reveal more than just their tits insomuch as their backgrounds, personalities and family lives are also exposed.

However, during this particular incarnation not only will tits be revealed, but fannies and bums, too. The production is designed as a period piece but, whereas the original production had been slightly coy with the nudity, this time around we are going full frontal.

Well, that gets the press going.

My character, Josie, is one of those London goodtime girls, a tart with a heart and lousy taste in men. Josie works in topless bars, which causes the *Daily Mail* to comment on my assets not being really adequate for the job.

I am thirty-seven, I am still very slender, I smoke my head off and I do yoga: I'm in great nick. The only thing that bothers me about taking my kit off in front of an audience is the fact that I have the skin tones of a jellyfish. During rehearsals I hire a massive wooden sunbed, install it in my attic and rotisserie myself inside it, pulling the lid down over my body until I start to slither around in my own sweat.

Healthwise, the tanning bed is one of my all-time regrets, that and the fags. I wish I'd used a bottle of fake tan, as I do now. But schoolgirl memories of streaky Tanfastic run deep and I decide to go for the real thing. I am the colour of Phoebe's hamster by press night.

My mother is in the front row; she blinks when I come onstage and begin to casually strip off while delivering my lines. I'm fine until I get down to my undies, at which point the bra refuses to unhook: I've got the strap twisted and eventually resort to pulling the original seventies Playtex number down round my hips and stepping inelegantly out of the thing. Then, as I wrench my knickers off, I hear my mother mutter 'Oh my God' and I struggle not to laugh.

The *Guardian* reviews my pubic hair. Seriously, the sentence goes something like this: 'Once one gets over the fact that Jenny Eclair's pubic hair grows like that naturally, one can concentrate on her performance.' Hahahaha. Back then I had very straight, glossy pubic hair, like a My Little Pony.

The reviews are OK, but not raves; the star of the show is very much the set, of which the *pièce de résistance* is a large plunge pool, set centre stage and big enough for all the cast to jump into for the finale.

As the show trundles on and the audiences dwindle, we get more reckless about jumping into the pool at the end of the show. One night, I attempt to dive-bomb my fellow actresses and my tampon shoots out into the nicely warmed water. Walking back to the dressing room, I tell Julie T. Wallace what's just happened and she marches me back onto the stage and instructs me to fish it out myself. 'It's no one else's job,' she says, being all strict and shining a torch into the pool while I do a fingertip search for a bloody Lil-Let. Julie is great, the whole cast is great, Lynne Miller is still a dear Camberwell mate and neighbour and I think we'd have all made really firm friends if the play hadn't closed four weeks after it opened!

Was it worth it? Who knows. A few weeks before the play opens, my agent gets a call asking if I'd like to take over *The Jack Docherty Show* and host a few episodes while he is unavailable. Everything is set for the opening of *Steaming*, the publicity, the venue, the posters. There's no way I can do both. I turn down the telly, and in my place a more or less unknown young gay Irishman takes over the *Docherty* job. His name is Graham Norton, hahahahahaha!!!!

What's that about being in the right place at the right time?

The truth is, of course, I wouldn't have done that job as well as Graham. Graham is born to do a chat show; he's a complete natural and one of the rare celebrities that I can think of who is genuinely happy in his very famous skin.

Graham is also one of the few people in show business whose success I genuinely don't begrudge, and, considering I'm genuinely the most spiteful and jealous person I know, that's quite an accolade.

What Am I?

As the nineties roll on, I become increasingly conflicted about who I am and what I should be doing. Acting and I are unfinished business, but it takes me a long time to finally admit defeat. The truth is, I'm just not that good; I'm not dreadful, I'm just meh!

However, in 1998 I decide to have another stab with a one-woman theatrical monologue for Edinburgh.

Mrs Nosy Parker is a cautionary tale about a woman who is very jealous of her posh neighbour who seems to have everything. But has she? Well, yes, she has a nice house, husband, child and another on the way, while my character lives in a council flat and has a son in a Thai prison on drug-smuggling charges.

Mrs NP inveigles her way into next door as a cleaner (I still have the pinny), shags the husband, but then has an emotional comeuppance when the new baby is born with a life-limiting illness. Inevitably the husband buggers off and the house and garden fall to pieces.

No prizes for subtlety here: I have always had a streak of the Victorian melodrama about my writing, and personally I think it's marvellous. Hmmmmmm? I am also quite good at pretending to get shagged over a recently polished bathroom sink. Oh, acting!

Before Edinburgh I brave the flight to Australia for the

Melbourne International Comedy Festival, which always takes place over Easter and is (or was then) a much smaller, cosier version of Edinburgh, where the organisers look after you, put you in great accommodation and ply you with Anthropologie smellies (still my favourite brand).

I have a strange relationship with Australia. While I'm there I never quite feel real; there's something odd about the water going the wrong way down the sink that gives me a sense of otherworldliness, an unbalanced sensation, as if I might fall through the earth's crust.

Once again, I feel crowbarred into my Perrier Award-winning persona.

Australian audiences very much demand the PVC jean-wearing ball-breaker and tend to look disappointed when I'm not constantly off my face, swearing and being a bit of a cow.

I try to live up to the hype, but Vanessa and Phoebe come over for a couple of weeks, so every night I have to peel off my mum skin, metamorphose into stage Jenny, strut around on stage for an hour, show off in the bar for another couple of hours, then creep home and get into bed with my nine-year-old daughter who smells of milk and Easter eggs.

I take her to the apartment swimming pool and encourage her to make friends with other children, but there are very few and they are rarely there for more than a night. Hello, new best friend, goodbye new best friend.

But we go to the zoo with the poet John Hegley and his family, complete with toddler daughter, and that evening Phoebe watches John's show.

I am on after John, and as I've never been able to watch another performer before I do my own stuff, I retire backstage and, as I construct my beehive in the dressing room, I can hear my daughter and Vanessa laughing in the audience and the guilt eases a little.

Phoebe is brought up on comedy and to this day feels duty bound to 'laugh properly' at gigs. She is very aware that a comic can't hear smiles and needs the reassurance of proper laughter.

I have very vague memories around this time of a second series of *Jenny Eclair Squats* for Channel 5. This time it's repackaged as *Jenny Eclair's Private Function* and is filmed at the Cobden Club, a private members' club in Notting Hill.

Peter Stringfellow is a guest and teaches us how to eat oysters, and in his honour we have a huge vodka ice luge made in the shape of male and female genitals.

We hold the series wrap party at Stringfellows strip club. Peter is an extraordinarily generous host; we have our own booth and politely clap the pole dancers without going anywhere near them. Peter is much maligned, but he made me laugh a lot. We are all creatures of our time, and his autobiography is hilarious.

The fact that I can remember so little else about these shows (apart from newbie Jamie Oliver turning it down) suggests that it was not a roaring success.

I cannot get telly right; maybe I don't find the right vehicle, maybe I can't decide who to be in front of the camera. Am I full-blown stage Jenny, or am I the other more reasonable, vaguely amusing woman who lurks in the background?

Maybe it's because I can tone myself down that I am offered a series of BBC Bitesize language programmes aimed at GCSE students. Or maybe the commissioning editor had been drinking at lunchtime. I am not a linguist; as previously mentioned, I can con my way through an audition for a German-speaking maid, and I passed O-level Latin second time around, but languages are not my forte and yet here I am teaching kids French, Italian, German and Spanish. Ha!

It's all done through my earpiece. A small plastic pea is inserted into my ear and when it comes to the foreign language bit I just mimic what the resident language expert has just said into my ear. Nothing really makes any sense, but occasionally we have regional food to go with the lingo and I enjoy a taste of my childhood in German week. Mmmm, wurst.

I found a clip from one of these programmes on the internet; there are two comments attached, the first one says, 'I can't stand this woman.'

It takes me a long time to realise that I'm not all that likeable on the telly. I don't have the easy appeal of Gaby Roslin and I'm not as controversial (or as beautiful) as Paula Yates. Unlike Jo Brand, I don't seem to be able to sell myself as 'funny' on-screen. Hence my second video, *The Platinum Collection*, filmed (twice) on my only day off from performing *Mrs Nosy Parker* in Edinburgh, is never released. 'The market for comedy videos has collapsed,' my agent lies kindly. What he means is that my first video sold so badly there's no point distributing a second. I'm heading for forty and feeling a bit washed up. Other women are pulling ahead.

Mel and Sue have a big success with *Light Lunch* on Channel 4, which soon moves to evenings. *Smack the Pony*, with Fiona Allen and my old mates Sally Phillips and Doon Mackichan, takes the comedy world by storm and rightly so. I feel like that old quote: always the bridesmaid, never the bride. There must be something else I can do. I seem to be someone who needs many strings to my bow in order to survive.

What's He Got
That I Haven't?

We have a millennium New Year's Eve party at Brunswick
Villas. Phoebe is ten and dresses up as a millennium
bug. She has always taken fancy dress more seriously than I can
ever be arsed to, though I think this peaks in her late teens when
she goes to a Halloween party as Nancy Spungen, takes her character too literally and passes out on a bathroom floor at 9 p.m.

This is the year my daughter will leave primary and start secondary school. I am potentially a deep embarrassment to her, but
she still has Vanessa and her dad, and they balance things out
a bit.

She loves me, I know this; she leaves me notes in crayon, 'I
love you, but I hate your job, why do you have to go away all the
time?'

'So that I can buy you stuff' is the answer.

I am forty in March 2000 and because I go away all the time
and Geof is still white-collar working at the *TV Times*, we can
afford to go to New York to celebrate. We land the day after my
birthday, on 17 March, in the middle of a snowstorm, which is
causing havoc with the St Patrick's Day parade, the cheerleaders'

legs have gone blue and the stretch limo that picks us up from the airport travels at three miles an hour through a blizzard.

We take Phoebe and Zack, who are both obsessed with Pokémon: all they want to do is buy and swap cards. We might as well have gone to Stevenage. However, I do remember taking the Staten Island ferry, seeing a brilliant Warhol/Basquiat exhibition and having a drink à la Dorothy Parker at the Algonquin. I wish I'd appreciated the trip more, but at the time I was a little blasé. We are very spoilt: we skate in Central Park, eat in diners and take photos of the kids in front of the golden doors of Trump Tower.

Careerwise, I feel pulled in different directions. On the one hand I still want to be a stand-up comic, but not exactly the same one over and over again; and on the other, I also have my first novel coming out.

I have David Baddiel to thank for this career move. In 1996 he publishes *Time for Bed*. It takes me a year to get round to reading it; in fact I'm reading it on the lavatory when I hear Princess Diana has been killed in a car crash and, weirdly, I still can't think of one without the other.

I am distressed about Diana and incensed by David's book. We are with the same management; if they can get David a book deal, then they can bloody well get me a book deal. What's he got that I haven't got? Well, a double first in English from Cambridge University for starters.

No matter. In 1998 I tentatively started writing my first novel and here we are, two years later, about to be published.

The book is called *Camberwell Beauty*.

I'm not sure what people are expecting, but I know what the book isn't: it isn't light, frothy or particularly funny, not unless you have a coal-black sense of humour. It is the cruellest thing I've ever written and a couple of years ago, when we finally get round to recording it on audio, I am shocked by its viciousness.

It's essentially the tale of two one-time best female friends and the disintegration of this friendship, the breakdown of a marriage and the burning down of a house. It's set on a fictional street in London, but very much based on Camberwell Grove.

In fact, one of the houses where I set a great deal of the action is now owned by Florence (& The Machine) Welch. I'm often tempted to pop a copy through her door, but it may freak her out!

I'm not sure quite what I think is going to happen once this book is published, but deep down I'd like to be hailed as a literary sensation; I want to win the Orange Prize (now Women's Prize) for Fiction, I want someone to buy the film rights, I want this to be a massive two fingers up at the world and at all those people who ever doubted me.

None of these things happens, but it's not a disaster either. The book is well written (for someone who got a D for her English A level) but the structure is convoluted and a lot of the characters are pretty unlikeable. Ha! I'm not keen on writing about nice people living nice lives; I like bad-tempered, complicated women, who make massive mistakes and take ludicrous risks. I wonder why.

In the summer of 2000 we take Phoebe on holiday to Italy and stay in a lovely old villa hotel in Santa Maria di Castellabate, which I will later rename Santa Helena di Castellabate for my second book, *Having a Lovely Time*, a title dripping with sarcasm. This is possibly the funniest of all the novels, but, again, only if you find things like food poisoning funny.

While on holiday, I receive the news that the then chancellor of the exchequer Gordon Brown has approved the casting of yours truly to be the new voice of family tax credits. The family tax credits gig is one of the best jobs of my career; all I have to do is sit in a booth and remind people to fill in their forms on time. Almost a quarter of a century on, if I hear a certain Django Reinhardt track I'm back in that booth and I'm still extremely grateful to Gordon Brown for the thumbs-up.

Some performers don't believe in doing ads. I don't have a problem. For me, voiceover work has enabled me to bide my time now and again; it has supplemented other projects and given me breathing spaces when I needed them. Oh, yes, and new bags, boots and fol-de-rols. I'm a teeny bit greedy. Over the years I've done Kellogg's Special K, a tofu ad, a government anti-salt campaign (terrible) and lots of voiceovers for various telly shows.

Shame they all dried up!

Growing Up

When Phoebe leaves her primary school, she cries so much she looks like she's got measles. I pay for a leaving party with another parent: it's a disco in a church hall, and inevitably it gets a bit out of hand and the police are called! The same thing happens on her eighteenth!

My daughter is a revelation to me. I suspect she is vaguely bright, but I don't realise how bright or how talented until we attend a parent/teacher evening, see some of her artwork and speak to her teachers.

'She should do the entrance exams to all the top girls' schools,' they advise. She gets into them all, but chooses James Allen's Girls' School in East Dulwich, which is happily the nearest and the cheapest. It feels like the end of an era: no more flogging into Chelsea, which, weirdly, I will miss.

Back in the nineties I used to regularly see Paula Yates down the King's Road, baby on hip and flowers in her hair. She dies of an accidental heroin overdose in September 2000 and I am devastated.

Paula was the prettiest woman I ever saw in the flesh. Some time in the early eighties she came round to my flat in Camberwell Grove to record a National Poetry Day item for *The Six O'Clock Show*, which she regularly co-presented.

I'm still working as a poet back then and as she walks up my garden path, her left breast (pre-boob job), small, natural and pert, slips out of her flimsy polka-dot dress.

When I point this out, she smirks, says 'How untidy' and tucks it back in. We meet on several TV shows after that, but I don't think she would ever recognise me on the street.

However, one day I'm in the foyer of the BBC when Bob Geldof mistakes me for his wife and taps me on the shoulder. This is in my beehive days; I'm standing with my back to him and when I turn around his face falls.

I am striking in my thirties, but Paula is in another stratosphere. She has everything: gloriously charismatic, funny and bright and then it just all goes to shit. What happened to her is monstrous and we are all complicit in her demise: we bought those papers, we read those stories and we couldn't take our eyes off her as she spiralled out of control.

Days after she dies, my second video, *The Platinum Collection*, which never got distributed, is scheduled to be shown late night on Channel 5. In the show I take the piss out of Paula (I was jealous and spiteful, and it was the nineties), delivering a line about her 'wearing a Little Miss Trouble T-shirt' and adding, 'I don't suppose she could get one that said "Super Slag and Crap Mum"!'

When you take the piss out of people who are more beautiful and famous than you are, you don't expect them to die.

Fortunately, my manager Richard Allen-Turner gets the offending line removed by Channel 5 before it is transmitted. But I still regret it; she didn't deserve what happened. I still think about her.

Maybe I am growing up?

I have a daughter at secondary school, but we still have Vanessa. I'm trying to be home more, but it's not enough and Phoebe is still too young to be left home alone. Things are changing but I am still ploughing the same stand-up groove, playing the ageing slag, but occasionally popping my lady author hat on and wanting to be taken seriously.

It's been five years since I won the Perrier Award and I'm not really sure what to do next. I'm no longer a jobbing comic; I don't do the clubs unless called on for a fundraiser, but I'm a regular on the touring and festival circuit.

At some point I end up at the Montreal comedy festival (Just for Laughs) in Canada, which I hate so much that for the first time in my life I feel suicidal in my hotel room. It's like a meat market and at no point while I'm there do I feel like I am inhabiting my own body. I am going through the motions and feeling angry. I am forty, I am sort of successful, but I feel like I'm treading water. I'm still a cool-looking woman, but it takes a lot of effort. My contact lenses get increasingly uncomfortable, constantly having to do my hair is a bore and the only thing I can do to keep my weight down (apart from the yoga) is drink more Diet Coke and smoke more fags. I feel I'm banging my head against a wall and yet I can't really complain. After all, I'm working, aren't I?

It's not just me that's not making the big time. It will take at least another couple of generations of female comics to make any discernible difference to the sexism of the industry. Right now, in 2000, it's still completely normal for panel shows to have men only line-ups. There are no women hosting quiz shows (still very few) and even the *Smack the Pony* girls aren't really getting the credit they are due.

At the BBC Comedy Awards that year the best of female comedy talent is represented by *The Royle Family* and *Dinner Ladies*; Victoria Wood wins writer of the year but otherwise the girls barely get a look in.

I think deep down I am very angry. I suspect things might not be fair, but I also think I might just be a bit shit. I guess this is what happens to a lot of women; gradually your confidence gets worn down and you start to doubt yourself. After so long in the business, what I finally realise is that you need the heart of a lion, the stamina of an ox and the skin of a rhinoceros.

Death and Vaginas

Xmas 2000: my germ-riddled brother brings botulism into the festivities and by mauling a buffet baked ham with his filthy bare hands ensures that everyone cops it.

I'm not saying my brother finishes Geof's mother off, but when she returns home post-Xmas visit she is in an enfeebled state, and after succumbing to a stroke one night early in the New Year she never regains consciousness.

When I ask my partner about his mother dying, he recalls driving to Dudley 'in a lovely grey Jag'. He sounds like he misses the car more than his mother, but I get it. Their relationship was strained; she guilt-tripped him and pressured him, she was tricky and manipulative, but I think the way she dies, without any suffering, is a massive relief to him. It is a clean break.

Sadly, when Marge dies, she takes the secrets of his long-lost brothers to her grave. The boys remain a mystery. What were they actually called, what did they like, who was the bossy/cheeky/funny/kind one?

Only she isn't buried. Marge leaves her body to medical science. Weirdly, the hospital is unwilling to accept it (rude) and demand legal proof of the gift. Eventually we find the paperwork alongside a load of cash stuffed inside a Hoover bag.

Meanwhile, my own parents are in their seventies and having downsized a decade or so earlier are living in blissful retirement in a long, low-ceilinged cottage in Lytham, which is very handy for Booths. They are so content they rarely bother with holidays; they don't have anything to get away from.

My father paints terrible watercolours and has a stab at conversational French. Meanwhile, my mother and her sister attempt to play bridge and drink coffee with their various covens.

I am an absent daughter, partner and mother. Phoebe starts her periods as I am getting into a cab to catch a plane to Melbourne, where I'm performing at the comedy festival again. 'Call Vanessa!' I yell at her as the cab pulls away.

Later, when she has counselling (like all fucked-up millennials), she no doubt tells her therapist about this, but what's a girl to do? I have a business-class ticket that entitles me to freebies in the posh lounge and I need all the time in there I can get.

The show is not quite ready, the theatre is too big, and I feel both exposed and fraudulent. I'm relieved to be doing only a couple of weeks and, once home, I desperately polish the material in time for Edinburgh.

In the end, *Middle-Aged Bimbo*, complete with me in a fabulous rubber pinstripe jacket on the poster, is a decent show.

I get a mini break from stand-up early in the autumn of 2001, when an old producer mate of mine, Mark Goucher, takes a risky punt and offers me a short run of *The Vagina Monologues* in the West End with Jerry Hall and Josette Simon.

I snatch at the chance even though when I saw the show with its creator Eve Ensler as a one-woman show, I found it cloyingly American and a teeny bit naff.

I keep my opinions to myself. It's West End, it's good for my CV, I might also meet Mick Jagger.

Opening night is 11 September 2001. On a blue-sky day in New York, planes are crashing into the Twin Towers.

Jerry Hall is in pieces. Her daughter Lizzie is in Manhattan modelling and, as it later transpires, 'saw the whole thing with her own eyes'.

We postpone opening night and resume the next day after a minute's silence.

Whatever I think of the 'Vag Mons' (or 'Twat Chat', as it's often nicknamed), it works. It has a kind of alchemy, especially when performed on a Bunny Christie set in a cute little West End chocolate-box theatre. Bunny Christie is a phenomenal designer, whatever the production; her work is worth getting off the sofa for alone.

I love watching Jerry glide onstage, Josette is pure class and I *do* get to meet Mick Jagger. He is very, very tiny: had I taken him home, my dad would inevitably say, 'That chap could walk under our kitchen table wearing a top hat.'

By contrast, Jerry is so tall that she cannot lie down on the floor of her tiny dressing room without opening the door and stretching her legs out across the corridor. Seeing her lying like this on a moth-eaten carpet, I wonder whether she has ever seen a rodent trap that close up before.

One night Jerry invites me to a party back at her place in Richmond. I pretend I have a really important meeting first thing in the morning and can't risk a late night. In reality I'm thinking, *How the fuck would I get back to Camberwell from Richmond?*

I will perform *The Vagina Monologues* with various casts on and off for years after this initial run. For a while I tour with Miriam Margolyes and Rula Lenska. I remember Miriam sidling up to me in the wings one night and whispering, 'I used to have the most luxurious bush, but now it's all fallen out,' which I found funnier than any of the lines in the show.

Years later I used Miriam's line as the inspiration for a joke in *Grumpy Old Women Live* about pubic hair falling out in middle age: 'It's called female pattern balding and the real dilemma with female pattern balding is whether to shave it all off or just comb it over.'

I also tour with Anthea Turner, who travels with cashmere blankets, posh scented candles and a case of decent wine in the boot of her Bentley. She is still married to Grant Bovey, who regales us all with stories of losing control of his helicopter in dense fog. Hey ho.

In some respects it's a relief to step outside the comedy world for a while. In December 2001, all the British Comedy Awards go to men, apart from best comedy actress, which goes to Jessica Hynes for *Spaced*.

I have been in this industry for twenty years and things have barely changed.

We are still not getting our fair share of airtime, we are still feeding men their punchlines, but it's considered completely normal and no one seems that fussed. After all, *The Office* is funny and there's a girl in that, whatever her name is.

Redundancy

One evening, Geof comes home waving two bottles of champagne – always an ominous sign. One bottle is cause for celebration, two means 'Let's get pissed because I've got something awful to tell you.'

My suspicions are right: he's been made redundant from the *TV Times*. An American company have recently taken over IPC Magazines and they don't want anyone over fifty.

I do not deal with this news well, despite the fact that I know he hates his bloody job and has been increasingly miserable for years. I'd still rather he stuck at it. I mean, what about me?

We can't both not have a job, Jesus! Fucking hell, I drink more of the champagne than he does, I mean, what about me? Oh yes, and Phoebe and the house?

Apparently, he has a payoff; he seems quite thrilled by this, but I feel sick. Geof is many things but he's not great with money. What will become of us?

My sister won't let us all come and live with her, even though she has a massive house half a mile away. Seriously, this crosses my mind, Geof, me and P living in my sister's attic.

After her divorce back in the nineties, Sara has married again, a barrister who becomes a High Court judge, at which point my sister becomes Lady Hart, which is annoying. Not that she ever uses it, apart from once in Nando's, when they are being arsey.

Oh God, oh God, oh God, I'm so used to Geof leaving the house first thing in the morning and then coming home in the evening, like something out of a Ladybird book, that I'm not sure how I'm going to cope with him at home.

He's soon going to realise that most of my 'working' time is spent smoking, drinking Diet Coke and lying on the bed 'thinking'.

I feverishly get on with writing *Having a Lovely Time*. Someone's got to bring home the bacon, not that we're going to be able to afford bacon; pasta then, it's just pasta from now on, pasta, beans and baked potatoes. God, I hate my life.

Geof, on the other hand, seems quite happy. He's not exactly poring over Sits Vacant in the papers, in fact the first thing he does is disappear off to Greenwich, where he volunteers to clean up some old boat.

The suits hang unworn in his closet, the ties are rolled away in his drawers, shirts no longer get taken to the dry cleaner's (no, I didn't iron them) and his shoulders drop.

I think I've underestimated how much of a slog he was finding his daily grind. There have been perks – an underground parking space on the South Bank, luncheon vouchers in the eighties and big laughs back in the days when magazine offices were full of cigarette smoke and people swigging Jack Daniel's at their desks – but as the world grew up and got boring, so did the job.

By the time Geof is made redundant he is juggling budgets and number-crunching and I've stopped asking if he's had a nice day because I know he hasn't.

While we tick over, I put my head down, get stuck into finishing the novel and mixing stand-up gigs with *Vagina Monologues* dates.

At this point I am still using a support act on tour, usually young bucks off the circuit who want to experience gigs outside the London club scene. Haha, most of them haven't got a clue what they're letting themselves in for! They join me at the start of the tour all bright-eyed and bushy-tailed but by the end they're bloated, bitter borderline alcoholics.

That's not entirely true, but at the time I have an excellent routine about support act cruelty, which I would never get away with these days.

Ex-support acts include Matt Lucas, Noel Fielding, Russell Howard, Russell Kane and Chris Ramsey. I'm not modern or generous enough to have a female support, a fact which embarrasses me now.

Matt has a massive asthma attack somewhere in Wales, Noel sleeps curled up on the back seat, like a teenage goat with odd socks on his feet. Russell (Kane) paces like a maniac before the show, Chris gets confused when I ask him to meet me at the Mal (I mean the Malmaison) and spends hours trying to find a hotel called the Mal in Manchester and Russell (Howard) is a bit too good for my liking!

One of my favourite support acts around this time is a boy with a very long neck who jumps on my comedy bandwagon fresh out of Cambridge.

John Oliver is an unlikely comic, swagger-free, feverishly intelligent and badly dressed. The three of us – me, John, our tour manager and forever mate Chris George – laugh ourselves sick around the country.

My audience often stare at John in silence and to cheer him up after a run of bad gigs I treat him to a ride on the waltzer in Skegness, which nearly breaks his swan-like neck. There is nothing to suggest back in those early days of the new millennium that John Oliver is on track to become one of the most celebrated satirists in the world. He lives in New York now, where he hosts his TV show *Last Week Tonight with John Oliver* and I don't feature on his Wiki page.

No matter: just shows how wrong you can be. I adore the boy, but I always thought he'd end up in accounting.

There is a YouTube clip of us together on a show called *Celebrity Diners*, where TV cameras eavesdrop on dinner conversations. I basically chain-smoke throughout, John orders the chicken, I opt for the kangaroo!

As I get older, the gap between my audience and my support act grows exponentially and both suffer. The newbies don't have the material to entertain my crowd, who turn their noses up at their antics, and in the end I phase them out, preferring to do the entire evening myself.

The last one is Ed Gamble, who is the first to admit he came unstuck in Tunbridge Wells.

Phoebe is now a teenager and no trouble, really; she is small and hard-working, with thin legs like my sister. The braces are off and she has a Rachel cut. There is a lot of whispering about boys with her friends, but not much action! She isn't half so slaggy as her mother. Geof is around a lot and him being made redundant is good for their relationship. He is always on hand to give her a lift and they remain close at a time when most girls think their dads are twats.

Vanessa is released from full-time duty to go to Chelsea School of Art but is on call to Phoebe when needed until she happily gets pregnant and has a baby of her own. Vanessa remains to this day a massive part of our lives; she knows more about the three of us than anyone else. She is the keeper of all the secrets.

Towards the end of the year, Geof reveals his master plan: he wants to buy a plot of land, or maybe something which he can knock down, and then build his own house. Christ, it's even worse than I imagined! Why can't he just get an art editor job on *Hello!* magazine and put me on the front cover every week? Honestly, some people are so selfish.

I bury my head in my own stuff, lalalala. Coming home from a holiday later that summer, possibly Corsica (nice, btw), Geof gets a call on his mobile at the airport.

He has bought a house, a house which he intends to smash into a hole in the ground. Oh shit.

Grand Designs

The house Geof buys with his *TV Times* redundancy money is a small fifties red-brick semi, with a garage that has been carpeted and used as a dining room. It is fantastically ugly. An old lady recently died there, and for many years after we receive her catalogues through the post, slacks mostly.

It's half a mile from Brunswick Villas. Phoebe will be nearer her school, but I still can't imagine us moving. I love our house; surely he can just build this bloody thing and then sell it? But the more Geof gets stuck into the project, the more I realise this won't happen. You can't expect a man to build a house and then assume he's going to allow other people to live in it. That's like asking a small child to allow some kid down the road to play with their new toy. It's not realistic.

Fortunately, proceedings are slow, so no decisions need to be made immediately – you've all seen Channel 4's *Grand Designs*, you know the drill. There is a terrible false start with a tricky builder, and for a while there is floundering over a massive hole, where just weeks ago a house stood with stairs and flushing toilets.

The site is on a bus route and not far from a primary school; kids just want to jump in the hole and it all feels a bit chaotic.

Eventually Geof assembles a new team which includes the architect Robert Dye, and a bunch of Australian, Polish and Russian builders.

Massive wooden hoardings are erected around the hole, Geof 'project manages' and I feign interest.

I have seen the plans, but I find them hard to translate. 'Gosh,' I say, meaning, *WTF?*

In later years, when Geof is working on extensions for his mostly female clients, he will make models of the proposed building work, complete with tiny plastic people, like contemporary doll's houses, and everyone gets the picture immediately.

Geof has swapped his Joseph suits for a hard hat and a pair of steel-capped boots and is more cheerful than he has been in years.

I try not to question anything and get on with my own life. *Que sera* and all that. Reading this back, I'm sounding almost reasonable. I'm sure I was a complete bitch about everything.

Fortunately, another West End theatre offer serves as a decent distraction. *Mum's the Word* was originally written and performed by six Canadian actresses in 1991, who suddenly found they had a mini global hit on their hands.

The premise is simple: six women sit onstage and talk about their experiences of motherhood. It takes over ten years for the show to open in London, and perhaps it missed its time slot?

I suspect the writing isn't strong enough for the West End. When I read the script, it feels like an Edinburgh show that has outgrown its own popularity, but I harbour these dark suspicions privately.

I say yes; of course I say yes. Imogen Stubbs, Patsy Palmer and Cathy Tyson have already said yes, and they are far better actors than I am.

The pop singer Carol Decker from T'Pau also says yes and Barbara Pollard, one of the original writers and Canadian cast member, comes over to complete the London ensemble.

Poor Barbara. This is a dream come true; she's made it into the West End, she is given the star's dressing room, she is an incredibly nice woman – she just isn't ready for the viciousness of the London critics. I think I'll leave the rest to the Guardian, who describe it thus: 'A show so toe-curlingly inane, reactionary and embarrassing that, by the interval, I was not only entertaining fantasies of mass matricide but considering the death penalty for those committing crimes against hilarity.'

Haha, to be honest, I'm used to being slagged off in the Guardian, but there are few things more embarrassing than a one-star review in a national newspaper. The audience, of course (mostly new mums who haven't been out since they squeezed new life into the world), love it, although when I catch sight of my mother's and sister's stony, embarrassed faces one matinee, I decide we won't bother discussing it after.

My dressing room is on the same floor as Imogen's; we become good mates. At the time she is married to Sir Trevor Nunn, and he is always very polite to me, but I can't help feeling he doesn't think I'm a suitable friend for Lady Nunn. Every night Trevor arrives at the stage door to take Imogen to dinner with friends. He's just finished running the National and seems at a loose end.

I'm just grateful to catch the bus home, slug back a glass of wine and get into bed. When Trevor and Imogen separate many years later, I feel relieved for her. No one needs to go to Sheekey's that often.

The show runs for three months and closes in June 2003.

I go back to the old routine, literally, dusting down the stage show and getting back on the road. Same old, same old.

Just before Xmas 2003, Phoebe goes to one of those underage discos London kids used to go nuts for, and I overhear her tell her friend Katy Trepass that she snogged a boy. I am listening so hard at the door I can hear Katy shout, 'But you said you'd wait for me!' 'I think it was the black top and the pearls,' my daughter responds. 'I think I looked sophisticated.' She is fourteen.

On the one hand I think, *Go, girl*; on the other, I want her to be eight years old forever. This is the start of it, isn't it? The late nights and the upset, the crushes and rejections. I don't know how lucky I am; she misses out on being a social media teen by just a few years. It's hard enough without all that crap.

Meanwhile, up the road, behind the hoardings, the new house is taking shape. A decision will have to be made very soon. We can't have two houses; it's not like one of them is in France, they're half a mile from each other.

Brunswick Villas goes on sale in the New Year.

I can still walk around that house in my head; houses are hugely important to me as a fiction writer. When I start a book I have to know where my characters live before I can make them do things. I have stolen many houses over the years, but, weirdly, Brunswick Villas has never made it into one of my novels, not yet . . .

In a bizarre twist, the couple who bought the Camberwell Grove flat off us over a decade earlier view Brunswick Villas. They have two children now and as soon as I see their little girl playing in Phoebe's bedroom I know she belongs there. They put in an offer and we accept it. Looks like we're moving after all.

By the way, *Mum's the Word* is still touring, so stuff the reviews, eh. I hope Barbara and her mates have earned a fortune out of it. I'm just rather glad I'm far too old to be asked to go back!

Oh Christ. Maybe they're writing a nana one!

Hello *Grumpy Old Women,* Hello New House

We will be moving into the 'other' house by the end of 2004, but before we even start to pack up fourteen years of domestic detritus, I decide to co-write another play for Edinburgh. I think I'm running away from reality.

Julie is up for it and full of ideas, and I decide to engage Chris George to direct. It's a gut instinct and even though he occasionally drives me bonkers I never regret the decision for a second. *The Andy Warhol Syndrome* is a sixty-minute monologue charting the rise and fall of a reality TV star, with a bit of transgender razzmatazz on the side. I, of course, think it's marvellous. The *Guardian*, on the other hand says . . .

> Beneath its surface wit ('Sleeping in a single bed – it's like practising for your coffin') there is absolutely nothing going on.

Hey ho, two stars is better than one and most of the other press is a great deal kinder. Weirdly, when the play has a short run at Riverside Studios the following year, a different reviewer from the same newspaper decides it's worthy of four stars!

It's a busy summer. Before Edinburgh, I need to complete *Having a Lovely Time* and squeeze in a weekend at Glastonbury. I'm covering the festival for Radio 4, interviewing comics, stall holders and stilt-walkers. I drag Phoebe along with me, even though she is worried about missing a day of school. I tell her I'll write her a sick note, but she's so scared of being seen on the way out of south London that she keeps her head on her knees in the back of the car until we clear the danger zone.

Because we are with Radio 4 we have a Winnebago/caravan thing. Phoebe and I even have a double bed. We share the van with the producers, who are both in their thirties and take care of Phoebe when I have to do a gig in the comedy tent. I have bad early memories of performing at Glastonbury in the eighties and I don't want my daughter to witness any defeat. It all goes surprisingly well, but I find a little of Glastonbury goes a long way and on the last day, when it's raining, I stay inside the van and watch Wimbledon on the telly. I hate Wimbledon, but I can't be arsed to stand in mud for Paul McCartney. Phoebe wears her wristband until it rots.

That year in Edinburgh I share a flat again with Stewart Lee. One night Imogen Stubbs comes to stay. Stew finds her in the kitchen in the morning in a white Victorian nightie and is reduced to a stuttering red-eared schoolboy. Ha!

Just before the packing cases arrive, I get a phone call from my agent asking if I want to take part in what they call a 'talking heads' show. These are TV shows which involve different people talking around the same topic, be that Channel 5's top magicians, the best adverts of all time or in this case, ageing. 'Hang on a second,' I interrupt, 'I'm only forty-three. How much is the fee?'

Four hundred pounds.

What can I say? I'm skint again, living from job to job and, because I'm weirdly superstitious about taking book advances, have yet to be paid a penny for the latest novel. Four hundred quid is four hundred quid. The show is called *Grumpy Old Women*, apparently, a spin-off of the successful *Grumpy Old Men* BBC series which, not having any skin in the game, I've never seen.

They would like to film at my house; that's not a problem, Brunswick Villas is an old pro when it comes to filming and over the years there have been many shoots in the place. She is photogenic and there's parking on the road outside.

I am bossed around by a large-bosomed, rather badly dressed woman who reminds me of a bigger version of my sister. I bristle. She wants me to wear a Santa hat. I don't feel we know each other well enough to be making these kinds of demands and tell her so. She puts the hat away and we crack on. Gradually, I relax. She is making me laugh, almost as much as I am making her laugh. This is unusual. I am stingy with my laughs. Who is this woman? Her name is Judith Holder; she is a TV producer who lives in the wilds of Hexham, which might explain the shoes. By the end of the interview session she has persuaded me to put the Santa hat on.

Without realising it, I've just made the most career-changing four hundred quid job I've ever done.

OK, so it's not like appearing during the Super Bowl half-time show, but . . .

That first *Grumpy Old Women* special is an instant Xmas classic and Judith is the driving force behind it. The reason why *Grumpy Old Women* is better than *Grumpy Old Men* on the box is entirely down to her. Judith provides the glue for the women's series. She films all the linking scenes in her own home, using her own friends and family, local supermarket car park, etc. Judith plays the grumpy everywoman, frazzled hair, to-do list as long as your arm, knocking on fifty and fed up. The talking heads merely add to this, and then Judith skilfully edits everything together. My most memorable comedy contribution to the Christmas special is simply forgetting what Jesus' dad is called.

The show is a hit, and the impact immediate.

I am suddenly recognised in the supermarket. Don't get me wrong: the paparazzi aren't exactly chasing me round the sauces and condiments, but there is a noticeable shift in the number of nudges, nods and whispers that follow me around my local Sainsbury's.

The programme airs on 18 December 2004 and we watch from our new home.

Over a hundred years separate Brunswick Villas from our new home, a smart black wooden box, with rubber floors and a great deal of concrete and glass. It will take some getting used to and a lot of our furniture from the old house is too bulky for its clean lines. Sometimes I have to swallow hard and try not to cry, but it has its own beauty and its own sense of calmness, and Phoebe, now fifteen, likes having the top floor to herself. I let it grow on me and now, twenty years on, I still get a thrill putting my key in the door.

For any neurotic parent of a teen, building a house on a main road is the best thing we ever did. The fact that we are on a night bus route and have a stop slap bang opposite the house helps me breathe more easily when she starts going out more.

Worrying about your child at night is the loneliest feeling. When Phoebe gets older and starts clubbing, I'd find myself crouching by the window of Geof's study, watching night buses roll up the hill, waiting for one to stop, open its doors and for a small bleach blonde to get off. At which point I would scurry back to bed and pretend to snore.

Just to give Geof and the architect Robert Dye some credit here, the house wins both a RIBA Award and a Manser Medal: both are big deals in architectural terms, especially for what is essentially a posh wooden shed on a busy main road in south London. Good work, lads!

Grumpy Takes Off

The BBC orders a series of *Grumpy Old Women*, and another and another. They seem to know when they're onto a good thing and it becomes achingly obvious that the programme has touched a nerve. Middle-aged women are being given a voice and guess who watches a lot of telly? Ooh, that's right, middle-aged women! These days the execs cannot stand this fact; they are forever chasing the 'youth market', who are off chasing a better time elsewhere.

Neither Judith nor I can agree as to who has the idea of doing a live version first. All we can remember is a meeting in a very dreary pub in Chiswick with a terrible lunch menu, where my agent and I sit opposite Judith and the head honcho of Liberty Bell, the production company that makes *Grumpy*.

By the end of the meal, a deal is on the table: Liberty Bell will give Avalon permission to tour a live show. Now all we have to do is write it, design it, cast it and get it up on its feet, whatever 'it' will be.

I know very much what I *don't* want it to be, which is what everyone will expect: a number of disappointed women of a certain age sitting on a stage, moaning.

If this is going to be worth doing, we need to confound

expectations. Fortunately, Judith has a long history of shiny-floor shows, producing Saturday night extravaganzas with the likes of Dame Edna Everage, so isn't averse to taking risks. However, with the live show being an unknown quantity, we are going to have to bring it in on a shoestring budget. Avalon don't want to lose their shirt, and no one has a clue whether it will sell.

A tentative seven-date tour is put together for autumn 2005. The venues include some of the usual regional favourites; seating anything from six hundred to around a thousand, it will be blindingly obvious if it fails.

There are absolutely no guarantees and, with Judith living in Hexham and me in London, we are going to have to write this via email.

We set ourselves homework, write around topics such as food, holidays, partners, kids, clothes and technology, and whittle away the material until the good stuff shines through. Richard Herring is brought in as script consultant and my mate Chris George comes onboard to direct.

In order to tidy the final draft, Chris and I go up to stay with Judith, who lives in a vast house which is so big it used to be a Barnardo's children's home. Judith is like a grown-up: she bustles about in a pinny and makes us a cheese soufflé in the Aga. There are fresh flowers on my bedside table and a little packet of biscuits; in fact the only downside of this 'work trip' is that she makes me go swimming at 7.30 a.m. and her towels, line-dried in the Northumbrian wind, are rough and scratchy.

Over the years we have become used to each other's lifestyle foibles. Judith likes the outdoors: like a Labrador puppy, she needs fresh air and regular exercise. I'm not that keen: I'd rather stay indoors and stare at myself in a mirror. She gets too hungry for lunch at 1 and is always trying to eat earlier, I'm a stickler for waiting. She craves sweet things, I don't, and she is a bit casual about wine supplies, which are vital to my wellbeing, e.g.:

Judith: 'Oh, I think I might have a bottle of wine somewhere.'

Me: 'What do you mean, you *might* have a bottle of wine? If you haven't got a decent bottle of Chardonnay chilling in the fridge right now, I'm catching a train and going straight home.'

If Judith comes to stay with me, she is always very suspicious as to whether I have changed the sheets. The answer is probably not. I'm a bit grubby like that. What I usually do before a guest arrives is pull back the duvet, give the bottom sheet a sniff, check for crumbs, old socks, sweet wrappers, etc., and convince myself it's good to go. When she questions the cleanliness of my bed linen, I remind her that I'm doing my bit to save the planet.

The casting for the first *Grumpy Live* outing is a tricky process. We need three women 'of a certain age' who are very different both in looks and in performance style. Obviously, I insist on being in it myself, which means just two more to cast, and eventually we hit gold with Linda Robson and Fascinating Aïda's Dillie Keane.

Linda inhabits the loveable down-to-earth, everywoman character that she is in real life and Dillie excels as the posh comedy giant that she is in real life. They are a brilliant contrast to each other and my job is to flit between them, playing the role of the naughty, sweary rebel. Between us we can cover a lot of comedy ground.

I'm not sure when it starts to gel, but by the time we do a rehearsal in front of a crowd of female staff members especially invited from M&S and John Lewis they laugh a lot and we start to enjoy ourselves.

It's very odd, realising you are in a successful show. Sometimes it takes a little while, but with *Grumpy* it is obvious from the first night. By the time we take our curtain call (gratifyingly rowdy) the producers are grinning.

We get a couple of rave reviews and the cast are immediately snapped up to do a much longer tour in the spring of 2006.

The show is a blend of three-way stand-up monologues and

sketches. We start each performance in silhouette at the back of the stage, dressed like three old-fashioned battle-axes, in old-fashioned raincoats (hiding individual costume reveals beneath) and head-scarves. We freeze while Al Murray supplies the voiceover.

V/O: In the time of HRT they landed, they
              had names like Jean, Marjorie, Wendy
              and Sheila, and they all had one thing in
              common, they were a bit cheesed off,
              some of them had had it 'up to here'
              and most of them were at the END OF
              THEIR TETHER.
                    Ladies and gentlemen – we present
              the invasion of ... THE GRUMPY OLD
              WOMEN.

SND – choirs of angels

Big swelling music, dry ice, the three figures come forward.

Huge applause.

WOMAN 1:   Is it me, or is it hot in here?

WOMAN 1:   Hello, everyone, I'm Jenny Eclair.

WOMAN 2:   I'm Linda Robson.

WOMAN 3:   And I'm Dillie Keane ... and please don't
           applaud us for knowing our own names.

WOMAN 1:   We're not that old.

The highlights of this first show include Linda wearing her nightie and falling off the back of a sofa, Dillie wearing a fabulous party dress which she can't fasten at the back because it's three sizes too small, and a monologue called 'Get Me the Manager' which strikes a nightly chord.

I just like saying 'Get me the manager' in Sainsbury's.

Let's say I've bought some fruit and the quality turns out to be substandard. I like to revisit the store with said fruit and by the time I get back there I'm all puffed up with self-righteous fury. So what if I park in the mums' and toddlers' bay? I've got bruised fruit, I've got rights! I'm a regular customer and I've got the Nectar card to prove it. And I'm building up steam now, ready to blow like a pressure cooker with a loose lid at the man in charge. No, I won't be fobbed off by Barbara the lady with RSI who sits at customer information because she can't manage a till any more, I want Mr Big. I demand to see the manager. Get me the manager. A small crowd has gathered, sensing blood. Get me the manager. And eventually the manager arrives and he's not a manager he's a boy-ager, he's about twelve, ha, and he only comes up to my armpits, so I go in for the kill. I use words like shoddy and inexcusable and I'm so furious he's got bits of my spit on his speccies. I threaten to take my custom elsewhere, humph, how would you like that, eh? And the thing is, he wouldn't like it, he's really apologetic and offers me some money-off coupons and a complimentary honeydew melon, and that's it! All the wind has been taken out of my sails; I can feel myself deflate like a punctured football. I've been beaten into submission by customer service, politeness and old-fashioned common courtesy. Which is a bit annoying when what you're really after is a hand-on-hip screaming match, and the worst thing is, you end up apologising to him, aaghhhhhhhh.

There's also the 'catalogue drop' which is a nightly audience favourite. Onstage we are discussing the thrills of catalogue shopping (it's 2005), including our favourite Lakeland catalogue, and enthusing about items such as the ingenious plastic banana guard, glow-in-the-dark drinks coasters and the incredible triple biscuit carrier – 'carries not one, not two, but THREE biscuits'. As we exit the stage, having reached a climax over various kitchen accessories, a net above the audience opens up and an avalanche of individual catalogue pages showers the audience below. Cheap but effective and the audience go mad for it.

The *Grumpy* Juggernaut

The *Grumpy* brand becomes a mini juggernaut. We even sell merch at the live shows: badges, T-shirts, mugs and tea towels. Everyone complains the T-shirts are too small. They are: no one has thought about our demographic properly. They don't want teeny-weeny navel-skimming skimpy little things; they want extra-large comfort T-shirts that they can curl up on the sofa in, eating crisps.

The original cast, apart from me, aren't available for the 2006 autumn tour of the live show, so we enrol Annette Badland and Rhona Cameron. I find the switch challenging: it's like changing classes at school and it takes me some time to get used to my new playmates. Rhona is monumentally talented but emotionally tricky, and for very good reason: her personal background is complicated and some of the stories she tells us make even my jaw drop. She is sober after years of caning it, but occasionally she loses her temper in hotels. I remember once seeing her appear in her knickers and a T-shirt at the top of a wide staircase in a northern hotel, carrying a plate and screaming about the tuna sandwich, which had just been delivered via room service. She was right, it was a crap sandwich.

Food becomes really important on tour; too many meals get

skipped and there are too many sandwiches and not enough veg going on. Rhona isn't the only one to have the occasional hotel meltdown: once I kick an empty mini fridge so hard I nearly break my toe.

Annette, on the other hand, is extremely professional; she is one of those actresses who can do comedy without being a comedian. Respect.

The show survives any amount of cast changes. There is even a run without me, when Britt Ekland is cast alongside Denise Black (ex-Kray Sister from all those years ago) and Dillie, who plays team captain. That woman is remarkable.

The original trio are reunited for a tour of Australia in the early summer of 2007.

I feel guilty about going. It's been a tricky year. In February, my sister's husband, Sir Michael Hart, QC, dies of lung cancer within a year of being diagnosed. Sara is widowed before she's fifty and our mother makes the mistake of criticising the handbag she slings over her shoulder for the funeral. 'It looks like a fishing bag,' she tells my sister, who snaps, 'It's an Ally Capellino fishing bag' before swapping it for something more funereal.

This death is devastating. It is a second marriage for them both and they are a very brilliant match. They also have Jasper, their ten-year-old son.

The sadness is unbearable, so I tuck it into a corner of my mind and try not to let the reality of the situation escape from its box. My sister will cope, of course she will – older sisters have to cope and she does – but I don't think I ever gave her the time or the kindness that I should have done, and for this I am deeply sorry. I find the idea of her being lonely in her huge house unbearable, so I don't let myself think about it.

Another reason for feeling conflicted about going is because Phoebe is doing her A levels (honestly, looking back, I'm a crap mother and sister). But I convince myself that she aced her

GCSEs without any help from me. Literally, when she got all grade As I was so shocked, I asked if she'd opened the wrong envelope. Maybe it's time to stop underestimating her?

In any case, I figure if it all goes tits up she can retake them. After all, she has decided to have a gap year before applying for university. I expect she will want to travel, which is all the rage back then, but she is allergic to MSG, so gives up on the idea of doing Asia and decides instead to audition for a drama foundation course. I trust her to deal with this on her own; she has an incredible brain, plus she can sing!

This is another revelation. The previous year she played Mrs Peachum in the school production of *The Threepenny Opera* (alongside her classmate Charlotte Ritchie, who played Polly) and sings so beautifully I can't physically get out of my seat in the interval. She doesn't get that from me.

The Grumpies fly to Sydney and Linda has brought her two youngest kids out with her. I think this will be a drag, but soon find Louis and Bobbie incredibly comforting. It's good to have them around: they are sweet and funny and bring a sense of normality to the proceedings. Sort of . . .

Judith has also flown out, having booked a big camper-van adventure with her entire family. She attempts to climb the Sydney Harbour Bridge but due to a panic attack has to be airlifted down (slight exaggeration).

We open in the huge Sydney Capitol Theatre and the reaction is muted; we need to make tweaks, so no more day trips for Judith. We beaver away in my little grey self-catering apartment and I try not to panic. We switch the end music to a Bee Gees number and add in enough Aussie cultural references to make the locals happy. It kind of works but I am always aware that we are not adored. Comedy in Oz is very camp: I think they might have been expecting a bit more of an extravaganza and I feel responsible for every line that doesn't get a laugh. By the time we get to Brisbane, my nerves are terrible. This manifests itself in the old tilting routine, only this time it happens onstage and I have to walk around the set holding on to anything that doesn't move so that I don't fall over. I'm back on the Valium.

At some point during the tour we have a few days off, and while Dillie flies off to stay with some friends somewhere exotic, me, Linda and the kids hire bikes for the day, take a wrong turning and end up cycling on a motorway. Juggernauts blare their horns at us and eventually we throw the bikes off a bridge and climb down to safety. We also accidentally take them to see a horror movie that has me, never mind them, under my seat. Those kids are unflappable, and Linda is a fabulous mother, apart from the time she leaves some smiley potato faces in the oven in an aparthotel in Sydney, which set off the fire alarm, necessitating a complete evacuation of the entire building and the arrival of the fire brigade, ha!

In Melbourne I hear that Phoebe has been offered a place to do a foundation course at both LAMDA and the Drama Centre. She chooses the Drama Centre. I am overwhelmingly proud of her, this small, determined girl/woman, and wish, like Linda's kids, she could be with me.

We finish the tour in Perth, which I find a mindfuck. Everywhere is closed by 9.30 and the Aborigines are treated appallingly. We are performing on a casino complex and are chauffeured nightly in a stretch limo with disco lights.

I miss home more than I ever thought I could. I feel a bit mad.

Australia isn't our only trip abroad with the show; we also do Finland and Iceland, but not with a British cast. The show is translated into Swedish (for Finland, as they speak both Finnish and Swedish) and Icelandic.

Judith and I find this incredibly thrilling. Somehow, we have managed to have it written into our contracts that we attend the opening night of any show performed in a foreign territory.

When we go to Finland, we swim naked in an art deco pool, which segregates the sexes because no one wears swimming costumes or trunks in Finland as they are considered dirty. Showering both before and after our swim, I feel very much at home – I've never seen so many women with my body shape. Loads of short, boxy women with small breasts and sturdy legs: these are my people.

The cast in Finland is OK but not a patch on the Icelandic cast. One of the Finnish actresses is too vain to be truly funny, but she is apparently the 'really famous one' (sigh).

Iceland is a different ballgame; all three women are hilarious, and Judith and I glow with pride when the entire audience rocks with laughter at the female pattern balding line. We might not speak a word of Icelandic, but we know exactly where they are in the script.

We are looked after beautifully on this trip, fed puffin and taken to see incredible waterfalls in a truck with wheels that must be six feet in diameter. En route to the airport, we manage a dip in the Blue Lagoon. Judith organises this; she is fantastic at making the most of every minute, which is great, because I am not.

Oh, by the way, Phoebe gets four grade As.

Art Imitating Life

S omehow in the middle of all this, I write another solo show, *Because I Forgot to Get a Pension*, which features the opening gag, 'I didn't really forget to get a pension, I just didn't think I'd live this long'. I am forty-seven!

The show takes a while to bed in, and unfortunately the comedy website Chortle reviews it on an off-night and I get one of the most vile, personal reviews of my life from Steve Bennett, who I have met since and seems a completely OK bloke, but on this occasion goes a tad overboard.

Have a read and you may well understand why I saw this and wept:

> You can do this sort of material with skill and honesty, as Victoria Wood has proved, but Eclair tackles it with the subtlety of a pantomime dame, perhaps in the hope that the volume of performance will hide the gaps in the material. [...] Eclair has become a caricature of her already exaggerated self, a bleached-blonde pterodactyl squawking away.

It's still up there on their website. That's the trouble with the internet: it makes crap chip paper. You can't just crumple it up and put it in the bin. I don't think any reviewer now would get away with such a vicious slagging-off of a performer, male or female. It hurt then and it still stings.

Weirdly, I remember the exact night. I knew there were problems with the show and, as always, I tried to overcompensate. Basically, I made the mistake of trying too hard, but at no point do I recall turning into a squawking pterodactyl. That said, maybe the review touched a nerve because I suspected he was right. As with many performers, self-loathing is never far from the surface.

Regardless of the Chortle review, I get the *Pension* show polished up and it tours successfully for eighteen months. There are some great lines in it, particularly about the joys of having a child in their late teens. Here's a taster:

When she was little, she used to tell me everything, gawd she went on and on and on, endless banal pointless rubbish and suddenly there she was about fifteen and it starts to get interesting, she went quiet on me and that's when you start snooping.

All of us women have got the snooping gene. It develops when you're a girl and you start looking for that piece of paper that proves you really were adopted but all you find is your mum's diaphragm and that freaky sanitary belt –

Anyway.

And there always comes the day when you find it … your daughter's diary. Now what you've got to remember is that there are different types of diaries: there's the slim handbag diary for dental appointments and meetings – dull; there's the food diary for calories eaten and how many sit-ups you've managed – dull; then there's the diary with the big fat padlock on, that's the one with all her secrets in, and what do you do? Decisions, decisions. Do you respect her privacy and walk away or hack it open and betray her trust?

Well, what do you think? I walked away, that's what I did.
I walked away and came back twenty minutes later with a
bread knife and hacked it open.

It's not entirely true. The last time I read my daughter's diary
she was eight years old and had written 'Mum is being a nightmare' and I have never dared pry since.

A lot of domestic anecdotes which I tell onstage are exaggerated for comedic effect, but over the years my family continue to
weave in and out of my stand-up. They have slightly heightened
stage personas, but they are very much based on reality: my sister
is boooy and doesn't use moisturiser, my brother is my mother's
favourite, my mother is stoic to a point of ludicrousness but lousy
with technology, my father is jokey and gifted me his knees,
Geof is put upon, but with hidden strengths, and Phoebe is a
cipher for all the jokes about motherhood that I need to get off
my chest. But the biggest butt of all the jokes, over more than
forty years of trotting around the stage, has always been me!
Me, me, me, me, me, me, me, which was the alternative title of
this book.

Like many performers, I have always been a complete mix of
arrogant egomaniac and snivelling bag of insecurity and self-
loathing, and when I was younger it took very little to swing from
one to the other: I'm great, I'm shit, I'm fabulous, I'm a failure,
etc., etc.

Around this time I am the answer to a £16,000 question on
Chris Tarrant's *Who Wants to Be a Millionaire?* I catch the pro-
gramme accidentally, having a rare Saturday night in, and I hear
Chris ask the contestant, 'Which British comic wrote the books
Camberwell Beauty and *Having a Lovely Time?*' I'm sitting there
thinking, *I know this one*, and the choices are Victoria Wood,
Meera Syal, Ruby Wax or Jenny Eclair. I'm on the sofa shouting
my own name at the screen, the man looks blank, even Chris

Tarrant looks confused. 'Meera Syal,' the man guesses, to which Chris responds, 'No, it's Jenny Eclair', at which point our loser mutters, 'Never heard of her.' Now, whether he did or not I have no idea, but that's what I hear in my head.

Big Ups, Big Downs

We film *Grumpy Live* for a Christmas DVD release in the summer of 2008.

Phoebe has spent the year at the Drama Centre and will be setting off for Oriel College, Oxford, to study English in the autumn. It was her English teacher who made her apply. Mrs Parkinson (mother of the brilliant actress Katherine Parkinson) told her to have a bash and so she does.

I get the news that she has a place after I finish recording my LBC Saturday morning radio show and cry, not with pride, but because I don't know if I really want her to go.

To me Oxbridge has always represented a blockage in the comedy system and I'm not sure I want my daughter to be part of it. The writer Michael Holden (ex-*Loaded*), who has been my sidekick that morning, sorts me out. I think he probably tells me not to be a silly cow and by the time I get home I am a lot more positive about it.

To be honest, she has to go to Oxford because she doesn't get in anywhere else. Ha!

One night, when I drink too much red wine, I email Warwick, or it may have been Bristol, to tell them she didn't need their stupid place because she is going to OXFORD. So that is grown up of me.

I love having a radio show on a talk radio station. I inherit the show from Sandi Toksvig, so big shoes to fill – joke, she's a size 3!

I basically witter on about the news with a guest co-host and various actors/writers who come on to plug their wares.

Michael McIntyre is a regular co-host. The Eclair-Powells saw him do a show in a tiny space at the Pleasance Theatre at the Edinburgh Festival some years previously, on a pissing-down Sunday night, and within seconds he has the audience rolling over like puppies for him.

I chat with loads of people. Grayson Perry is a guest. I make him draw me a horse's head, which he does in biro on the back of my typed-up running order. I have it framed for safety. Prunella Scales pops by and is marvellous, talking about a play at the King's Head, but very distracted and constantly checking the contents of her purse. Some years later, when I hear she has early dementia, this all makes sense.

I love my LBC job, but dislike the management. Not the producer – Tim is lovely – but the big bosses are mean. For Xmas, we presenters each get a tin of Quality Street with our names written in biro on small white stick-on office labels; so cheap, so unimaginative, I slag them off on air.

I think my days are finally up when I accidentally cause a grand's worth of damage by carelessly swinging a suitcase in a fit of temper outside the premises and smashing twelve square feet of sheet window glass, complete with LBC logo. It shatters like a car windscreen before theatrically tinkling out all over the pavement. Understandably, I am asked to contribute financially to the damage and not long after I am 'let go'.

Fuck 'em.

Anyway, where was I? We are filming *Grumpy Live* at the Richmond Theatre, it's a happy occasion, even though it means it's time to put that show to bed. Once it's on DVD, it's curtains for touring.

Lovely Bobbie Girl and Louis turn up with Linda. Louis has been doing his GCSEs and he's so fabulously grown up and talks excitedly of having a big night out to celebrate the following evening. The next I hear of this big night out is on the news. Louis is out with his mates when they are set upon by a gang off the Caledonian Road and, in the ensuing row, Louis's childhood friend Ben Kinsella is stabbed. Ben dies in Louis's arms.

Imagine the trauma. It's heartbreaking. So many young lives shattered.

Those responsible are soon found, charged and imprisoned. The Kinsellas set up a charity against knife crime in Ben's name, but will obviously never fully recover, and the tragedy puts a terrible strain on Linda's family.

That Louis is now a fantastically talented singer-songwriter, selling out massive gigs, is a huge testament to him and the friends and family who got him through a truly horrific time.

I cheer every time I hear that boy's name.

As for Linda, there is no one I would rather bump into anywhere, be it a TV or radio studio, or simply out on the street. The woman is a queen.

Judith and I decide to further capitalise on the success of *Grumpy* by writing an annual for middle-aged women. Based on the *Jackie* magazine of our youth, we call it *Wendy* and hire a model to play our 'everywoman' cover girl. The book is full of cartoon love stories, horoscopes, letters, problems and quizzes, all skewed towards the perimenopausal and beyond market. We even have some nice colouring-in pages and photos of 'fellas we fancy', including Phillip Schofield because I'm not sure back then if even he knew he was gay.

Wendy is great, but it's too expensive for our market; we wanted it to be the size and price of a *Beano* annual. But the publishers know better: it retails for £18.99 and consequently it doesn't sell as well as it should, which is such a shame. If you ever see one in a charity shop, nab it.

I stumble on a review of the book in one of the broadsheets which reads 'Far more amusing than it needs to be'. FFS: this review will never cease to enrage me. It's completely indicative of how dismissive certain elements of the press have been about my entire career, and, to be frank, it pisses me off.

The book is published in the autumn of 2008, when I am temporarily living in Derby, doing a rehash of *The Killing of Sister George*, which has bizarrely been chosen as the reopening production for the Derby Playhouse. It's a bonkers choice: they needed to go for something a lot more family-friendly, like *The Sound of Music*.

Don't get me wrong, I love the play. I auditioned some years back for the part of Childie, with Miriam Margolyes playing June Buckridge, aka Sister George, the drunken old lesbian, in the West End and didn't get it. This time around I'm playing the drunken old lesbian. Life, eh!

I'm not really good enough to pull this off and the director, the brilliant Cal McCrystal, suspects this from the off and tries all sorts of tricks to make it different/possibly hide my theatrical inadequacies. If I'm honest, some of these ideas don't really work for me and I am confused about how to do it.

Yet again, the tiny cast of three is entirely female and entirely delightful, the people of Derby are genuinely warm and there is a Marks & Spencer within five minutes of the stage door, which is a massive silver lining.

We get three stars from the *Guardian* – and I think they are being generous. My agent comes, and pronounces the production 'a waste of time'.

Phoebe phones me during freshers' week: she has been to a foam party and come out in a massive allergic rash – Jesus.

I miss Geof's sixtieth. I think my agent is right.

Oh well, with any luck the *Grumpy Live* DVD will be a monster hit. It isn't. Lee Evans is top of the comedy chart, followed by Michael McIntyre, bloody buggering hell.

We are all at home for Xmas. Just before the end of term there is an outbreak of mumps in Phoebe's college and when we pick her up she is hamster-faced. Mumps is a notifiable disease, and you are not allowed out of the house with it. Effectively you are in quarantine for at least a week. Apart from her fat neck, the rest of her is extremely thin. Alarm bells go off in my head, especially when she admits to hating Oxford.

We tell her that if she still hates it at Easter she can leave, and then concentrate on trying to get some food down her. Physically my daughter takes after my sister, who is naturally slight, whereas my brother and I are prone to beefiness. This natural slightness, plus even just a couple of weeks of controlled eating, soon tips Phoebe into unhealthily skinny. As an ex-anorexic, I worry whether it's genetic.

The jury's still out on that one, but having a mother with controlled eating habits and food 'rules' can't help. I'm grateful that the disease never quite gets its claws into her, and she manages to pull herself back from the brink, but I know that on several occasions it has been a close thing.

Grumpy Rides Again

New Year 2009: Phoebe goes back to Oxford and something clicks. She finds her tribe of fellow misfits and theatrical/comedy types and starts learning how to be happy there. Good, that's one less thing to worry about. Only I won't stop worrying about her . . . ever.

Motherhood is terribly painful, and it doesn't get any easier. I'm glad I only had one child. I couldn't cope with the anxiety of any more and, anyway, I suspect she would always have been my favourite and that's not really fair, is it?

Avalon suggest Judith and I write another *Grumpy* show, which is a kind of terrifying prospect, but the political and financial state of the country provides an incentive. In 2009, the UK is officially in a recession. To be honest this recession is global, but the country loses faith in Labour and Gordon Brown's odd nervous tic becomes more obvious. It's a sort of half-gulp affair, as if he has a cough sweet stuck to the roof of his mouth. I find it transfixing.

It's been two years since Brown took over from Blair and comparisons between the two can be petty. Brown doesn't wear Paul Smith ties, he wears ties that look like they come from one of those old men's shops that sell shooting sticks and spotted hankies on a high street in Argyll. But surely this is no reason to force a general election?

Our second *Grumpy Live* show is titled *Chin Up Britain*, and the artwork is reminiscent of Second World War propaganda posters.

We have a brand-new line-up for this show, and this time I am joined by Susie Blake and Wendi Peters. Susie is old-school showbiz. Her grandmother, Annette Mills (by all accounts, a bit of a goer), wrote 'Boomps a-Daisy' and was the presenter of *Muffin the Mule*, a 1940s/1950s children's television programme featuring a wooden mule called Muffin. Annette's brother was the actor John Mills, and she is the aunt of Hayley and Juliet Mills, who are actually around Susie's age. Susie has a huge theatrical CV, but telly-wise is best known for playing the patronising continuity announcer on *The Victoria Wood Show*. She has also done a couple of stints in *Coronation Street*, as has Wendi, who played the monstrous Cilla Battersby-Brown for a number of years.

Both Susie and Wendi are musical and can't understand why I find something as simple as swinging my arms and marching in time totally impossible.

For the poster and programme cover, the three of us are photographed wearing a sort of 'Mum's Army' military uniform, complete with saucepans and colanders on our heads. The show is a call to arms, a plea to the country to put their shoulders back and get on with it. It's a bossy kind of show but it fits with the times.

We mix our pipe-smoking military look with floral pinnies, so that we are a cross between the armed forces and domestic goddesses.

The set is clever, a forces think-tank HQ disguised as a Cath Kidston-style kitchen, complete with Welsh dresser, kitchen table, etc. Everything in the kitchen doubles up as something else. The washing line becomes a skipping rope for an alternative

Grumpy Olympics, the kitchen table a catwalk runway, campaign charts roll down from the top of the dresser, and at the end of the show the shelves light up for a section entitled 'Kitchen Disco'.

There is a lot of bunting, and all the props are handmade, including a fabulous pair of knitted breasts. For the curtain call, we reappear onstage wearing miniature planes strapped to our heads and perform a choreographed fly-past à la the Red Arrows, our tiny planes streaming vapour trails of coloured smoke.

The show is designed by Susannah Henry and directed by Owen Lewis. The regions love it, but the West End proves snottier.

We have a run at the Novello Theatre in the summer of 2010, and I appear on *The Graham Norton Show* to plug it, sharing a sofa with Kurt Russell, who very generously laughs at everything I say. I suspect he thinks I'm either funny or mad.

We open in that strange limbo time of a hung parliament following a general election, the ousting of Gordon Brown and the eventually chummy love-in between David Cameron and Nick Clegg in the Number 10 rose garden. The coalition can't come fast enough for our script, which has been in a state of flux for weeks.

Whereas business on tour for this show is brisk and we enjoy sell-out crowds from Edinburgh to Exeter, ticket sales in the West End are sluggish.

The show sits slightly uncomfortably among the usual West End dramas and full-blown big-budget musicals, and although this is reflected in the cheap ticket prices, it's still considered an oddity and some nights we struggle to fill the stalls. Matinees are even worse. Yet again I seem to be in a West End flop. This is getting to be rather a habit!

We slash the ticket prices to a tenner, but it doesn't seem to make any difference. Every night when I catch the bus home from the Strand back to Camberwell, I am joined on the 176 by throngs of overexcited theatre-goers who have just spilled out of the Savoy Theatre, clutching programmes for *Legally Blonde* starring Sheridan Smith. I put my head down all the way to SE5.

I write a little book as a side project to this second *Grumpy* show. *Chin Up Britain* (with a bit of help from Judith) is a tiny lavender-coloured guidebook to keeping one's head in a time of crisis. It's stuffed with piss-taking advice about saving money and beautifully illustrated in a post-war ladies' magazine style. OK, so it's not going to win the Booker Prize, but it's a handy little loo book, even if I sometimes forget I wrote it! It's mostly about how to feel rich and successful when you are skint and feeling like a failure. For example:

> Feel better about where you live, simply by giving your house a name rather than a number. Changing your address from 15 Sydenham Road to 'Flitcroft Hall' will cheer you up no end. It might be the same two-bedroom maisonette on a busy dual carriageway that smells of feet and kippers, but so what?

> Request a finger bowl in KFC.

> Refer to your parents as 'Mummy and Daddy'. Only really rich people do this, you will sound like a twat, but you will sound like a twat with money.

Getting Worried

The West End sales for *Chin Up Britain* leave me feeling anxious. I am forty-nine years old and occasionally I panic about not having a proper job. I have never had the kind of employment that comes with pension contributions, holidays or sick pay. I am still winging it at almost fifty. What if this all goes wrong?

The life of a freelance can never be plain sailing, but as you inch closer to middle age you suddenly realise how thin the ice can get and yet you skate on.

Since Geof left the *TV Times* we are both freelance; maybe Phoebe will do something sensible and become a dentist. Then I remember she's not studying dentistry – she's doing English, which is basically just reading books. Oh Jesus, what will become of us?

Geof's nice little sideline in doing up derelict houses with his mate Simon (two ex-crack dens in Brixton made very chi-chi to date) comes off the rails in the recession of 2009/10, when the banks won't lend any more money for risky projects, and Geof switches to designing extensions for other people.

His timing is spot-on. No one is moving but everyone wants more space, and there are a lot of local clients looking to push up, push back and push sideways. Geof's speciality becomes the glass box kitchen extension (complete with bifold doors) on the back of a Victorian semi. He is brilliant at his job, but he isn't business-minded. (Neither of us is, that's why we don't have joint accounts. We'd be forever pinching each other's money.)

I go to see a man at the bank to talk about a pension, but he draws a pie on a piece of paper and explains that, even though I will be putting all the money in the pie, I won't get to eat all the pie, or something. My head has been going lalalalala ever since he picked up his pen. I leave without a pension plan, lalalalala, but I do nick his pen, so all is not lost.

I do not come from money, but I come from northern middle-class comfort. There was only one patch in my parents' life, when my father left the army, that I felt poor. But we weren't, not really, we were hard up.

My parents weren't spenders and I have inherited the capacity to close my purse sharpish when needs be. Fortunately, I like baked potatoes.

I find it pretty easy to cut back and I have always saved when possible. I am like a child who enjoys a fat piggy bank, because it makes me feel safe and I have a terror of not having enough and outliving my savings. When times are lean, I stop buying lattes and carry my own peanut butter sandwiches around in an old Tupperware.

To be honest, I get very little joy from spending money in restaurants. That said, Geof and I are partial to a pre-theatre hot dog from Five Guys! Personally, I find eating in smart restaurants tastes better on someone else's expense account.

I've been in the business for a very long time. I know how things go. There are the Prada handbag days and the Tesco carrier bag days, but no matter how often you tell yourself it's normal for your career to flatline occasionally, when it happens you are never really prepared.

Grumpy 2 will not tour again. After the poor ticket sales in the West End, the producers are nervous about taking it back out on the road. Instead, I will do another solo tour.

I feel slightly exhausted by this. Occasionally there have been times in my career when I have felt like a dancing bear. While men my age are being rewarded with nice sit-down panel show gigs and afternoon quiz shows, I am not. Not then, not now. And although we've gone a long way in redressing the gender balance on panel shows, for some reason there is still this mad discrepancy when it comes to the big shiny-floor shows, TV quizzes and game shows.

Why are there no female equivalents of Graham Norton's chat show, why does Stephen Mulhern get all the cushy afternoon gigs, why did they blow the opportunity of giving *Countdown* to a great female presenter and allow Anne Robinson to louse it up instead?

I do quite a lot of shouting at the telly and have developed a habit over the years of not watching shows that I think I should have been invited on and haven't. Hence I've avoided watching *Have I Got News For You* for over twenty years! Oh, and 8 *Out of 10 Cats*, they can do one, too.

It's hard not to get bitter occasionally, but in the case of funny women there's a casual misogyny aimed in our direction that affects all of us, so I get angry, not just on my own behalf but on the behalf of everybody else.

In fact, I think the generation of female comics who have been overlooked more than any of us are the women who came along in the ten years after me. Loads of them deserve to be bigger names than they are. I would count Lucy Porter, Jo Caulfield, Zoe Lyons in this group. It's all about timing, innit.

The first wave of British female stand-ups consisted of Victoria Wood and French and Saunders, with the likes of Ruby Wax, Tracey Ullman, Sandi Toksvig and Helen Lederer alongside.

My generation includes Jo Brand, Hattie Hayridge and Josie Lawrence, who became well known on telly, plus the remarkable Lily Savage, of course. But from the mid-nineties there is a dearth of new female comedy faces on the box, until *Smack the Pony* arrives in 1999.

For many women in comedy the door isn't opened often enough or for long enough and it's shocking how much talent gets left out in the cold.

The invitation to the inner sanctum of telly fame and riches that will last you a lifetime is quite arbitrary. In recent years Sara Pascoe and Sarah Millican have definitely made it, but it's only Katherine Ryan who has hit the really big time. Here's a fact: however successful some British female comics are, we are not performing solo shows in arenas. In fact, the only woman currently gigging in arenas is Rosie Ramsey, wife of Chris Ramsey and co-presenter of the podcast *Shagged Married Annoyed*, the live version of which sells out Wembley.

Instead of taking *Grumpy* out again, I write a solo show called *Old Dog, New Tricks*. The poster makes me laugh; my face is superimposed on the body of a show poodle who is busy doing tricks. I buy a hula-hoop; I shall make my stage entrance hula-ing my hoop.

My agent isn't keen on this image; he thinks people won't know it's me, what with the poodle quiff. I ignore him and set off by myself in the autumn of 2010.

Old Dog, New Tricks

Something goes wrong with *Old Dog, New Tricks*. I'm not getting bums on seats. It goes like this: I arrive at the venue and the management greet me with the dreaded words, 'We've moved you into the small room for tonight.' Sometimes I get demoted to the bar.

My career seems to be going backwards. One night I find myself playing the tiny studio in the basement of a town hall, while Greg Davies strides like a colossus on the main stage above my head. The ceiling reverberates with the sound of his feet and a thousand people laughing at his jokes. Hold on, two minutes ago I was one of the judges on a comedy awards panel that gave him one of his first breaks!

I can't blame the poster, not when it was my idea.

I limp around the country, feeling wounded and washed up. I'm also embarrassed. I keep wondering what my audience say to each other after sitting in a half-empty auditorium. The show is good, but loads of people are doing good shows and the competition out on the road is fierce. Some of the places I am booked to do are being used by younger, bigger names as warm-up venues. I feel like I'm constantly being reminded of my position in the comedy league. Right now, I'm not even third division.

There are also new girls on the block. Miranda Hart is the biggest breakthrough comedy star of the decade, with her extremely well-written, fantastically cast and brilliantly performed sitcom *Miranda*. Sarah Millican is on the rise, as is Shappi Khorsandi, both of whom shine on *Live at the Apollo*, which, try as my agent might, will not offer me a slot.

As I have got older in this business, I have become horribly aware of the existence of lists. Each channel has lists of people they want on their TV shows and lists of people who they are genuinely not interested in. I was once listening to *Woman's Hour* when the female producer of *Have I Got News For You*, Jo King (yup, truly), was on, defending the lack of female comics on the show, saying that 'lots of funny women turned the job down'. At this point I emailed *Woman's Hour* to say that I had never been asked, never mind given the opportunity to turn it down, and the presenter (possibly Jane Garvey) promptly read this email out. Jo King (I mean, honestly) squirmed and bluffed and ended up saying that I was an 'acquired taste'. Meanwhile, I sat at home and blushed, alone and utterly humiliated.

Quite often in my career I'm reminded of the day I went to play with Sheona Norris when I was about nine, and when she went to the loo I snooped through her diary. One of the entries read 'Jenny Hargreaves is not as popular as she thinks she is'. Hahahaha, you're not kidding.

In the autumn of 2010 I feel as popular as the girl in the Lee and Herring sketch, the one who 'smelt of Spam'.

Coincidentally, 2010 is the year Victoria Wood is interviewed by the *Guardian* and admits to feeling undervalued and unwanted by the BBC, who had demoted her 2009 *Victoria Wood's Midlife Christmas* special from Xmas Day, which she had been promised, to Xmas Eve without even bothering to tell her.

If Victoria is finding the industry tough, no wonder I'm struggling.

Is it my age? The menopause is yet to be fashionable, and recently at a charity dinner Jeffrey Archer actually tells me to my face that I should accept that I'd had a good innings and give in gracefully. 'What about my mortgage?' I squeak in response. But I don't think he understood the question.

In November 2010, Geof, Phoebe and I go to Hastings for the funeral of our friend Angie. She was fifty-two and cancer snatched her. I need to explain Angie, because the longer she is dead the more I wish she was alive. I wish she could have lived longer, so that I could have been a better friend. I hope she knew how much we all loved her.

There are very few special people in real life. When I think of Angie, I imagine her as an illustration in a children's book of fairy tales, a circus trapeze artist, a mermaid, a princess with long yellow hair and a big nose. Her life was a triumph, her death, and that of her new husband only three weeks before her, is a tragedy. It is unbelievable that two people who married in the summer of 2010 should both be dead by Xmas.

I first meet Angie in the early eighties. She is part of the art school mob that I hang out with; she paints murals that still exist all over London and dances around bonfires in men's leather lace-up boots. She is honey-skinned, with a pile of straw-coloured hair; she wears Victorian white nightgowns and ancient velvet coats. She is the most beautiful of all my friends and they would all agree.

She and her partner Simon have two honey-coloured boys in the years following Phoebe's arrival, and, along with other friends with young families, we drive knackered cars to the seaside and smoke and drink and spend New Years and birthdays celebrating together, eating sausages and cheese and mounds of pickled red cabbage and baked potatoes, the heap of babies wriggling around on the floor, getting bigger every year.

Simon and Angie move out of London, first to Norfolk, then

to Hastings, their marriage breaks down and Angie has cancer, which, after a great deal of treatment, she survives. But then comes another cancer and this time she refuses yet more chemotherapy. She writes poetry, keeps bees and gives up meat and processed food but I think, deep down, she knows she will die.

On a beautiful summer's day in 2010 she marries Len wearing a gold satin dress, in a sunlight-dappled garden by the sea, and that evening, as we walk back to the car, me, Geof and Phoebe, a white barn owl swoops against the denim-blue night sky and I instantly think of death.

Len dies first of a swift and merciless pancreatic cancer just months after the wedding and Angie follows him three weeks later. To this day it shocks me. I wish I'd been less selfish and held her hand more.

The day after her funeral is a Saturday and I'm in the bath, crying. Phoebe has left to go back to Oxford, so when my mobile rings I presume it's her having forgotten something. But it's my agent Richard, phoning on a Saturday morning, which is weird. The first thing he asks is 'Is your passport up to date?'

'Yes.'

'They've offered you *I'm A Celebrity*. You have thirty minutes to make your mind up: the flight leaves for Brisbane tomorrow night.'

'What about the tour?'

'We can reschedule.'

I tell him I need to ask Geof and Phoebe's permission before I say yes, but when they don't have a problem with it, I think, *Fuck it*.

I can't face the reality of my own life right now, so I might as well run away. The idea of being 35,000 feet above sea level, away from everything cocooned in business-class luxury, suddenly really appeals.

I say yes.

Jungle Madness

The deal I am offered turns out to be less than a third of Sheryl Gascoigne's fee! This is not a favoured nations (i.e. everyone gets the same) scenario: you are paid according to your celebrity worth. I'm a lightweight, which is reflected in my pay cheque. Honestly, I'd have done loads better if I'd been through a messy mud-slinging divorce/a personal drink 'n' drugs hell and/or had a decent pair of tits/nice bum. Fact is, I'm a dumpy small-breasted, flabby-arsed fifty-year-old who wears glasses even in the shower.

I am also not guaranteed a place on the show.

I am being flown out as back-up. They are expecting a high walkout rate, the weather is grim and people are already fed up, but if I do go in I will be a late arrival, traditionally not a great start.

I drink, sleep and eat chicken satay sticks on the flight over. It's a Malaysia Airlines flight and the flight attendants are perfect tiny dolls. Once I land in Brisbane, I'm met by sniffer dogs and slightly bored paparazzi, who are very obviously just going through the motions, click, click, click.

Beyond customs, my *I'm A Celebrity* wrangler, a nice curly haired gay boy, who's drawn the short straw of looking after me, takes me to a faceless hotel. The weather is moody, I am very jet-lagged and struggle to stay awake over my dinner. I have the Moreton Bay bugs, which are sort of like lobster. When in Australia and all that.

Then ... nothing. I have to stay in my room, keep my head down and order room service while they decide what to do with me. Nice gay boy keeps in touch, but, although I've recently joined Twitter, I'm not allowed to play with it. I read and watch telly, think about the unfairness of Angie's early death and wonder whether I've done a stupid thing in coming out here.

Before I go mad with homesickness and boredom there is a flurry of activity. I am driven to another hotel, served a slap-up lunch and informed that I am going into the jungle. Craftily I swipe a bread roll for future emergencies.

Once I'm dressed in my jungle gear, I secrete the bread roll into one of my breast pockets, which gives the impression of having one boob slightly bigger than the other. Well done me. Apart from the wonky tits, I look like my dad in my shorts.

I channel my dad a lot in the jungle. I've seldom felt more like him. He weirdly influences how I behave. I find my inner 'gung ho'.

The other late arrival going in with me is Dom Joly, he of the big phone and *Trigger Happy TV*.

Things you may not know about Dom include the facts that one of his middle names is Romulus, his Canadian wife Stacey is an utter treasure and he knows every capital city in the world. We are friends to this day.

The two of us are helicoptered (a first for me – loved it) to the 'jungle' and we have to canoe to some little island, where our mission is to win stars for the camp by staying the night in a snake-infested hut. Oh, great. I fucking hate snakes, but I go full Derek on it and cope better than Dom, who is prone at times to be a bit of a snivelling ninny over the sheer number of the bloody things.

Task finished, and with a respectable number of stars collected, I lie in my sleeping bag and nibble the bread roll from my breast pocket. What on earth have I let myself in for?

The next day, still wearing yesterday's knickers, Dom and I are helicoptered to a clearing some distance from the camp. Nigel Havers and Shaun Ryder have been dispatched as the welcome party. Neither are particularly delighted to see us: I mean, it's not exactly like we're delivering pizza. My heart sinks a bit and by the time we have trekked down to the camp making desperate small talk, I have a migraine.

I don't often get migraines, but when I do I need to lie in the dark and puke up. I spend my first night in camp doing just this. I throw up and I throw up and I throw up. My radio mic is splattered with vomit; I haven't got a toothbrush yet. This is not the way to ingratiate myself with my fellow campers. Everyone rightly keeps their distance and I prepare for an early elimination.

My wooden-framed bed is on the outer edge of the camp. From this vantage point, I can see and hear everyone. My closest sleepmates are Sheryl Gascoigne (highest paid, first out), who is a poppet and so pretty I can't take my eyes off her, and Shaun Ryder, who is less pretty and already covered in festering insect bites.

Shaun calls me 'geezer bird'; he respects my potty mouth and northern roots. He thinks I'm tougher than I am.

I'm not tough but neither am I 'self-delusional', a 'bit thick', 'conversationally boring' or just plain 'odd', like some of the other contestants.

Not everyone is insane, difficult, weird or self-obsessed. I am fond of Britt Ekland. I'd met her before when she guested on my LBC show and talked about Peter Sellers being cruel. She told me a story about how he had bought her a watch, but because she didn't wear the outfit he wanted her to wear, he took it off her wrist and stamped on it.

I think certain men possibly defined Britt's life for too long. She is a fascinating person in her own right, but hearing her talk around the firepit I get the impression that even her father hadn't been very nice to her. In fact, the more I listen to people talk about their childhoods and their parents, the more grateful I am to June and Derek for their no-nonsense common sense, their uncomplicated affection and complete fairness.

Britt is scared of going to the dunny at night, so decides to stop drinking any liquid in the afternoon so that she won't need a wee in the dark. This is obviously a bonkers idea, but she can't be persuaded otherwise. Inevitably she dehydrates to the point of kidney infection, for which she is seen by a medic, treated and left to sleep it off. She burrows so far down in her sleeping bag that we cannot see her head. The cameras simply move around her, and nothing is said. I don't think she even gets up for Ant and Dec; perhaps she can be seen in the back of the shot when they come into camp, like a cocooned caterpillar with a UTI.

I also really like Nigel Havers. He is so dishy and suave and everything you want him to be. He is charming and funny and good to chat with, but sadly he pulls out of the camp after we are asked to shove electrodes down our pants (or some such nonsense) as he's worried about his pacemaker conking out. I miss him when he's gone. He's a civilising force.

Some people irritate me. Lembit Öpik is a silly man: I rename him 'limpid prick' in my head. He has squirrelled away some rolls of toilet paper in case people are 'profligate' with it. This is the word he actually uses. I can't imagine what he thinks he's going to gain from this action, that when the camp runs out of bog roll he will suddenly appear as the saviour of clean arses and we will do his bidding. At the time he is dating a twenty-one-year-old woman who also works as his PA. Later Geof tells me that when he gets chucked out he and his girlfriend spend a lot of time at the hotel pool, staging lovey-dovey antics for the press. Yuk. He is intellectually a terrible lightweight and a complete charisma-free zone.

Equally idiotic is Gillian McKeith, who is famous for being a poo doctor. The fact that she has two extremely nice daughters is a credit to . . . someone. She is moany and boring and 'faints' all the time, particularly when she is called on to do a challenge, hence the public keep voting for her and down she goes again.

She is too frail for the job. I try and stay away from her because she brings out the bully in me. I am glad when she is voted out. Apparently she smuggled herbs into the camp in her pants, which is an upsetting thought.

There are camp mates I barely recall – a rapper who disappears without trace, the Olympic athlete Linford Christie, who doesn't like cold water and . . . no, can't remember anything else. Nice enough chap, good legs.

We also have a swimwear model in the mix, a perky American blonde who had spent time in Hugh Hefner's Bunny Girl luxury home, which was by all accounts covered in dog shit as most of the resident Bunny Girls kept small dogs that shat everywhere. It's difficult to understand, in 2024, how a man such as Hugh Hefner was ever looked up to and revered, that his was a lifestyle people envied, living in some mansion surrounded by semi-clad beauties, who apparently vied for the chance to sleep with an ancient bag of jizz.

Again, judging from various conversations, I get the impression Kayla's dad has been tricky, too! She is fine in the camp; I just find the whole swimwear model cliché slightly dull. We do a challenge together one day which involves being dunked (in our swimming costumes) in horse shit, so that's 'fun'.

While writing this, I Google Kayla Collins to see what has become of her. I check on her Instagram account and discover she is now a brunette mother of five. I hope she is happy.

Alison Hammond is a late, late arrival. She turns up in a crate.

I hope it might be a kangaroo, anything to relieve the boredom. Poor Alison jumps out, full of beans, but no one gives her the attention she could do with. She tries her best to have fun, but by this stage we are set in our ways, we don't have the energy for new introductions, she is wasted on the camp. I like her a lot; she really suffers with maternal guilt and at one stage she breaks down over an insect challenge. She worries that seeing his mum eat bugs will upset her small son. I feel for her, safe in the knowledge that my daughter is more or less an adult and has better things to do than watch this show. In any case she doesn't have a telly.

I get a video message from Phoebe quite late on in the game. From the footage it's easy to see she is trying hard not to look hungover! Bless.

It's pretty obvious from the get-go that Stacey Solomon will win the show. She is a complete one-off: she wakes up grinning and has endless energy for anything. We have one row, when she tells me reading books is a waste of time. When I try to explain why it isn't, I feel 103. She is a sweet, sweet, golden-hearted woman and I am completely unsurprised by her continuing success. Alison and Stacey have done the best of all of us: maybe being nice actually works? Oh dear, bit late to try it now.

Coming Out

As predicted, Stacey Solomon wins the 2010 series of *I'm A Celebrity* by a landslide, Shaun comes in second and I'm third, which pisses Dom off, haha. He is fourth.

By the time I am voted out I've had enough, and in the final feast challenge I'm defeated by the idea of eating an eyeball. We all have our limits. For me, it's an optic nerve and I am delighted that my time is up. Mentally I'm starting to wobble.

Geof has been staying at the Versace Hotel, which is weirdly very nineties and stuffed with terrible furniture and framed black and white fashion photos which start repeating themselves down the corridors!

I am very dizzy when I get out. I think it's panic; the old tilting problem happens and I'm given some lovely Valium to stop me falling over.

Geof meets me on the slightly rusty rope bridge for all that reunion nonsense and we hug self-consciously. I'm delighted to see him but can't wait until we can be alone and I can start bitching. Safely in our suite, I have three baths, one after the other, and a mediocre room service steak. Sorry to ruin anyone's posh hotel fantasies: let's just say the Versace is very comfortable in a time-warp kind of way, sort of like staying with a very rich old nana, but that steak is nothing to write home about!

I feel sorry for whoever has to clean the tide mark round the bath when I eventually get out. I do my best with it, but it needs scouring powder.

Geof has made friends with Dom's wife, Stacey, but tells me there are other 'friends and family' he actively hid from when journeying to and from the camp. He is not the most sociable of men and the daily coach trip is several hours each way. He has been getting up at 4 a.m. every day, while trying to keep his business in London going from a completely different time zone. His phone bill when we get back is in the thousands.

We are flown home first class, which is glorious and not something I've experienced before or since. There is a bar in the middle of the plane – an actual bar where you can go and have a drink. How marvellous. Everything has been paid for; that flight could go on forever as far as I am concerned. We land in snow at Heathrow.

Geof and I are both surprised at how well I seem to have done. Neither of us can imagine who has voted for me, certainly not my family who don't go in for phone voting, though I think my dad may have had a go. That said, my parents are relieved and quite proud of me, even though I don't think either of them can see the point of the show.

Turns out I'm big with primary school-age boys, who think I'm funny and brave. Back in Camberwell, they swarm around me in the supermarket asking for my autograph.

Typical: I've gained a whole new fan base of kids who are far too young to see any of my live shows, or buy me a drink for that matter.

OK! magazine approach with an offer for a family photo shoot and interview. I rope in my nephew Zack, so that we look like more of a normal family rather than the odd little trio that we are, and we're assembled to look human in various parts of the house. It's all part of the game. My agent is thrilled with me. I think he may have cried: he usually does when I surprise him and do better than he expects.

I enjoy Xmas at home. The jungle diet has done its job and I am able to pop myself into a psychedelic vintage little dress. I have lost over a stone, mostly from trudging miles to challenges. What people don't realise when they watch *I'm A Celebrity* is that most challenges are some distance away, like miles, and en route you pass a sort of graveyard of previous challenges – broken bits of wooden structures, clearings full of what looks like derelict oversized children's playground apparatus. It's not just the UK that uses the site: it's shared with all the other international productions. The place is littered with bits of broken shit, basically, and when it rains the mud smells bad.

Oh, yes, and the stone walls surrounding the camp, they're fake, they're made of polystyrene and hide a rat run for the cameramen. Sometimes if you stand in the right spot you can hear blokes behind the fake walls eating crisps.

One of my abiding memories of the jungle experience is sighting a giant wild turkey on the outskirts of the camp. I mean one of those massive black Thanksgiving-style fuckers, with a huge red wattle and matching snood.

I mean, WTAF?

Another night a poisonous toad comes jumping into camp and suddenly there's a flurry of black-clad bush rangers bearing down on the undergrowth with torches and sticks.

I'm not sure I was ever insured against poisonous toads.

Reality TV and Panto

I'm *A Celebrity* is my introduction to the world of reality TV shows. Once you do one, it opens up the door to more reality TV shows. Now, some performers think this is the kiss of death. Haha, well, good for them, well done to anyone who manages forty years in the business without doing any kind of celebrity reality show. I've done loads and mostly been quite crap at them.

I do particularly badly on *Celebrity MasterChef*, for example. Gregg and John see straight through me and I am deservedly first out, having muddled my quantities of sherry vinegar while attempting a tarragon chicken dish I'd once eaten at a friend's house. I must have asked for the recipe while I was a bit pissed, with inevitable results. Gregg Wallace actually pulled a face when he ate it, like a child being force-fed a terrible school dinner.

I also sign up for *Splash!*, which is a bonkers ITV show that the critics hate but which rates well enough to get a second series. Presented by Gabby Logan and Vernon Kay, it's a diving show that involves celebrities risking spinal injuries in order to amuse the British public.

I sort of love it and for a while I dream of diving in my sleep. We are mentored by the utterly divine pocket-sized Tom Daley and his Olympic training team. I am utterly hopeless but eventually manage to tip myself head-first off a three-metre board while more athletic participants somersault backwards off the ten-metre board. Jo Brand, who is judging, calls me a 'flying prawn' because I am wearing a pink swimming costume. In reality, I have the grace of a small car falling off a cliff.

Penny Mordaunt, the Tory MP who ended up carrying the big ceremonial sword thing at the coronation of King Charles in 2023, is in the same series. On the night of the recording, she does a massive belly flop which must have hurt her pride as much as anything else. You can still see it on YouTube. Ha!

People sneer at reality telly shows but I've had some extraordinary experiences while doing them. *Strictly* is, of course, the big one, but I've got fat chance (literally) of getting on that, not being currently on the BBC's wish list. Channel 5's *Dancing on Ice* has had a sniff around, but at my age I think I'm too much of a risk. No one wants to see a woman in her sixties break every bone in her body.

I do, however, jump at the chance to do *The Great Celebrity Bake Off: Stand Up to Cancer*, because I get to go *in the tent* and touch all the things. I also win, but only because I'm up against baking idiots, including ex-support act Russell Howard, gorgeous model and basketball player Ovie Soko, who manages to look cool wearing white towelling ankle socks with slides, and Louis Theroux. Theroux really wants to win, so I am delighted when I beat him and get my star baker pinny (which I wear for painting).

Weirdly enough, after appearing on *Celebrity Bake Off* I am auditioned for the co-presenting gig when Sandi leaves. I lose out to Matt Lucas, but I know I came close because the production company send a big bouquet of flowers and a card on the day Matt is announced, saying 'Next time'. Only 'next time' they give the gig to Alison Hammond, and I don't get a look-in!

My other celebrity TV pinny is from *Celebrity Pottery*

Throwdown, which I am beyond thrilled to get asked to do in 2022. This is my all-time favourite. Being in a pottery studio with weepy Keith and co. is one of the highlights of my year, even though it is weirdly both knackering and nerve-racking. The actor James Fleet rightly wins, but I like to think I may have come second, and the pinny is proper quality, as designed by weepy Keith. To be honest I knew I hadn't won when he remained resolutely dry-eyed while judging my wares!

The other opportunities offered after *I'm A Celebrity* include panto, which many contestants find themselves signing up for the Xmas following the jungle. It's a kind of tradition.

I am lucky. I'm offered *Cinderella* in Richmond, which is a bus and train ride there, plus a courtesy car home.

Sadly, I am cast as the Fairy Godmother and with this being a traditional panto in a posh London suburb there's no mucking about with the script and absolutely no swearing.

I'm not really cut out for this role. The costume is a huge lilac affair, reminiscent of those seventies crinoline dolls that sat on top of lavatory cisterns with a toilet roll hidden coyly up their skirt. Every time I turn around in my tiny dressing room I knock something off my dressing table. I have to walk down corridors sideways. I'm reminded of being my sister's fat-arsed bridesmaid. It's not as if the frock is new, either: sewn into the back of the neck is a label with the name Sheila Ferguson (ex-Three Degrees) written in laundry marker.

Originally, I'm meant to sing the number 'Spread a Little Happiness', even though my agent has flagged up my musical difficulties before signing the contract. The musical director tells me not to worry; apparently, I can 'talk/sing it'.

Only I can't, I can only murder it. When we rehearse around the piano, some of the company babes who are present in the rehearsal room look anxious, a couple cry, the pianist thinks I might be joking. I'm not.

The next day we get a phone call from the production company announcing that the song has been cut. I could have told them.

Panto is nuts. For me, it has become a measuring stick of tiredness: you can be tired, really tired, and then you can be panto tired, which is a state of exhaustion somewhere between fucking knackered and dead. It usually kicks in on a three-show day. Imagine having jet lag while dressed up as a Marie Antoinette lookalike, for six weeks.

What I like about doing this panto most is having two live Shetlands onstage. Nice to be sharing the boards with creatures more likely to shit themselves than you are, and they do, frequently.

I also make a friend. My Cinderella is the actress Kellie Shirley. We still meet up. Meeting new friends when you get older, and you're as suspicious as I am, is a rare bonus. Kellie is one of the few women, apart from my own daughter, who I like to hug.

The other job I get as a result of doing *I'm A Celeb* is *Loose Women*! I know, right . . .

A Sit-Down Job at Last

*L**oose Women* is a very divisive show: some people really love it, while some people really despise it.

Personally, I think it will make a nice change from constantly flogging my arse off on tour. The studio is on the South Bank, which is my side of the river, meaning it takes me twenty minutes to get from door to door first thing in the morning, in a posh courtesy car, too.

It's like a proper job. I never get offered jobs! And it's sitting down! Sitting down, once or twice a week (depending on schedules), talking and getting home in time for a late lunch! Bingo, that's my kind of job!

You also get your hair and make-up done and clothes especially borrowed and styled for you.

The stylist is called Bertie; she and a couple of the runners, Matty and Daisy, are soon my firm favourites on the show. Bertie understands my body shape and taste, and the young runners are a laugh.

But sometimes I am out of my depth. There is a shared history between some of the other girls, deep loyalties and forgotten feuds, big nights out and tabloid tittle-tattle. I'm never sure how much of myself I'm meant to give.

I am also slightly scared of Denise Welch, which sounds silly now, but in 2011 she is still drinking and can be erratic. Denise has completely turned her life around since, and the whole *Loose Women* vibe seems much kinder and more mature. But back then I am anxious not to get on the wrong side of her. Both she and Coleen Nolan are long-standing panellists and gossip columnists' favourites, as is Carol McGiffin, a funny, bright woman with some politically odd views.

Oh dear, I don't like confrontation as much as people would like to assume, but the whole point in being on a discussion show like *Loose Women* is to have opinions.

Well, here's the thing: sometimes I don't know what I think. I mostly think somewhere in the middle is about right – neither this nor that. I don't have hard and fast rules, I find it quite easy to change my mind, I'm easily persuaded by other people's arguments, I can usually see both sides. To be honest, I can be a bit wet.

I'd rather be allowed to just be funny, but that's not the remit and anyway there are already lots of funny ladies taking turns on the panel, so I can't push too hard. I'm a newbie. Everyone wants to be funny, apart from the anchors who lead the discussions; these are the sensible head girl types, such as Andrea McLean, who is a poppet.

I also get on well with Janet Street-Porter (hilariously bossy), even though she can be intimidating, but then maybe I am, too? In my own way.

Although they are scrupulously fair with the dressing rooms rotation and we all have a turn in the shit one, there is a subtle hierarchy within the show. This becomes apparent in myriad different ways, from petty things like who gets which make-up chair/artist to slightly more annoying incidents.

One night in December 2011 we are all invited to the National Television Awards at the O2. It's a big do. I cobble together an outfit at home, before meeting up with everyone at the studios, where we are due to be ferried down the river to the awards in a water taxi.

It's only when I pitch up at LWT that I suddenly realise that some of my workmates have been in make-up and wardrobe for hours, being primped, laced and zipped into fancy hired frocks.

In a fit of contrariness, I have deliberately gone against the whole glam bollocks, and from my own wardrobe I've chosen a silver box-shaped dress which I have teamed with green tights and green shoes. From the knee down, I look like a fat Kermit the Frog. Inevitably I make the 'worst dressed' lists in some of those bitchy magazines, the ones that get off on pulling women apart and taking photos of celebrities looking like shit.

It's not a good night for me. That morning I'd received a dodgy mammogram result and I'm awaiting a further check-up (all fine in the end – water-filled cysts, apparently), which has freaked me out and I'm on edge.

The O2 is a terrible place and there doesn't seem to be anything to eat; we don't win and afterwards I can't find my supposedly pre-booked car to take me home. Instantly I feel all paranoid and a bit mad in my ugly green tights. Everyone else has got into their cars and gone. I strop around, on my own, trying to work out where the bloody tube station is, until my car eventually arrives. I don't think doing this show is very good for my head.

But for all the misgivings I have about doing the programme, there are plenty of really enjoyable moments. Alex James from Blur comes on and remembers seeing me die on my arse doing an after-dinner speech at a cheese convention in a hotel down Park Lane. Genuinely one of the worst gigs of my life, I escaped via a service lift and slunk out through the kitchen onto a back alley full of stinking bins.

Some years after this, Alex and I meet again when we are

booked, with a load of other chancers, to do a cooking show on-board a cruise ship. The show is called *Battle Chefs*, and Alex and I end up touring a custard pie factory together in Lisbon, wearing blue plastic shower caps on our heads and feet. Even Alex, who is naturally very sexy, cannot pull this look off. He is also very hungover and feeling guilty for having got very pissed the night before with the Olympic long-jumper Greg Rutherford. Who is a complete gent, btw.

I digress. There are perks to doing *Loose Women*. I have plenty of time to get on with writing my third novel. *Life, Death and Vanilla Slices*, which turns out to be my mother's favourite, is set up north and the story reveals itself to me as I write it.

Writing novels is very frustrating. I'm not someone who can plot the structure beforehand and then just embroider around it. I start with a house and some people in it, and they tell me who they are and how they are related to each other and, in an un-bearably wanky kind of way, the characters tell their own story. I'm sorry if this sounds precious, but it's the only way it's ever worked. Every time I try to plot a story before I start, it fails.

Life, Death and Vanilla Slices is the story of maternal favourit-ism, sibling rivalry and a missing teenager. I am proud of it: it feels like a grown-up book. I'm desperate for it to do well. Publication is set for the summer of 2012. Huzzah. I'm on telly and I have a new novel coming out. Go me!

I am recognised on the street, my bank balance is piggy bank fat, any stand-up shows I do sell well, but . . . I'm still not entirely convinced that *Loose Women* is really what I should be doing, but it's just so convenient and easy.

Turns out it's not just me who has doubts: the powers that be also think I'm a square peg in a round hole. I'm not sure what annoys them about me most. But I understand why they might find me frustrating. I don't play the game completely, I'm happy to be an outsider, hanging around on the fringes of the gang.

Loose Women is not the be-all and end-all of my career; it lags behind the writing and the stand-up. None of my family watches it, my mother thinks it's silly and is probably a bit embarrassed by it. I doubt my sister has ever watched it in her life.

Early in the summer of 2012 I'm in Blackpool with my friend Clare, doing research for an article I'm writing about the resort's bizarre charms (I'm a fan of the place), when I get a call from my agent. We are in a cab en route to the train station: '*Loose Women* won't be renewing your contract after the summer break,' he tells me.

I turn to Clare and say, 'I've lost my job.'

They don't give any specific reason, but, of course, there was that incident . . .

The Incident

The incident is a silly thing, and I don't think it's the only reason why *Loose Women* let me go. However, I do think it is another nail in my coffin.

Other nails include occasionally trying to talk about art and culture, when apparently no one is interested, especially when I defend modern art and get cross when people pull faces.

By the way, I think the whole vibe of *Loose Women* has changed for the better over the years and on recent guest appearances I've been struck by how much classier it is these days. Sorry, but that's how I feel. The production team has changed and there's a slightly nicer atmosphere these days. I'm probably being defensive. I'm probably trying to hint that they only sack me because I'm too bright for them, but deep down I know that's not true! Let's face it, I'm not exactly Mary Beard – I don't spend my time on the panel dropping Latin bon mots and quoting Shakespeare!

What I do, however, is something that is very childish and silly.

Let me set the scene. The corridors at LWT studios are covered in large framed portraits of their most popular stars. All the big names are up there, grinning down at the also-rans and wannabes.

Now, one of my problems is I should never be trusted with a pen. On this occasion I have a biro and in an idle few moments before the show, while hanging out with Janet Street-Porter, I scribble on some of the glass-fronted portraits. I draw a handful of pubic hairs on the Welsh opera singer Katherine Jenkins's thighs (she is wearing a gown which is split to the crotch) and I draw a blue ball bag coming out of Alan Titchmarsh's trousers. Janet and I have regressed into idiotic sniggering schoolgirls. It seems harmless enough; the graffiti is not permanent, it comes off with a lick and a quick rub – I'm using a weedy biro not a magic marker – the markings are very subtle and you have to look very closely to notice them. We are still giggling in the morning meeting and, in front of the rest of the girls and some production staff, I'm quite open about what I've been up to.

A day or so later I receive a phone call warning me that a story has broken in the *Daily Mail*, which paints the incident in a much more sinister light. According to the paper, we have defaced the portraits of prettier, younger women because of our rabid hag-like jealousy. Hold on, what 'women'? What about the blue ball bag hanging out of Alan Titchmarsh's trousers? Nope, that isn't mentioned. The *Mail* twists the facts about who has been drawn on; in the photograph, Alan is standing next to Myleene Klass, ergo (Latin) we have defaced Myleene Klass.

I am hysterical. Fortunately Phoebe is in the house and reminds me that I haven't killed anyone, but even she is a bit cross with me. I'm in my fifties, FFS.

However, she and Geof rally round, while flowers and letters of apology are sent to the injured parties. I try to explain that Myleene Klass wasn't actually involved, and we should be saying sorry to Alan, but apparently this will confuse the issue.

To give Myleene her credit, when approached for comment she says she thinks the whole thing is hilarious. Go, Myleene. Katherine, on the other hand, is *furious*.

I'm an idiot. The paper savages both Janet and me, but I was the one with the pen. To be honest, ITV are very good to let me work out the rest of my contract, but I think my card is marked the day the story breaks. Janet, on the other hand, is still there!!!

Writing this, I feel quite embarrassed about the incident, and looking back I can see why people might think it spiteful.

Fortunately, my mother is incredibly good about it. Despite never having watched the show and not being a fan, she is completely on my side, to the extent that some years later when Katherine Jenkins performs at Lytham Prom on the green opposite my mother's flat, she closes the windows so that she can't hear 'that woman caterwauling'.

Maternal loyalty, however misplaced, should never be underestimated. Thanks, Ma. She always did give me the benefit of the doubt.

Back to the Boards

When one door closes, write another stand-up show, give it a title, tour it, take it up to Edinburgh, repeat until you die.

And so I write *Eclairious*, which rolls around the country and even manages a trip to the Melbourne Comedy Festival. It's a good show containing traces of cynicism, which I think are entirely justified.

Great to be gigging again, been off the road for a while. Failed my MOT, leaky undercarriage, problems with my steering (pissed), illegal levels of gassy emissions from the rear end.

Good to be back. I'd just like to say travelling round the country gives me great joy, but actually it gives me varicose veins and a fatty liver. I'm like an ageing comedy goose, waddling round the country: hello Pizza Hut, hello Nando's, hello late-night chippy, hello mini bar, hello Type 2 diabetes.

Anyway, as I say, I haven't been doing much stand-up – took a break to spend some time with my family, 'til I realised they didn't want to spend more time with me.

I look great on the poster, so great that when I play my home town of Lytham St Annes, my mother doesn't recognise my face on the billboard outside the theatre.

She says she will come and see the show, but in the end she bottles out. 'I couldn't bear it if people didn't laugh,' she admits. Some of her friends brave it. One or two may still be talking about it!

It's 2012: my father is living in a nursing home about a mile away from the cottage in Lytham. My mother visits twice a day until it gets too much, at which point she cuts it down to every afternoon. Pa can no longer walk and is doubly incontinent, but he is cheerful and compos mentis and the staff love him. He is funny and friendly; in the morning he spends his time doing terrible pencil crayon drawings and in the afternoon he and June do the crossword puzzle in the *i* newspaper. Before June leaves she supplies him with biscuits in case he gets hungry in the night and makes sure his back scratcher is within reach. This is old-age love.

I think my father views his stay in the nursing home as a difficult posting; his army training kicks in and he copes. He has always been able to make the best of things; he is not a whinger, although he is repulsively graphic about his bowel movements.

My mother copes, too; after all, she still has Aileen. Her sister lives round the corner from the nursing home and will often pop in to see Derek in the morning. Then, when June has done her afternoon shift, she will go and have a cup of tea with Aileen before she goes home. June is still driving, but Aileen's deteriorating eyesight means that she has given up her car. My aunt is a widow now and the two sisters rely on each other a great deal. All their friends keep dying. My mother says, 'I'm never out of that bloody black skirt.'

I have a joke in my stand-up set about staying with my mother during this period. 'By the time I've got out of bed, she's up, dressed, made soup and been to a funeral.' And on occasion it's true.

Phoebe has left Oxford and is devastated when she doesn't get a first. She is so upset that I take her to the Royal Vauxhall Tavern where we spend the night with Chris George, Vanessa and Julie watching our Aussie mate Bob Downe perform his all-singing, all-dancing human Ken (as in Barbie Doll) impression. Paul O'Grady is in the dressing room when we go backstage for a chat. He is beyond kind to P, who has never forgotten it.

A year on, she has an apprenticeship at Battersea Arts Centre, where she is learning all the tricks of running a venue, including cleaning toilets and making coffee. I hope she is better at cleaning toilets than making coffee.

She lives at home for a while, but it doesn't really work. I am over-anxious and, having been away for three years, she wants to come and go as she pleases and not answer hysterical phone calls from her mother at 2 a.m.

Behind my back she is writing scripts and is accepted onto a playwriting mentoring programme at the Royal Court Theatre. I snoop around her bedroom until I find a scrap of a writing exercise; when I read it, my heart feels calm. This is what she is meant to do. I just have to leave her to get on with it.

We all have to get on with it; there is no golden ticket and I am still getting mistaken for Su Pollard. I seem to spend my entire career stepping sideways. I keep moving but I never get very far. I know I am comparatively successful, but not compared to the people that I compare myself to. Unsurprisingly, show business is full of insanely jealous fucked-up people. I know this for a fact because I'm one of them.

At fifty-two, I am very, very menopausal. This manifests itself mostly in anxiety and fury. I am expecting hot flushes, but they don't arrive. Where are my hot flushes? I am incandescent about not having hot flushes. I feel like fighting everyone.

I see a doctor at my local surgery. He refers to my vagina as my 'downstairs'. I want to punch him. He is very, very anti hormone replacement therapy.

I go privately (thanks, Helen Lederer, for the phone number), get an HRT prescription and feel better within three days of taking the pills and rubbing in the magic gel. Eventually, I convince my surgery to put this scrip on my NHS tab, and I've been on it ever since. Hair and nails have never been better. These days they grow at such a rate I could well be part wolf.

Thank You, E. L. James

In 2012, a book is published which provides comedy fodder for every stand-up in the land. *Fifty Shades of Grey* by E. L. James is the gift that keeps on giving. It's a novel about the relationship between Anastasia, a young female graduate, and a wealthy business creep called Christian who introduces Anastasia to a lot of kinky sex. According to Wikipedia this style of erotic fiction is categorised as 'dark romantic literature'. Hmmm, IMO it's a good old-fashioned dirty book stuffed with lashings of bondage.

Thanks to the huge success of this book, every comic has an 'alternative porn' routine. This is mine:

Anyone at the back secretly reading *Fifty Shades of Grey*? I've read it, didn't do much for me to be honest: forget the S&M, the only thing that really turns me on these days is an M&S meal deal, main, side, pudding and wine all for a tenner, oh yes, I should coco.

How many people read that book and how many people read my book? Yes, not enough smut in mine, obviously.

And that's why I've decided to jump on the mummy porn bandwagon. My next novel will be titled *Fifty Shades of Beige*, which is about a woman who can only orgasm over a Farrow & Ball paint chart.

Yes, it's a new genre of clit lit – property erotica written for women who dribble on estate agents' windows and fantasise about off-street parking.

Just written my first chapter. As I say, it's about a woman called Melissa, who gets sexually aroused by desirable property, and her developer boyfriend Giles. Sometimes Melissa makes Giles wear a hard hat in bed – sort of fetish thing.

Giles showed Melissa a picture of a potential barn conversion in the Dordogne, 'How do you feel about renovating that?' he breathed. Melissa bit her lip and trembled, aaaaaaghhghgh, desire flooded through her veins, all the way down to her lady guttering. She wanted it very badly, so badly that she was dripping like a badly wrapped parcel of mince in the fridge ...

The *Fifty Shades of Grey* phenomenon is so widespread that when Avalon suggest we write our third *Grumpy* show, Judith and I opt for the aforementioned title, *Fifty Shades of Beige*. Bingo, now all we need to do is write the rest of the show.

Fifty Shades of Beige

*F*ifty *Shades of Beige* is our best *Grumpy* show to date. This
cast consists of me, Susie Blake (from *Grumpy 2*) and
newbie Kate Robbins, and the show is so popular that we tour it
for three years.

Kate and Susie both have equally fascinating but very different theatrical backgrounds. Kate's mum was Paul McCartney's
cousin; her dad was a club comic, Mike Robbins, aka 'Nearly a
Gentleman' – by all accounts a hugely charismatic man, who,
together with Kate's beautiful mum, ran the pub where Paul
McCartney first performed with John Lennon!

Comedy and music are blended in Kate's veins. Her brother
is Ted Robbins, comic, actor and radio presenter; her eldest
daughter is Emily Atack, actress, jungle queen and telly star,
whose equally gorgeous sister Martha is a theatrical agent, while
Kate's son, adorable George, has dabbled in TV production work,
and her three sisters are singers/actresses/artists. Kate and her
sisters are all lookers; when they are all together, I call them
Kardashians of Flitwick, the village where most of the clan live.
There is so much talent in that family, from impressionists to
fantasy cake bakers, that it could be sickening if I hadn't met and
immediately liked them all.

Susie's family is equally theatrical (as mentioned previously). I know nothing of her father – he has long been absent – but her mother Molly (still alive during the run of this show and in her nineties) was a well-known artist and Susie draws beautifully, too. In fact, the three of us are quite an arty cast; we carry sketchbooks around with us on tour and try not to mind when Susie's pen and ink drawings are the best.

A trio of women is always hard to manage and occasionally there are tears and slammed dressing-room doors, but there is also a huge amount of camaraderie, laughter, post-show drinks and crisp-eating. The *Grumpy* hire car at the end of a tour looks like it's been ferrying toddlers around.

This show is magical onstage: it strikes the right balance between daft and making a point. The designer (Susannah Henry again) excels herself, and we start the show hidden inside a shed accompanied by a great deal of dry ice and the music from *2001: A Space Odyssey*. As the music rises to a crescendo, the shed collapses to reveal Susie, Kate and me wearing boilersuits with buckets on our heads, à la spacemen. The gist being that we are travelling the galaxy (in a shed) to spread the grumpy word (mostly common sense), only to discover that we have landed in Stevenage/Cheltenham/wherever we happen to be playing that night. At this point, it's helmets off and on with the show.

In the interval we have a costume change and begin act two with a middle-aged female spy sequence, introducing the possibility of Jane Bond, who is able to go about her espionage business completely unseen, because who takes any notice of middle-aged women?

For this sequence we are in macks and black Velcro trousers which we peel off after the routine to reveal the three of us in onesies. Onesies are big at the time of this show and the sight of three women of a certain age in massive Babygros works every night. It's the ideal costume; we don't even have to do buttons up. The onesies have snap fasteners down the front, and all is well until mine goes into a tumble drier on a hot-air cycle and massively shrinks. The following night when I whip my black trousers off after the Jane Bond sequence the audience laugh more than they ever have before. I don't think anyone has witnessed such a massive camel's toe onstage before, and no amount of wriggling and tugging will unclench it.

Fortunately, I have a spare, and we buy an emergency back-up, but the costume reveal will never be quite so funny again and I'm slightly tempted to wear the tight version just for the laughs. But considering I'm in danger of doing myself a gynaecological mischief, the child-sized onesie is recycled.

Grumpy 3 tours for so long that our last outing coincides with the lead-up to the Brexit referendum. No one I know and like is thinking of voting for Brexit – oh, apart from my mum, who dabbles with doing the wrong thing, because she lives in a *Daily Mail/Telegraph*-reading constituency and she's easily led.

Sara, Ben and I tell her in no uncertain terms that if she votes out she can forget about spending Xmas with any of us ever again. Harsh, but it does the trick, unless she secretly rebels at the ballot box. I hope not.

As a Londoner, I can't see any advantages in leaving the EU, and guess what? There haven't been any. It's been catastrophic for all sorts of reasons and all sorts of people. And I'm not sure the country will ever recover.

It's tricky on tour to recognise that not everyone agrees with you. While performing in Devon, we drive past fields sporting massive UKIP posters and when we attempt to bring the subject into the show we are met with a prickly response. In Manchester there are some actual boos and very quickly we realise that our audience is more politically mixed than we presumed and that it's a bad idea to bring contention into the auditorium. The referendum is dividing families; we don't need the audience turning on each other. Tactfully, we drop this particular hot potato and, although we are horrified by the result, the show goes on.

Showbiz in Your Fifties

Surprisingly, I work a lot in my fifties. I keep expecting the bubble to burst, but it seems that as long as I keep my head down and keep slogging, then the scrap heap can wait. It's there, though, just out of sight. I can smell it, like a compost heap.

Telly is still elusive. I crop up as a guest on various bits and bobs, disgrace myself on quiz shows, perch on daytime telly sofas to publicise my wares, but I'm fully aware that the likelihood of scoring a big TV gig diminishes by the day, and I try not to mind.

Who am I trying to kid? I'm fucking furious, particularly when one male comic after another gets a nice cushy travel programme. Shit, fuck and fucky shit. I'm also aware that suddenly more women are actually getting the attention they deserve, and even though this is a great thing, I feel like I may have missed out. The new girls on the block are twenty years younger than me.

Is there an age when you are supposed to abandon your ambition? I keep waiting for this to happen, but it doesn't. I'm as jealous as I ever have been, with an extra dollop of bitterness.

Radio is more welcoming than TV, and in 2014 I'm commissioned to write a series of six fifteen-minute monologues for Radio 4. I casually ask the producer whether I can perform them, but she laughs and says, 'I can get much better actresses than you.' She is right. In the end I write seven series of *Little Lifetimes*, until a new commissioning comedy boss decides I've hogged the airwaves for long enough and drops the show in 2022. I can't say I haven't had my fair share: there are around thirty of these broadcast monologues and a few more in a published collection called *Listening In*. Over the years we have some of the crème de la crème of the British acting scene performing these mini dramas, including names such as Lesley Sharp, Lesley Manville, Imelda Staunton and Harriet Walter. My producer Sally Avens is right: there are lots of actresses who are far better than me, and watching them work is always a thrill. Lesley Manville does hers in literally two takes.

It's hard to pick a favourite, but Vicki Pepperdine playing a teacher who goes berserk in the staffroom on the day she retires after a long career teaching in an all-girls school makes me howl with laughter, and I realise how lucky I am to have this parade of extraordinary talent willing to perform these short stories for crap money!

Even people who can't abide me or my stand-up find themselves enjoying *Little Lifetimes*, which must be infuriating. Ha!

By this stage in the game there is an obvious divide in my writing: there is the funny stuff and the less funny stuff, which includes the radio work and the novels. Some of the less funny stuff is not really funny at all, although a streak of black comedy runs through all my fiction. My characters tend to be flawed women who do terrible things which tend to have consequences in later life.

Moving is my fourth novel, published in 2015 and set in the house my sister once lived in on Kennington Road, a tall Georgian number with too many stairs. The inhabitants, however, are entirely fictional.

My lead narrator is an elderly woman, Edwina, who is coming to terms with the fact that she must sell her oversized house, and as she leads a young estate agent around her crumbling home, the past, and what happened, is revealed room by room.

It is a book that breathes quickly and easily on its own. It almost accidentally manages to come together; I don't have to fight with every chapter. Or maybe I'm looking back with an ease I don't feel at the time. Richard and Judy choose it for their book club, which means more shops stock it and it sells pretty well, popping onto the *Sunday Times* bestseller list for a week or two, which gives me a massive boost.

I'm not the only one writing my arse off. Phoebe's debut play opens at Theatre503, a tiny black box of a space above the Latchmere pub in Battersea. *Wink* is a sudden mini hit, the re views are wonderful, it sells out its entire run and is nominated for four Off West End awards, including Most Promising New Playwright. She's on her way and her father and I are disgustingly proud.

My mother makes it down to London to see the play. There is no disabled access, so she stumps up the steep narrow stairs, one step at a time, calliper clacking, and makes it to the top. She is eighty-six and has been a widow for less than a year.

My father died aged ninety, three weeks before Xmas 2014.

A few days before he dies, my mother knows something is wrong because he can't be bothered to do the crossword in the *i* newspaper. She calls me while I'm onstage and I ring her back in the interval. 'He's behaving very oddly,' she says. 'I'm not sure he recognises me.'

My father is dying. I cancel any work I have and head north, meeting up with my mother and siblings in Derek's bedroom at the nursing home.

My father has a tube down his throat. I kiss his big old head; he might be dying but he is not diminished. He feels very present, even though he isn't conscious.

The waiting lasts a couple of days. My sister and I sleep over on the floor, while Ben takes June home to get some rest. And on it goes, it can't be much longer. We are all too exhausted to talk so we put the television on, an old episode of *Lewis* plays in the background. A man falls off a roof.

Hours later, I write this in my notebook:

My father's hands are grey, he rattles deep and gurgles
Hard, in his mouth is a tube to stop him biting his tongue – he
heaves and fluid fountains though the tube
My sister hits the panic button – a small domestic siren
My mother – 'what did you do that for?'
My sister, 'don't tell me what to do'
Me – 'don't speak to Ma like that'
My brother – 'stop it you two'
The nurse comes – Wynne – clears his airways with a pipe like
the dentist
Lewis on in the background, it's an old one – someone has
fallen off the roof,
'Turn that thing off' – my sister,
Wynne feels for the beat in his throat,
My brother tells my father to 'sleep', we are all there, my
mother, my brother, my sister and me
He does what my brother tells him,
There is no beat
I hug him, kiss his old face,
My sister and my brother do the same,
The nurse goes to tell matron,
'What's happened?' asks my mother.
That is how unbelievable it is,
Even though we have been waiting since Friday.
The gigs I have cancelled are rescheduled.

Bra and Pants Saga

We persuade June to sell the cottage and move into a flat right in the centre of Lytham, where she can walk to a Sainsbury's Local within three minutes. Once upon a time, these flats used to be the local baths where the three of us swam as kids. I don't approve of converting swimming pools into flats. Where are children supposed to learn not to drown? But it's ideal for June: it even has an underground car park, where she regularly scrapes her car along an inconveniently placed pillar. My brother wraps the pillar in blankets, which doesn't thrill the residents' committee.

June is resistant to the flat's charms; the fact is she misses Derek, she misses their old life, the idea that she might be lonely is unbearable. 'Getting old is not for cissies,' she says. She is smaller and thinner than she used to be, and yet no one has ever suggested that she be fitted for a new calliper. She has two National Health monstrosities, which are increasingly hard work. We go private and have a lightweight alternative specially made for her, but it's too late; her muscles are now so weak it's not really stable enough for her, and every day she must Velcro-strap herself into her antiquated leg irons. I could spit.

Back in London, selfish as ever, I am juggling *Grumpy* shows with writing a new solo show.

As usual, the title comes first, followed by the poster/artwork shoot. The show title is easy. *How to Be a Middle-Aged Woman (Without Going Insane)* is a no-brainer, but as for the poster, I am bereft of ideas. I know I want something different, but I have no idea what that might be. I want reality rather than any airbrushing, and at the last minute I pack a pair of Ugg sheepskin slippers along with half the contents of my wardrobe and head off for the shoot. Instinctively I know the slippers are the key to this 'look'.

I like the make-up girl, I like the photographer, but nothing is really taking off. I try wearing something dressy, with the slippers as a sort of afterthought, but it's not enough. Or is it too much? An idea comes out of nowhere. I return to the dressing room, strip down to my underwear and slippers and re-emerge to finish the shoot.

My bra and knickers don't match – good, the white bra and big black knickers, plus the sheepskin slippers, is just the look I'm after: bit pasty, a bit dumpy, but, to be honest, a hell of a lot less pasty and dumpy than I am now!

At the time of this shoot I'm still doing a bit of yoga now and then, and I'm hanging on to the very last remnants of the super-toned ashtanga bunny that I once was. I am a chunky size 14 middle-aged woman in what looks like utility undies. Sexy? No. Funny? Yes.

Not everyone finds this poster amusing. A stranger comes up to me at a mate's party and slags it off to my face. 'I can't imagine what you were thinking,' she squawks. 'It doesn't do you any favours!' 'Good,' I respond.

I plug the show on *Loose Women* as we are now on good enough terms for me to be happy guesting, and opinions are divided. Some women are so horrified about the idea of a bra not matching the pants that I make a joke about ambulances legally not having to take you to hospital should you get run over wearing non-matching undies. Some people genuinely don't know if I'm joking. I conclude that the world divides into women who have lingerie and those of us whose knicker drawer looks like Lost Property.

We benefit from a nice piece of free publicity when Transport for London threaten not to allow the poster on the Underground. Thanks, TfL: you've just handed us a nice little controversy on a plate. Apparently young women in bikinis being 'beach-body ready' is one thing, but a middle-aged woman in her scraggy knick-knacks is potentially obscene. This objection is overruled and London commuters are treated to me smirking at them in my pants on their daily travels.

My old mate Chris George comes onboard to direct the show and agrees to tour manage, too. It's his idea that I start the show à la the poster and walk onstage wearing a white bra, black pants and the slippers. Predictably, the audience go mad for it: it's the easiest laugh I've ever got without actually doing anything. My first line after the laughs subside is: 'Have you ever had that dream, where you're not wearing any clothes ... Shit, I've done it again.' At this point, I slip into some clothes neatly hidden behind a chair and it's on with the show.

A highlight of How to Be is the 'cunting bunting' section, which is Phoebe's idea. Everyone in the audience gets a piece of triangular bunting with the pants and bra pic on the front and during the interval they're invited to write the things that piss them off most about getting older. A surprising amount are about wanking.

When the batteries run out on your vibrator before you've finished yourself off

When the arthritis flares up mid-masturbation

Empty toilet rolls on top of the cistern (many, many of these)

My mother insisting I know who she is talking about when I left Wales thirty years ago

The invention of Viagra, boo!

Other people's children

People who don't close the toilet lid before they flush the lavatory and then complain when rust spots appear on their radiators (plumbing engineer)

We take a shortened, hour-long version of the show over to the Melbourne Comedy Festival in the spring of 2017. Geof comes, too, and we have a really happy time, see some great art, catch trams to the beach and find a favourite bar where we eat and drink after the show. It's called Self-Preservation and it feels like it.

I feel secure about the show, the bra and pants gag works just as well in Oz as it does in the UK, I sell well, the reviews are good and there are moments when I finally feel like I know what I am doing.

Then the problem of what to do next rears up again.

More than anything I would like to be offered a job that doesn't involve me inventing everything from scratch. Every time I finish one project, I can't help feeling I'm being sent back down the mines to hack out another.

Listening In, the collection of Radio 4 *Little Lifetimes* monologues, is published a couple of months after we get back from Melbourne. In a fit of madness, I ask to do the illustrations and front cover myself, hence they are terrible. It's such a shame, but considering the BBC own most of the rights to the stories (apart from the seven that I write especially for the collection), I barely get paid. Doing the illustrations, however bad, is my way of getting some fun out of it. I sort of regret it now, especially the front cover: it's fucking awful. Hey ho, the collection goes more or less unnoticed, which is a shame.

Maybe the terrible front cover puts everyone off? Oh dear.

At the end of June 2017, Geof and I get married. I know, right. I wasn't expecting it either.

Wedding Bells

'**I** fucking hate weddings, I've never seen a fascinator I haven't wanted to stamp on. Ideally I'd like to run through John Lewis's bridal department with a blow torch' – Jenny Eclair

Here's the thing. Engagement announcements make me feel queasy and weddings make me clench my fists. I have never had any desire to be a bride, I never had the floating-down-the-aisle fantasy. I grew out of all that nonsense by the time I was about eight and have been amazed ever since by the sheer volume of people that still buy into it.

My pet loathing is the destination wedding, not that I have ever been invited to one: the idea of flying hundreds of thousands of miles to share in someone else's supposed 'happiest day of their life' makes me feel furious. Any wedding that demands excessive time, travel or expense is a complete no-no. Yes, you are important to me, but not so important that I feel I have to buy a new pair of shoes and book an Airbnb.

Is there anything more demanding than a wedding list? Anyone who is instructing me to buy eight matching cereal bowls from John Lewis is asking for a second-hand ocarina from a market stall (look it up). Personally, I also think that if a marriage doesn't last as long as the guarantee on any of the wedding gifts, those gifts must be returned to sender.

As for elaborate hen and stag nights, just stop it; stop the bottomless brunch shit and the poxy pink, brain-numbing prosecco and please don't ask me to wear anything penis-shaped on my head.

See what a miserable old bag I am?

My problem is that I am slightly phobic about organised fun, and you only have to spend ten minutes on Mumsnet to see what a hysterical can of worms the whole wedding business has become.

Weddings these days are a money-spinning industry, like baby showers and wellness, hence the insane epidemic of scented candles. There are even candles for a gentle menopause. Oh, do fuck off.

I'm also not good with rules of any kind, vows, his side/ her side, seating plans and speeches by people who are crap at making speeches.

Basically, the idea of being held hostage in some fantasy of the bride and groom's creation makes me feel very hostile indeed.

Which makes the decision to get married very tricky.

To be honest, it is my financial adviser's idea. He comes round and talks to me about death duties and the government taking even more money off me as a single woman than if Geof and I got married. Grrrrrrrrrrr.

Now, if there's one thing that bores me more than weddings, it's the thought of paying more tax than necessary, even when I'm dead.

Don't get me wrong: I don't mind paying tax, but not more than my fair share.

I propose to Geof, who isn't keen, but gradually we both come to the conclusion that as it has to be done, we might as well enjoy it, up to a point.

It's very important that we don't get married in a church, because that would be a nonsense. We hire the glass box extension
in the garden of the South London Gallery, which offers a few
set wedding 'supper' options (it's not fucking 'breakfast'), plus
booze, etc.

My sister offers to buy us a cake and we invite thirty friends
and relatives. On the day we get married, Geof boils me a breakfast egg and writes 'Happy wedding day' on it.

I buy new shoes: they are cream Aladdin slipper things with
gold lobsters embroidered on the front, and team them up with
a pair of M&S elasticated-waist baggy trousers, a black chiffon
sleeveless top and a cream lace jacket, which I bought for a posh
corporate a couple of years previously. Phoebe will wear the pink
dress she bought for her friend Katy's wedding with her silver
ankle boots and Geof decides to wear something nice, without
any brown sauce down his front.

The venue allows a few of us access in the morning and we
decorate the place with massive white balloons, white bunting,
peonies and fairy lights.

Chris George is in charge of the music, Phoebe has written a
speech, Geof and I will say a few words, my niece Daisy is going
to sing and play the ukulele and Phoebe's boyfriend, Tristram,
will headline with his guitar and sing a few Bob Dylan numbers.
Bingo.

After we have tarted up the venue, we take my mother to the
Dulwich Art Gallery to see the John Singer Sargent exhibition,
which she loves, although we have hired her a wheelchair, which
she hates.

She and my aunt have come down from Lytham, the two sisters, June in her late eighties and Aileen in her nineties, sharing
the twin-bedded spare room down the road at my sister's. It makes
me happy to think of them talking into the night together.

The ceremony is at 6.30 p.m. The sun is still shining, Phoebe walks me down the aisle, lots of my favourite people are in the room; sadly the bloke doing the actual ceremony gets a ridiculous fit of the giggles, which makes me quite cross (not a great bride look), especially when he continues to snigger throughout. I mean, WTAF? I am scowling for the duration of the service.

Happily, I am cheered up by the ring, which is designed by our friend and neighbour Alex Monroe, and consists of a dainty golden band studded with tiny diamond daisies. This is a complete surprise and I am delighted, both by the ring and the fact that it fits perfectly.

I don't give a ring to Geof. He has the hands of a bear!

We have a burrata starter, something with chicken for our mains, cake for pudding, followed by speeches, live music, chatting and laughing, and we are all out by 9.30 (such is the deal). It's a lovely summer evening and Geof and I are home by 10 p.m., just in time to watch *Love Island*. So that's romance for you.

Two days later we fly to Porto for a five-day honeymoon, in a lovely apartment with a view of the sea.

I do not return pregnant. I am fifty-seven years old. I can't imagine getting married any sooner. I feel I am just the right age.

I haven't actually changed my mind about weddings. I still can't utter the words 'husband' or 'wife', I have never, ever called myself Jenny Powell and a year later, when civil partnerships became legal for heterosexual couples, I am a teeny bit pissed off that we'd jumped the gun!

Dry Fanny Creams and Other Pharmaceuticals

Peop le say to me, 'Why did you do that advert?'
And I say, 'Because I wanted to break down the taboos and the stigma surrounding vaginal atrophication . . . [pause] and it was quite a lot of money and I wanted a new sofa.'

In 2018 I get an offer I can't refuse: would I like to be the face of Vagisan moisturising cream?

People are very coy about dry fannies. For example, there is no product on the market called simply 'dry fanny cream', which is all anyone really wants. One day we will live in a world where men and women are confident enough to walk into a chemist and say, 'Large tube of dry fanny cream, some itchy bum ointment and a large pack of his and hers incontinence pads, please.' But we are not there yet. Discretion is a word that makes me feel a bit twitchy; it is why a woman's vulva or vagina is referred to by some manufacturers as her 'intimate area'.

We've come a long way with body positivity, and how we talk about periods and the menopause, but we still play nicely around vaginal dryness, even though 50 per cent of women over fifty suffer to some degree. Apparently it's one of those taboo topics. Hmm, who says so?

Sometimes, I reckon ad companies create fictional media taboos that don't exist in real life, so that they can feel a bit superior when it comes to their supposedly 'taboo-busting' ad campaigns. As if to say, 'Look how modern and cutting-edge we're being.'

Vagisan is owned by a very well-established German pharmaceutical company; it's a good product, I have absolutely no problem advertising it and the commercial is nicely shot on a pink velvet sofa, which is specially made for the occasion!

The ad makes the papers for being shown in a pre-watershed *Coronation Street* ad break.

Predictably, some people (most of whom don't have vaginas) are appalled. Objections fired at me personally on Twitter consist mostly of being 'put off meals' and cries of 'not in front of the kiddies'. It's such a boring knee-jerk reaction and the majority are from blokes with football team profiles. Yawn. Men who despite being 'tough guys' are weirdly squeamish about ageing women. I think we disgust them so much they are actually frightened of us.

It's all very tiresome. A few women join in, apparently repulsed by the idea of my atrophied vagina. I say nothing, and hope karma works her magic and that in later years they are dealt an itchy, dry fanny that keeps them awake and scratching through the night, hahahaha.

And just to set the record straight, personally I don't have a particularly dry fanny. It's probably average for my age. I'm also extremely continent, unless I sneeze violently, but on the flip side I'm a bit deaf (genetic on father's side) and have recently been diagnosed with chronic dry eye disease.

Sadly, there is no magic cream for dry eye; once you've got it, you've got it. Tbh, I'd rather have a dry fanny than dry eyes, but loads of us with both eyeballs and vaginas have both – great.

When I first start experiencing itchy dry eyes, I assume it's an infection, use a load of over-the-counter meds, to no avail, and end up panicking and paying to see a private ophthalmologist, which, thanks to the Vagisan money, I can.

He is sympathetic but firm. I have dry eye disease. Too much screen time, being a woman of menopausal age and forgetting to blink frequently enough have all contributed to the condition and all I can do is use the drops and the ointment. Well, yes and no; for starters, not every brand of drop works for everyone so there is a great deal of trial and error before finding your optimum drop. I use the Hylo range – the blue bottle suits me best. Any dry eye drops containing preservatives are a complete no-no for me, so read the labels if you're a fellow sufferer. I also have to use an ointment at night, loads of it, squirted into my eyeballs before I go to sleep. The next step in my eyecare regime might sound odd – it is a trick I was taught at Moorfields Eye Hospital. There, among millions of quid's worth of surgical equipment, a doctor suggested I use clingfilm.

So I do. For a good five years now I have been filling my eyes with dry eye ointment (a bit like a runny vaseline in a tiny tube) before covering my eyelids with two-inch squares of clingfilm. Once stuck to the skin around my eyes, this acts as a sort of moisture chamber which protects my eyeballs from drying out overnight.

It's boring and a hassle, and when I'm on tour the staff who pop in to give my hotel room a once over must wonder why I have a roll of clingfilm on my bedside table. Oooh-er missus and all that.

I also have a procedure called LipiFlow every couple of years, if funds allow. This is a laser heat treatment conducted along the eyelids that releases the gummed-up meibomian glands (all rather technical and expensive), but if you can afford it, I really think it helps and it's completely painless. In fact, it feels like someone is pouring molten honey along the rims of your eyes. I'm sure one day this treatment will be accessible in every high street optician, hopefully sooner rather than later and at a price everyone can afford.

Dry eyes, dry fanny.

There's a lot of desiccation involved in getting old generally. As we age, we basically run the risk of turning into overcooked turkeys; there isn't a bit of us that isn't bone dry. In one of the *Grumpy* shows, we had a great line about shin dandruff. Judith wrote this one:

'Come the winter, when I take my tights off there's a blizzard of shin dandruff.'

What a marvellous line. Sometimes the joke is worth experiencing the thing that triggers it!

Goodbye *Grumpy*, Hello *Older and Wider* Podcast

We risk taking a fourth *Grumpy* show out on the road in 2018. In some respects, I wish we hadn't. The appetite for the show has dwindled and ticket sales are bewilderingly disappointing. I feel really guilty, and responsible for the number of empty seats wherever we go. Fortunately, the cast are uncomplaining. Dillie Keane, original cast member of the first *Grumpy* triumph, has been round the block for even longer than I have; she's been there and knows how to cover up the bruises. Lizzie Roper hasn't done the show before, but if she is disappointed by the response, she doesn't show it. They slog on: even when I get food poisoning in Newcastle, at one of our rare sellout shows, with over a thousand people in the audience, and start chucking up into the wings, they slog on. Three times I leave the stage to vomit. A stagehand follows me round with a bucket of sawdust, which reminds me of kids puking up during assembly in primary school; there were always little puddles of sawdust sick dotted around.

The premise of *Grumpy Old Women to the Rescue* is that the grumpy old women have retired and are living on a tropical island – cue Hawaiian music, leis, etc.

Typically, the ladies find paradise a bit boring and start craving rain and dog shit, at which point an emergency SOS (à la *Charlie's Angels*) summons them back to reality to sort out the usual crap the world has got itself into.

The promise of some Harvester vouchers clinches the deal, and the ladies do a quick change behind a tiki bar, returning to the stage dressed in their superwomen alter ego costumes – Menopause Woman (me), HRT Girl (Lizzie) and Hatchet Face (Dillie) – and then it's on with the show.

Despite plenty of highlights, the show lags in places and neither Judith nor I know exactly how to fix it. Looking back, I think the franchise has simply run its course. We do one national tour and call it a day.

I look back on these shows with huge affection. I work so often by myself that having friends to play with onstage is quite a novelty. Everyone brings their own something special to the stage: Dillie simply wearing a pair of shorts is a masterclass in physical comedy, Susie doing an unapologetic pole dance in her sixties, Kate belting out a big number into a garden hose, Wendi trying to get out of a bean bag, Linda getting apoplectic about the number of bags she ends up carrying. Just a brilliant collection of game female performers, who are happy to wear stupid costumes and never once say, 'No, I don't think I want to try that.' They wear badly fitting party dresses and stand in a B&Q shed with buckets and colanders on their heads without complaining.

The shows are big on headwear: smoking aeroplanes, papier-mâché planets and even a see-through umbrella masquerading as a jellyfish.

I owe so much to so many who worked so hard on these projects: the set, sound and lighting designers and particularly the tour drivers, the poor sods who put up with us bitching, gossiping, insisting on stopping at garden centres, getting lost in motorway service stations (Kate Robbins) and having to go back to the theatre/hotel for forgotten cardigans and phone chargers. Who kept driving through the night while we swigged post-show wine on the back seats, dropped popcorn all over the place and made them stop for chips.

It's sad when you know something has had its day, but it's even sadder when you don't.

It isn't long before Judith and I find another opportunity to work together.

2018 is the year of the podcast boom. Everyone and his dog (literally) starts recording one. Originally Avalon approach me to fly one solo, but the idea of sitting in a studio mumbling to myself is upsetting, so I suggest roping Judith in and carrying on the *Grumpy* voice in a more lo-fi way. I'm not worried about Judith's performance abilities; she is a bossy, opinionated, confident woman in her sixties, eminently capable of holding her own while chatting with me in a tiny cupboard tucked away down a corridor in Avalon Towers.

The proposal is that we meet fortnightly and record two shows with our newly appointed producer, Daisy Knight. Daisy looks like she's just left school, but it's soon apparent that, as the mother of two young boys, she's not going to take any silly nonsense from us two, and quietly and skilfully she manages to edit together our ramblings.

In the beginning we have guests, but considering the podcast has yet to be monetised, we can't pay them. Fortunately, people are used to not being paid when they're plugging stuff on all sorts of shows, from *Woman's Hour* to *Lorraine*. But I still find it embarrassing to ask people to flog out to Kensal Rise without so much as a cab fare. Also, considering no one knows about this pod, it's hardly going to make a difference to whatever they're trying to push. There's a lot of 'doing it for a favour' going on, but gradually we start finding our rhythm and the need for guests dwindles.

Judith and I are very different. I think our audiences align themselves with one or the other. I am the slightly naughty younger sister, whereas Judith is the capable Girl Guide figure who occasionally goes wildly off the rails and does surprising and mad things. Judith lives in the country in a thatched cottage with massive gardens and many outbuildings; I live in south London on a busy bus route in the small wooden black box that Geof built! She is outdoorsy and keen on walking, fresh air and exercise, I am not.

We both have male partners who are of the same vintage, and daughters ditto. Our common ground includes books, art, gossip, rage, ageism and food. Judith is greedier than I am and a much better cook; I am lazier than Judith but I'm also bendier. We are chalk and cheese but also fish and chips. We are very different, but we go well together. *Older and Wider* is an informal version of *Grumpy*, we are very indiscreet and tend to overshare.

The week Daisy starts producing our podcast she is also at the helm of another brand-new pod, *Shagged Married Annoyed*, with Chris and Rosie Ramsey.

Q: Which one of these pods is now so popular it does arena tours?

(Clue: It's not ours!)

That said, over the past couple of years we have branched out into live shows, which are not suitable for broadcast, insomuch as they are shows and not just the podcast onstage. We play hypochondriac's bingo complete with prizes, read excerpts from our corona lockdown diaries and share slides of the audiences' 'hobby clap' (the good stuff, including a massive pastry penis and a self-built shed) and 'hobby crap' (the utterly shit stuff, mostly ceramics). And the glorious thing about bringing *Older and Wider* to the stage is that, so far, we are only doing matinees, huzzah! At last, I can be home in the evening and sit in front of the telly like a normal person. I'm also loving the freedom that performing a non-scripted show gives me; we have a running order but no actual cues. We just go onstage and have a ball.

Fiction, Fact and Phoebe

My fifth novel, *Inheritance*, is published in hardback in August 2019, set in London and Cornwall, plus a touch of Southend, because I can't resist an esplanade. It revolves (once again) around a house, this time a large, recently renovated clifftop villa, and the family who have owned it over the years. There is a tragedy at the heart of the book: a child drowns and the consequences of this accident reverberate for years to come.

It's also a tale of the cuckoo in the nest, be that an adopted little girl or the co-habiting girlfriend of a man who is too old to be living with his parents. The story begins in 1950 and ends in 2018, and I really enjoy writing about the refurbishment of 'Kittiwake', the Cornish house perched on the cliff. I'm always much happier writing about sofas and dinner plates than I am about trees, and have a lovely time browsing interior design websites, choosing curtains and rugs for my fictional home. Vicariously, I spend a fortune.

Inheritance performs respectably, but we all know the true sales figures will be revealed when it's published in paperback in twelve months' time.

I am proud of this book but scared of how I'm ever going to write another.

There seems to be an expectation that I can just keep churning out projects, another show, another book. The fact is, if I don't keep churning these things out, I have no paid work. Apart from a small weekly column in the *Independent* online (which, sadly, doesn't last more than a couple of years), I am completely financially on my own. The podcast runs at a loss until we eventually start getting adverts four years after we started, by which time we owe Avalon, who produce the show, a hefty sum. I'm not complaining, I just want people to realise that just because you are working doesn't mean you are getting paid. I can't tell you how many people genuinely don't realise that telly appearances for plugging your wares do not come with a nice fat fee. You do them because it's part of the game. Unfortunately, people also expect you to wear new stuff; woe betide you wear the same top too many times on the box and no, I don't get given freebies! The truth is, the shirt I am wearing on the cover of this book was loaned and taken straight back to Boden.

Sometimes I crave a real job. Not a real job in an office; let's face it, as 2020 approaches I'm getting on for sixty and more or less unemployable. I can't do spreadsheets, I can't stop swearing, if anyone told me what to do I might tell them to go fuck themselves and sometimes I spend hours just lying on the bed looking at my phone.

What I mean by a 'real job' is a long-running telly-presenting gig, or a radio-hosting number, a showbiz job with a regular wage and – ooh, I don't know, maybe holiday pay. I have never had a paid holiday in my life; however, I have been to places for work that I'd never have otherwise seen, so swings and roundabouts, eh.

Inevitably, I start writing another book, because this is what I do when no one offers me a prime-time telly slot. I strap myself to my filthy, germ-riddled keyboard and type.

I embark on my first non-fiction for a while, *Older and Wider:*

A Survivor's Guide to the Menopause. It's a clever move because it means I can cash in on my menopausal experiences before I'm too old to call myself menopausal. Let's face it, sixty is the cut-off age. At sixty you've got to face up to the fact that you are post-menopausal. In 2019 I'm fifty-nine, at the tail end of it all, but still entitled to write a book about it. Now that's what I call timing.

I consider myself a bit of an expert on the menopause, having written a lot about the condition for my stand-up shows. I'm also pretty passionate about it, the misconceptions and its many varied physical and mental side-effects. I want the book to be both a bit of a hand-hold and a bit of a laugh. There is so much gloom around the menopause that I want to lighten things up a bit. I decide the book will be chaptered alphabetically, for example, 'E is for EMPTY NEST: It's not until your children leave home that you realise quite how long a packet of cereal can last.'

I leave out any long-winded medical stats and instead concentrate on the many pluses of not bleeding through your pants every four weeks.

The guide discusses hobbies replacing your sex life, avoiding polo necks, mood swings and getting your shit together (writing a will). It also includes a great chicken thigh recipe and the barcode for a useful pair of Marks trousers.

I ask Judith permission to use the *Older and Wider* title and she generously agrees; we are still podding weekly, still not getting paid and she knows I have a mortgage to pay.

The guide is a culmination of everything I have learned about being a menopausal woman in my fifties, which, on reflection, I have rather enjoyed. As I say onstage, 'The menopause is the only excuse you're ever going to have for shoplifting and behaving like a hysterical nutcase. What's not to like?'

The book writes itself and I'm looking forward to showing it off when it's published in 2020.

Incidentally, it's not just me who has been scribbling away. In

2019, Phoebe, now living with her boyfriend in New Cross, has secretly entered a play for the Bruntwood Prize for Playwriting. The Bruntwood is an international playwriting competition, with a fat cash prize and lots of opportunities should you win. The great thing about it is that you have to enter under a pseudonym; the whole process is completely anonymous, which, if you are in danger of being called a nepo baby (fuck this, btw), is a massive bonus. Over the months leading to the awards being announced, the longlist dwindles down to a shortlist. My daughter is on this list: she has written *Shed: Exploded View*, a play inspired by the artwork by Cornelia Parker. Parker's work hangs in Tate Modern; it's an extraordinary installation by one of our leading living artists, featuring a shed blown up by the British army and painstakingly reassembled in mid-air on wires. These fragments are lit to create extraordinary shadows. It seems the play (which I don't read before it's submitted) is about relationships exploding for whatever reason. Yeah, I know: she's quite a lot cleverer than me and doesn't often resort to fart gags (not that she's averse).

As a finalist, she is invited to the awards ceremony held at the Royal Exchange in Manchester. The event is live-streamed.

Geof and I watch in our separate studies. We are too nervous to watch together. I gird myself for her disappointment. She is wearing a red leopard-skin dress, my lovely, clever girl. As soon as they begin to describe the winning play, I know it's hers; it couldn't be anyone else's. She walks to the podium, makes a speech and her father and I sob. The award is announced on Radio 4's seven o'clock news: it's a big deal and potentially career-changing. My heart almost bursts; she has worked so very hard and I love and admire her so much. Not only has she won some cash, the play will be staged in 2020 at the Royal Exchange and she is offered a writer's residency at Banff University in Alberta, Canada, plus meetings in LA. Next year will be hers for the taking.

The Final Family Xmas

We all go to my sister's place in Wales for Xmas 2019. The farmhouse is not glamorous, but it's big enough to sleep the entire family and there is plenty of land to roam away from each other. My mother will be taxied from Lytham with one of the nice Whitesides taxi drivers. She is ninety now but still capable of sitting in the kitchen, peeling sprouts and giving us braised red cabbage instructions.

On the day of her ninetieth birthday back in May, I phone her up and ask how she feels about it. 'Well, I've beaten Tom Wolfe,' she replies.

My sister has converted her study into a little bedroom for June on the ground floor, near the spare bathroom at the back of the house.

As my mother lies in her bed drinking tea in the morning, she is overlooked by a large and terrible painting that I gave Sara for her sixtieth. My mother glances up at the highly coloured nude and mistakes the naked lady's breasts for fried eggs. This is not as insulting as the paying guests who stayed in the valley and found the thing so objectionable that they turned it to the wall, so as not to 'upset the children'.

I've been painting on and off for a while now, and being

creative in some way other than writing is increasingly important to me. I dabble in classes when I can and feel more at peace drawing than doing anything else. I did Art A level at school back in the day and got a D; I haven't improved, but I know it's good for my soul.

Geof and I have always taken refuge in galleries and he's so incredibly knowledgeable that, without really trying, I've kind of absorbed a lot of information. Art is my 'thing' and it feels good to have a 'thing' that isn't work. Sadly, both Geof and Phoebe can draw better than me, which is annoying.

We have a good time in the valley, apart from when I fall out with my nephews for watching football on Boxing Day and, after a massive row, flounce off into the fog, hoping to disappear long enough for them all to get really worried about me and send out a search party. Unfortunately, I have to give up on the idea after about three minutes because I've forgotten my phone and my coat, and I'm too bored and cold to go missing for long.

My mother is surrounded by her children and five grandchildren. She looks happy, but sometimes she also looks vague and now and again she gets confused about which door leads to which bit of the house. We all notice, but we don't talk about it. After all, she was driving up until recently, until a cataract op didn't have the desired results. She's fine, completely fine. We are all fine: 2020 is going to be great.

Hello, Covid

On New Year's Eve 2020, Geof and I stay in. I make some terrible meal and at midnight we go up on the roof to watch the fireworks in the distance.

Everything is normal, not exciting but normal.

In January I record the first few episodes of series five of *Little Lifetimes* for Radio 4 with a bunch of brilliant actresses including Amelia Bullmore, Monica Dolan and Anne Reid.

In February, I sign up for a bread- and marmalade-making class in nearby Dulwich Village. After all, I am approaching sixty and this is how I roll.

I take a friend who is a TV set designer and we talk about the weird virus in China; she doesn't think it will come here, neither does my mother. 'Well, it might come to London,' she says, 'but not to Lytham.' As if being leafy and having a windmill can stop it. For a while, my mother views Covid as an undesirable trying to gain access to a private golf club: if it's not wanted, it's not getting in.

The bread (soda) and marmalade (Seville orange) are a triumph, but, being a natural catastrophiser, I worry about the virus. I think it's on its way.

A week or so later we celebrate my daughter's thirty-first

birthday at the lovely Delaunay restaurant near the Strand (btw it's since been taken over by a conglomerate and I refuse to set foot in the place).

'Where is everyone?' my daughter ponders, tipping oysters down her neck. The place is dead, and the waiting staff look anxious.

At the beginning of March, I host the Romantic Novelists' Association Awards ceremony, and everyone is self-consciously bumping elbows and giggling at the ridiculousness of it all. After all, life can't just stop, can it?

Two days before my sixtieth birthday, on 14 March, I take a train to Penrith to do a literary festival. *Inheritance* will be out in paperback in a few months and I'm plugging it as much as I can. There is a lot of talk about the virus and, after my event, all the other authors due at the festival cancel. I am their last guest.

On my way back to London the train passes through Preston, and it strikes me that I should get off and visit my mother, but I don't. I want to go home: it's nearly my birthday and we are going to see the Picasso at the Royal Academy. I'll see her soon, I decide, and stay on the train.

I turn sixty on 16 March. The plan is that I am going to spend the next five months writing a show about being sixty and start touring in September.

I've done the photo shoot for the publicity (weirdly flattering) and approved the poster design. I decide to call the show *Sixty!* (*FFS!*) but haven't a clue as to what the content will be.

At the Royal Academy some of the East Asian visitors are wearing masks; this is incredibly alien to us, but not to them. In many countries people wear masks as a matter of course. The Academy is huge and there aren't many people viewing the Picasso exhibition. The show is phenomenal.

We have lunch in a chi-chi little place opposite the Academy's rear entrance (phnargh). A young Italian boy on the next table coughs and everyone tenses. 'It's not the virus,' his mother assures us. But we have all seen the reports from Italy and we sit as far away as we can. Phoebe and I have the sea bass.

That evening we have a local pub supper with my sister, nephew and his girlfriend. By the time we get home, all the West End theatres are preparing to go dark.

I also get a text from my next-door neighbour, Barbara; she sends me birthday wishes but also a message to say her husband Colin is on a ventilator in King's. He has the virus.

We suspected as much. The night before we'd seen an ambulance arrive outside their house and the paramedics wore full hazmat suits. Suddenly this thing is very close.

Colin dies on 18 March. He was in his early eighties, a hugely strong ox of a man who loved his cruises, cricket and family. He and Barbara were the best of neighbours; they put up with us building the house, rallied to the rescue when we had a flood and regularly delivered home-made buns for Geof. Colin is among the first 150 people in the UK to die of Covid.

There is talk of a circuit-breaking lockdown, maybe for as long as two weeks. I order some silicone gloves from the internet and start wearing them on public transport. Hopefully, because I live so close to King's, people will think I'm an absent-minded surgeon who has forgotten to remove her gloves post-shift. Sales of hand sanitiser go through the roof and the weather is beautiful.

Into Lockdown

The entire country goes into lockdown proper on 23 March. I have left it too late to visit June. I persuade myself that she's fine: my mother is a coper. We set up a veg box delivery, but she insists on doing any other shopping herself, 'otherwise I won't get out of the flat'. She is almost ninety-one, has one kidney and poor eyesight; her sister is registered blind and is three years older. Neither are advised to shield. Her cleaners are allowed to visit as long as she stays in another room. Helen and Gayle become vital to my mother's wellbeing; we owe them enormous thanks.

Suddenly all my work stops. I'd been making a BBC documentary about the effectiveness of activism through crafting, which is immediately put on ice, and the fifth series of *Little Lifetimes* is completed by actresses working from home studios.

The one thing I can continue doing, apart from writing, is the podcast.

For a couple of episodes, Judith and I attempt to record it via voice notes on our phones, which is ridiculous and sounds bonkers. Happily, within weeks we are set up with proper mics and Daisy manages to produce us remotely on a platform called Cleanfeed, which is similar to Zoom but has a superior sound quality.

The weekly pod becomes incredibly important; it's the only time I feel like I'm connecting with the wider world, and we get a huge number of emails from listeners telling us that it's helping them to laugh through these strange times. Tbh, I think it's helping us just as much as them, if not more.

Like many families up and down the country, my siblings and our various offspring hold bad-tempered Zoom quizzes during which everyone cheats and various relatives flounce off in a sulk. We window-visit Phoebe in New Cross and I brave the supermarket once a week, scavenging food for us and for Barbara next door. Those initial supermarket trips are traumatic: the queuing in the car park, the fury at the non-mask wearers, the lack of choice on the shelves, the fear of it.

My autumn tour is cancelled as soon as it becomes apparent that lockdown isn't going to be the two-week deal that we'd hoped for, and that life isn't going to just snap back to normal any time soon.

Financially I'm OK. I have enough writing commissions to see me through, and considering I won't be going on holiday I don't have any major expenses to factor into my budget. I stop buying clothes and spend my diminished earnings on food and art materials, and set myself the task of doing a thirty-minute sketch a day. Sometimes I give up after ten minutes, having done little more than scribble, other days I can spend a couple of hours, happy as a pig in shit with my paints.

Before long the entertainment industry finds ways of getting telly shows made and one of the most ingenious series to come out of lockdown is *Grayson's Art Club*. Filmed remotely in Grayson Perry's studio with his wonderful wife, the ceramicist and psychotherapist Philippa Perry, this is the first art show on telly that really is for everyone. The country joins in, and the resulting artworks are not only visually great, but tell a story of our times. It's hugely popular and I am knocked out to be asked on as a guest. This involves filming the process of me creating a piece for the show on a small table in my sitting room. The camera kit is delivered to the door, Geof helps me set it up and I use oil pastel crayons for a small interior study of a corner in my house. I want to do something that reflects how much of our lives are now being spent indoors. I mostly draw my sofa.

Not that people aren't going out. The Covid spring is beautiful and, although we are rationed to an hour of exercise a day, the local parks are heaving. The world seems to divide into those who feel they must jog/run/skip/hop and jump through this weird ordeal and the rest of us who potter and occasionally stroll. I do not hate lockdown: there is a weird sense of rehearsing for retirement about it and I genuinely believe that, apart from the health risks, it's much easier for the over-sixties than it is for young people. I start writing stand-up about it, e.g.:

I reckon if you're going to be stuck in a pandemic for over a year, I've come to the conclusion that lockdown was officially easier for the over-sixties. OK, so we might have been more at risk of dying of Covid but we could legitimately stay at home and do jigsaw puzzles without dying of shame. Pity the young people used to going out clubbing and taking ket every night, suddenly reduced to staying indoors and trying to find all the edges to a thousand-piece puzzle of Durham Cathedral. 'Kill me now.'

And it's not just jigsaws that made getting through the pandemic easier. There was a lot of other stuff about lockdown that really didn't bother us. For starters, there was no home schooling for us – my daughter's thirty-two, I've done all that. Some of my neighbours had school-age kids. At the end of the first lockdown they'd aged about seventy years. They looked like they'd been exhumed. Up at 7 a.m. teaching their kids their times tables, meanwhile next door we weren't getting out of bed 'til midday. The only thing I got up for was the Amazon delivery. What is it today, darling? It's a new jigsaw. Ooh, what's it called? It's called Cats Playing in Positano.

And the gyms were closed [big shrug].

Lockdown gives me plenty of time to write the new show. I just can't perform it, not yet.

I can't even get on a bus; public transport is reserved for key workers. This is particularly galling as I have just received my over-sixties Oyster card (a perk of living in London) which entitles me to free public transport outside of rush hour. Sometimes I sit on my sofa, watching empty buses rolling up and down the hill outside my house, thinking, *If it wasn't for this pesky pandemic, I could be sat on the top deck of the 176, going all the way to Penge for nothing.*

Mother Worries

My sister and I visit June as soon as we are legally allowed. She stands in the hall, smaller than I remember, and when we ask if she is pleased to see us, she says, 'You have no idea.'

This is very typical of June, who, being northern, is not prone to gushing, but I can tell she is pleased. She is delighted, in fact, and she seems fine, older, a bit thinner, but still capable of bringing her two daughters breakfast in bed – I'm joking.

Lytham never held much appeal to me as a young woman – I couldn't wait to get out of the place – but having turned sixty I can suddenly see its charm. The green is free of dog shit, no one has spray-painted genitalia on the pristine white windmill and they have done a lovely job on the promenade. There are benches for 'a little sit-down' everywhere and you can cycle safely for miles along the front; not that there is a bike at June's, or a car for that matter: Ma is no longer driving. Nor can she see to read the paper either and has cancelled her subscription to the *Daily Telegraph* (no bad thing, I hear you mutter).

Reading books is also a problem.

This makes me sad. My mother and aunt were 'once upon a pre-Covid time' members of a hilarious book club, which basically took months to read any chosen novel, possibly because they all tried to borrow it from the same library. I attended one of their meetings; the book was very much ignored, but there was a huge discussion over how everyone took their coffee and the variety of biscuits on offer. At the end of the session, a hoo-ha ensued over whose coat was whose, considering they were all very similar and heaped in a pile on a spare bed. 'Mine's a camel,' one woman kept repeating.

June is a reader by nature, so we load up an iPad with Audible favourites, but she keeps forgetting how to use it. We laugh and I write some jokes about old people and technology.

'I bought my mum an iPad,' I say, rolling my eyes. 'I don't know if anyone has had any experience of dealing with technology and a nonagenarian, because for all the trouble this fucking thing caused, I might as well have bought her a python.'

Then she tells us how she has pulled her Alexa out of the wall because she 'doesn't like it talking back to her' and we notice a large burn mark on the kitchen work surface that never used to be there. It's her eyesight, we mutter, and I paint lines on the hob in silver nail varnish to make it more obvious when it's on and off. It's concerning but there's nothing to worry about, not really, not yet.

When does a niggle of doubt become a sense of dread? With June there is a sudden dramatic deterioration over the summer. We visit again in August and manage to nag her into a second-hand wheelchair. My sister and I take her out on the prom in St Annes, we have scampi and ice cream, but when June gets home she is very tired. We think she might have sunstroke; she isn't 'all there'.

The next day she seems fine, and we leave her to it. June has always rallied, and she has her trip to see an old army friend to look forward to. A taxi is taking her to visit her friend Diana in Wiltshire. As the trip approaches, Ma gets very uptight about packing. When I speak to her on the phone, she always seems to be checking the contents of her case, ticking off everything she has decided to take. I presume she has just lost some confidence due to lockdown.

The day before her mini break, she is walking down the backstreet to the shops and she falls. Paramedics are called, but she refuses to go to hospital, so they bring her home. Later that evening her sister rings her and, realising she isn't making much sense, decides to take a taxi to check up on her. Aileen is ninety-four; she takes her nightie and stays with June, who is 'disorientated', which must have been very frightening. According to Aileen, June wakes up in the morning and seems completely fine, even offering her sister a cup of tea in bed.

Only she isn't fine. The family tom-toms start beating and Sara, Phoebe and I drive up.

'If it's a walking stick, why isn't it walking?' my mother sniggers from the sofa. We all exchange glances.

Something is wrong here, off-kilter. She is a radio station that keeps tuning out.

Maybe she's had a stroke, just a tiny stroke. The kind of stroke you can make a full recovery from. Eventually I manage to get through to a stroke specialist on the phone, who asks a series of questions. 'How is her vocabulary?' he enquires. I explain that sometimes she is very lucid; earlier she'd commented on the Japanese anemones in the garden.

'Japanese anemones,' he repeats, sounding worried.

'Yes, in the garden,' I reply.

'So she's seeing things.'

'Er, no.'

'Soldiers.'

'Pardon?'

'Japanese enemies, soldiers in the garden.'

Oh Jesus, I feel like we're all going mad.

Could it be concussion?

She is taken to Blackpool Vic for a scan: nothing comes up. It's not concussion and the specialist rules out a stroke.

We are confused. It's pretty obvious we can't leave her; she becomes more vulnerable by the hour. We make enquiries about some home care, but it's not going to be enough. She would need live-in help.

Finally, someone suggests phoning the matron of the nursing home where my father stayed for the last three years of his life. Caroline, the matron, pops over. June knows her and behaves as if it's a nice social situation. She begins using her telephone voice. Caroline is incredible with her. She asks a few questions and susses the situation immediately. June has dementia, and she isn't going to get better. She will never live independently again.

What the fuck do we do? Does one of us give up our life in London and take on the responsibility of looking after a woman who is so suddenly changed?

And how do we decide, flip a coin? We aren't trained, we aren't even particularly nice.

Matron makes the decision for us, without us ever having to ask: she offers a room at the Delaheys, but we need to decide quickly.

Phoebe goes back to London and my brother comes up.

We pack the same bag June was going to take to Wiltshire, only she isn't going to Wiltshire now, she is going to a large de-tached red-brick house a couple of miles down the road, the one with the big fish tank in the entrance hall.

'It's just for a little while,' we lie, and June is quite content with the idea that after her fall she needs a couple of weeks of being looked after. The old June would have seen right through this rubbish.

My brother drives the short distance to the Delaheys. This is really happening. He parks the car in the drive.

Due to Covid restrictions, we are not allowed to accompany Ma into the home.

The sight of my mother disappearing behind the front door is something I will never forget.

The three of us go back to June's flat and have fish and chips. This all happened so fast.

Guilt and Fury

Do I feel guilty about the fact we solve the problem of June by 'sticking' her in a home. Yes and no. I wish it had never happened, but I am glad she is there. I know she is safe, the nursing home and staff are familiar to her, she likes them, but, even so, after a couple of weeks they have to hide her suitcase because she keeps packing to go home. This is heart-breaking. We tell her more lies about being safer from the pandemic where she is, and in some respects this is true. Throughout the entire Covid saga, the Delaheys doesn't lose a single patient to the virus.

Occasionally we manage quite good chats on the phone, and there is never a moment that she forgets who we are, Sara, me and Ben. This is comforting, but I cannot see her in the flesh: it's window-waving only. This becomes farcical, due to the home's triple glazing. I cannot communicate with my mother through the glass. On one visit I climb onto the windowsill and yell at her through a slightly open window while all the other residents in the conservatory wonder why the fat woman outside is doing a failed Spiderman routine. It is exhausting.

Visits get easier when I land a telly job in Manchester in November 2020. It's before Covid testing kits, so, like everyone else involved in the show, I have to quarantine for two weeks before we start filming, then I'm driven in a Covid-safe car (Perspex screen) to Manchester, where I live in the Hilton for a couple of weeks.

The job is nearly perfect: I even get a clothing allowance, which is a first. It's a life drawing show, for Channel 4, so right up my strasse, but with a twist.

The twist is what makes me feel uncomfortable and the clue is in the title. The show is called *Drawers Off*, and the twist involves all the competing artists taking it in turn to get their 'drawers off', i.e. being a life model for the day.

I question the need for this from the start, arguing that it will limit the pool of willing artists: someone my age or older could be a shit-hot painter but think getting naked on telly is a bit silly. That's because it is a bit silly; it's not necessary. 'What if you're a teacher or a copper?' I argue, but I am shouted down. The format is the format and there are plenty of people willing to do what the format requires. I still think it's stupid, but I'm desperate to do an art show on the telly, so desperate that I'm prepared to overlook this obviously daft attention-seeking quirk.

To give the production company their credit, they do it as tastefully as possible. The lighting in the studio is lovely and nothing floppy or gonady is dangled in front of the cameras. It's still daft: if you need a life model, get a life model. They know what they're doing, they can hold a pose properly, and for longer. It's a job; don't do the professionals out of a job.

Despite my reservations, I adore making this show. I'm teamed with the art practitioner Diana Ali and even though we have to keep Covid distance regulations on- and off-camera, we become good buddies. The backstage facilities are very basic, and we have no hair or make-up artist to help get us camera-ready. This doesn't bother me: I can do my face with my eyes closed, but it sets a precedent for future telly jobs, which I don't approve of.

Some of the artwork produced on *Drawers Off* is glorious,

some of the life modelling less so. Quite a few of our artists enjoy the process, others loathe it and their embarrassment is palpable.

Manchester is in level 3 lockdown for the duration of my stay at the Hilton, which means everything is shut, including the pool, gym, bars and restaurants. I have a small fridge in which I keep my daily Chardonnay rations and some snackage. I am fed breakfast and lunch at the studio and my supper is arranged online by a runner, usually from either Nando's or Wagamama. I can't be bothered to experiment and my tomato allergy, which manifested itself in my late forties and gives me mouth ulcers after eating any red seeded fruit, makes eating takeaways tricky.

I am not lonely, I've spent too long on tour to get homesick, I have a big room and all my toys. I listen to audio books, set up a little painting corner on the work desk, have a bath after supper and get into bed to do my prep for the next day.

This is not showbiz, as some would have it, but I'm completely content. I'm on the seventeenth floor and when I look down from my huge windows, the silent city below seems to be under some kind of spell.

Drawers Off manages two series, broadcast in 2021 and 2022 (both the year after they are filmed), before Channel 4 pull the plug. Losing this job upsets me hugely and I am furious, furious that they have managed to fuck up a perfectly good idea by not honouring the art enough. In the first series, they cheapened it by making the contestants pose as life models and in the second, despite employing proper professional life models, they ruin it by adding a terrible cheeky-chappy voiceover, which upsets me so much that when I first hear it I lie face down on the floor and bite the carpet.

Thinking about it now, I am still angry; art is so important to me and to so many others. Who cares if most of us are destined to be crap painters all our lives? That's not to say we don't take it seriously. I don't mean that an art show shouldn't be good fun, especially when everyone involved is an amateur, but making something supposedly 'more accessible' by taking the piss out of it is tiresome. Fucking hell. I'm still *fuming.*

While staying in Manchester I am driven to Lytham every week on my afternoon off to window-wave at June and check up on the flat. During one of my visits to her flat, I pick up an old navy leather cross-body bag which I think I'll find useful. I like wearing it; it makes me feel connected to my mother.

I'm wearing this bag the first time I am allowed into the home. It's the spring of 2021, I am fully masked up with a negative Covid test. I wait anxiously in the conservatory while they go and fetch June. I'm fatter than I was pre-Covid and Geof has been bleaching and cutting my hair, with the result that I have a bright yellow mullet. Will she even recognise me?

Later, when I recount this anecdote onstage, I describe myself as looking like a fat Limahl from Kajagoogoo.

Anyway, a nurse brings June in, who takes one look at me, points and very clearly and concisely says, 'That's my handbag.' Thus proving that there are some bits of the brain that dementia cannot reach.

It's a brief and wonderful moment. For a few seconds she seems like the old June, but then she is gone again.

2021: The Year of the Mask

I start writing my first Young Adult novel, *The Writing on the Wall*, in 2021. It's a funny old time: we are in and out of lockdown, wearing masks, having jabs and waiting for life to return to normal, which it sort of does, but not really.

People are becoming divided over the pandemic, and I have to come off Twitter for a while after saying publicly that 'I can't see why people who don't want to wear masks on the tube don't sit in their own separate "cunt" carriage'. It takes a fortnight for that one to calm down!

At least we can see friends and family more, and work, although heavily restricted by pandemic guidelines, is coming back.

There is the second and final series of *Drawers Off* to film (weep, gnash), and the stand-up tour *Sixty! (FFS!)* is back on for the autumn.

The prospect of going back out on the road is surreal. I've had so much time off stand-up that I feel panicky about it.

Writing a book is safer!

The idea for *The Writing on the Wall* lands weirdly out of the blue. In a nutshell it's about two fifteen-year-old girls who share a bedroom, many decades apart. It's simple: Helena occupies the bedroom in the seventies, while Hermione arrives in the same house in 2018. How do they meet? Time travel, of course. Hermione catches a bus to town after newly arriving in the neighbourhood, and, hey presto, she is back in the seventies, meets Helena and their adventure begins. Obviously, there is more to it than that. Hermione can't catch any bus back into the seventies: it only works if she walks through the graveyard on the way to the bus stop. One day, while walking through this graveyard, she sees her seventies pal's name on a gravestone. Can Hermione travel back in time and save her friend's life? I know, right; you'll have to read it if you want to find out.

I set the book in the house where I grew up, 49 Blackpool Road, and I am very happy revisiting my past, rifling through the contents of my old chest of drawers and remembering all my vinyl records, the colours of my nail varnish (Miners Murky Mauve), my yellow ball of Kiku talc and collection of *Jackie* magazines. Helena is basically me and Hermione is based on Phoebe, but with a much trickier upbringing. Helena is needy and attention-seeking, Hermione much cooler!

Talking of Phoebe, she manages to have two plays out in the spring and summer of 2021. *Harm*, a one-woman play about how toxic social media can be, is staged (in line with current Covid restrictions) at the Bush Theatre in London and filmed for BBC 3. *Really Big and Really Loud* is a fabulous kids' show, which tours with the company Paines Plough in their travelling yellow bubble theatre tent. I see it in a park in Brixton and have the best time with a bunch of eight-year-olds.

By the summer of 2021 we are starved of a holiday and spend ten days in Cornwall.

Geof and I love Cornwall; if only it wasn't such a pig to get to from London. We love St Ives and Penzance, with its fabulous Jubilee outdoor pool and St Michael's Mount and all the public gardens and houses to snoop around.

It's the sort of calm before the storm. The tour is approaching and before that *Older and Wider* has its first live gig. For some reason we are jumping in at the deep end and performing our inaugural show at the big old Latitude Festival.

OK, let me just say this: I hate performing in tents, especially in the middle of a hot day. The sound quality is always crap and it's really hard to hold the audience's attention. There's always too much going on elsewhere: why should they sit down and listen when they could wander off and get their hair braided, see that Icelandic indie hip-hop band, eat another falafel.

Judith talks me into it; she even hires an upmarket camper van with all mod cons, including a washing-up bowl. She also promises me some kind of mini Sani Loo that comes with its own zip-around tent. I can't say no.

There's a lot of Covid paraphernalia to deal with before we are given our festival wristbands and, despite being mostly outside, it still feels risky and I'm not sure how comfortable I am being among big crowds.

It's a messy but enjoyable gig. We bribe the audience to stay with packets of lettuce seeds, and those who know the podcast actually sit on the floor like primary school children at story time. After the gig we drink some wine, have dinner and Judith wanders back into the festival throng with her daughters.

I decide that even though I like Damon Albarn, I can't be fucked to watch him on a screen while standing in a field. So I go back to the camper van, heave myself onto my sleeping shelf and listen to my audio book!

Judith hardly drinks, but on this occasion, high on adrenalin, she makes an exception. It's a rookie error and in the morning she is so hungover that she throws up three times into the washing-up bowl.

Realising I am nowhere near match fit for a tour, Avalon book me onto a 'comedy cruise', which leaves Southampton and floats around Southampton without actually going anywhere for three days. Having done *Battle Chefs*, I am an old hand at cruise ships, but I have an uneasy night in my cabin knowing I won't be playing to my usual crowd, which by this point in my career consists mostly of women around my age wearing striped Breton tops. As I say onstage, 'looking out at my audience is a bit like looking out at a busty menopausal *Where's Wally?* convention'.

I am due to do two shows in the theatre the next night and the set I have worked on is a hybrid of old material with some of the new show thrown in. The first show is pretty awful and I hide in my cabin 'til the next, when I give myself a talking to and perform better in front of a less ancient/boozier crowd.

The experience is the kick up the arse that I need: the new show is not ready, and I need to stop titting about. I haven't been working hard enough. Lockdown has made me lazy, and I've rather enjoyed dossing about, drawing and painting, going for walks with Geof and generally taking it easy.

The truth is, I have a massive idle streak that I have fought all my life to beat. I think what drives me is the suspicion that if I let all the ambition go, I might not get out of bed. It's the dreaded Nana Hargreaves in me.

But surely in your sixties there has to be a middle ground? Sadly, finances dictate that I get back on the road. I can't actually afford to potter forever.

But Covid has taught me some valuable lessons: I'm less scared of not working, I love being at home, I love Peckham Rye, I love flowers and blossom and birds, creating daft things on my kitchen table, listening to audio books, but, most importantly, how it makes me realise how lucky I am to have Geof.

Geof is a white-haired gent now, with a proper beard and moustaches (imagine if Father Christmas had a really stylish brother). He has left the building design and project management game behind, because he is too old to go up ladders in a hard hat, and too old for clients who want a grand design on a thruppenny-bit budget. He will still do consultations and draw plans for the occasional local client, but he has another business now, selling twentieth-century original prints and posters. It's mostly an online concern, although we sometimes do fairs where I play his lovely assistant and people look at me and ask if I'm that lady who runs the dry cleaner's in Streatham.

Geof has always had a good eye and he knows what he's talking about. Lockdown sales are surprisingly good, thanks to all those people who get bored with looking at the same four walls while being furloughed and decide to spend their wages on art rather than a holiday.

Funny how 'furloughed', a word we'd never really used before, is suddenly so common (not that us freelancers know how it feels to be furloughed!). We are left very much to our own devices; I decide that pottering will have to wait. I need to find my gig legs again.

My Millionth Show

Sixty! (FFS!) is my millionth show. OK, so it isn't, but in the autumn of 2021 it's the latest of very many.

As the title suggests, it's about turning sixty, but turning sixty during a pandemic puts a new spin on it, and, like every other comic in the land, I've got my 'Covid content'.

Hence one of my opening lines:

Good to see you in real life. Don't get me wrong, Zoom is great for stuff like Xmas with the family, that mute button is a precious thing, but not for gigs …

My favourite line, about the pandemic arriving in time for my sixtieth birthday, goes like this:

I mean, happy fucking birthday. Just what every woman wants, an airborne killer disease, oh yes, and by the way, now that you're sixty you're automatically in a higher-risk age category. That's right, you're more likely to die.

And there's me thinking the biggest risk to turning sixty was the danger of buying some Nordic walking poles and a gilet.

In the second half I come back onstage wearing a gilet, with a pair of Nordic walking poles, accompanied by the King's Singers belting out 'The Happy Wanderer' – 'I love to go a-wandering', etc. – which gives me huge joy every night.

I do my first night in Leicester's tiny Y Theatre and feel like crying when the audience applaud the walk-on.

It's such a relief to be back onstage: Zoom gigs tried to be a thing, but they never really worked. Neither did the attempt to stick comics on a stage in a field or car park while people sat in their cars listening to a live link on their phones.

Comedy comes in many shapes and forms now, and the internet has created stars out of people who have the skills to use it to their advantage. Instagram, Twitter and TikTok are brilliant for those making social comment, playing characters or simply biting the hand of the media platforms that feed them, mostly by taking the piss out of online influencers. I follow lots of these performers; are they stand-ups? Does it matter?

My stuff suits a stage and an audience, I like the whole rigmarole of making an entrance and exit, the interval breather, the post-show glass of wine. I'm old school.

But I also believe that doing the podcast, which takes the pressure off doing 'jokes', because it's not punchline reliant, has made me a better stand-up. I trust my instincts more and I've found that, after years of being shit scared of improvising, I'm enjoying it more and more.

I'd never dare make up an entire show on the spot, but now and again I find I can let go of the script and muck about for a while. However, I'm wary of becoming self-indulgent; there are too many comics who are over-enamoured of their own flights of whimsy and forget to make any gags.

I'm glad comedy keeps changing, it forces you to experiment, but deep down in my comedy bones I will always be someone who enjoys standing in the wings, waiting to hear my name being announced and walking out into the lights.

I'm also very good at touring, possibly because I've been doing it for more than forty years.

So for anyone who fancies the idea of spending three months mostly sitting in the passenger seat of a hire car, here are my Essential Touring Tips:

Hire a tour manager driver who you like and doesn't freak out in a blizzard.

Good tour managers don't smell and always fart outside the car.

Make sure you have some toys for the journey, plus a phone charger, so that if the worst comes to the worst you can scroll through Instagram looking at people who aren't sitting in traffic on the M25.

Have something you can do in the car. I buy tapestry kits and, once completed, I send them off to the prison charity Fine Cell Work (one of my favourite charities) to be made up into cushions. I've done loads – you should see my brother's face when he gets one for Xmas, hahaha.

Make sure you have plenty of snacks and drinks in the car. Sadly, I've had to stop drinking Diet Coke after it triggered too many incidences of cystitis. These days I stick to water, still and cold, and Pink Lady apples.

I also keep a bottle of post-show Chardonnay in the glove box. It fits perfectly. And don't forget paper cups, otherwise you will be swigging from the bottle at midnight and people will talk.

Know your service stations. Marks and Waitrose franchises have completely changed the world of touring; once upon a time it was Ginsters or nothing. My tour manager, Chris George, once bit into a Ginsters breakfast buffet bar in the car and the smell lingered for weeks, like a diseased pig on fermented coleslaw.

Occasionally you will come across a Leon – nice. Pret outlets are also rare, but do the best coffee.

Do not queue for coffee anywhere. Always use the machine in WH Smith, it's quicker and tastes better. Don't ask me why, it just does.

Most theatres will have a filthy microwave backstage. A carton of soup shared with your tour manager is a good idea in winter.

Always have an emergency sandwich about your person.

Beware large bags of potato-based snacks; they are very moreish.

Finally:

Do not finish every show with a cartwheel when you are too old and too fat to cartwheel.

I slide back into touring with ease, and whenever I'm near enough I stay at June's. It's strange to be in the flat without her. I keep expecting to find her in the kitchen. All her things are still there, the white Meissen in the hall dresser, the vases she made in her pottery classes, the raffia mats on the dining table.

My mother is deteriorating. In November, with gigs in

Liverpool and Chorley, I take the train north and Phoebe comes with me. She has recently opened her third play of the year at Reading Rep. Co-written with Owen Horsley, *Dorian* is described by the *Guardian* as 'a riotous homage to queer culture' and given four stars by the paper (more than I've ever had from the *Guardian*).

She is exhausted and moans all the way about how queasy the train is making her feel. 'Pendolino trains,' I remind her, 'always do that, it's the way they tilt on the tracks.'

We see June, which is sad. She is immaculately groomed, but is distracted and endlessly searches her handbag for something she will never find. We also nip up to see the illuminations, but my daughter is off-colour and that night, catching sight of her curled up on the sofa, something odd crosses my mind. I chase the thought away; she's not drinking, but then she barely does, I'm the white wine queen. Phoebe takes after her father; she doesn't have an addictive personality.

Less than a month later she comes round to tell me that she is indeed pregnant. She sits on the floor in my study and I try to get down to hug her but having sort of broken my neck doing pretend cartwheels onstage it's all very awkward. She has just come from King's; there are some doubts over the viability of the pregnancy, but weirdly she isn't panicking. I think she knows this is going to happen.

I am much more neurotic. Geof and I are delighted but anxious: what if, what if, what if? This is beyond our control. The baby is due in July and I do not relax for the next eight months.

The Neck Job

A t the end of my *Sixty!* *(FFS!)* touring show I have been
faking a little cartwheel, more of a bunny hop than the
full wheel but, even so, I am too old and too heavy to bunny hop
and I have put too much pressure on my neck and shoulder. I
know that I've done something awful when I roll over in bed one
day and something seems to snap.

The pain is indescribable. I am taken to King's, which is five
minutes from my house, at just after midnight in December 2021.

We are in that lateral flow test period of Covid, and I sit in
A&E, wearing a mask, and wait. There are around thirty others,
all in various stages of distress, also waiting. At about 3 a.m. we
all settle down for a sleep. Some of us lie on the floor, there are
no staff and collectively we all give up. It feels like some strange
kind of bomb shelter. I am downwind of someone who smells like
they might have trench foot.

At 8 a.m. I walk out. I feel insane.

Over the next week I begin to lose mobility in my left hand,
I take silly amounts of painkillers and, finally, a physio tells me
I need an operation as soon as possible, before the damage be-
comes permanent.

I pay to go under the knife, and the sleepover in a private

hospital feels like a mini break. The telly in my room is tuned to an Arabic station and I am offered wine with my dinner. I have a cheeky Chardonnay and mix it with my intravenous fentanyl driver – this is the life.

Because the hospital is more expensive than Sandy Lane in Barbados, I leave the next day. They supply me with lots of lovely pain relief and warn me about the side-effects. Obviously I do not listen, and consequently almost die of faecal impaction. Trying to have a post-op poo is worse than childbirth, but within a month I'm back onstage talking about it: 'So there I am, crowning a ten-pounder without gas and air, in the end I have to stage an intervention: I go for home forceps delivery . . . and I'm never using those salad servers again!'

This is the joke I get out of this experience. Sadly, it's not worth the 8K the op cost me, and I still don't have full mobility in my left hand, which means I can't knit (not that I ever could) or dismantle a Yoyo baby buggy either, which reminds me: why are babies' buggies such twatting shits?

Christmas is an odd one. I'm fresh out of hospital after my neck op and feeling rather fragile. Turns out it wasn't broken, but I did have to have some discs shaved down that were pressing on a nerve, and I now have a proper old-fashioned scar down the back of my neck, which I obviously tell people is the result of a shark attack.

The new Omicron variant scuppers our Xmas plans: half the family are down with it and June's nursing home closes its doors to visitors. It all feels a bit back to square one.

That said, secretly Geof and I quite enjoy having a quiet Xmas dinner together. We just have a chicken crown, baked potatoes and frozen peas! Ha! Onwards everyone, bloody onwards.

Onwards and Arrivals

Podcast Judith beats me to grannyhood when her daughter gives birth to twin boys in March 2022.

Phoebe is also expecting a boy, which is something I have to get my head around. I'm slightly scared of boys. Despite being the kind of woman who has fought very hard to be heard in a man's world, I have always loved being a woman. In fact, I think being a heterosexual man must be rather dull. I like female things and I worry a boy won't want to sit down with me and colour in.

'Marmaduke is a great name,' I suggest, but apparently it's nothing to do with me, hahaha.

Thinking hard about this unknown, as yet unnamed baby, I gradually realise that a boy will be a good thing. Phoebe and I are almost unnaturally close and look weirdly similar; another girl might feel the pressure to be just like us, a kind of mini Babushka doll. It wouldn't be healthy. A boy is a clean slate, I decide, and wonder what he will look like. Babies are about the only thing these days that you can't send back; everything else you can parcel up and get rid of. You get what you're given with a baby.

Knitting booties is out of the question, considering a) my left hand no longer functions properly, and b) I've never managed more than a blanket square. So I concentrate on working instead and all knitting duties are taken up by P's old nanny Vanessa who is a ninja with a needle or a crochet hook.

There are the edits to finish on *The Writing on the Wall*, some bits and bobs of telly, a travel show with Rosie Jones and another with Sandi Toksvig, and more tour dates.

I catch my first dose of Covid when we are meant to be flying off to Stockholm for my belated sixtieth birthday treat. I am now sixty-two and yet again the mini break gets cancelled. However, a month later we are on a plane and on our way to Stockholm.

FYI, wine is terrifyingly expensive in Sweden and not sold in normal supermarkets! You have to go to a bottle shop or spend £50 in your hotel! Still, the art is great and we have a very nice time. Phew.

In May, we buy a pram. The bump is big now, Phoebe is thirty-three but in the baby department of John Lewis she looks like a pregnant schoolgirl.

My mother is quite confused about the baby. She thinks it's mine and urges me not to travel 'in my condition'. Seems mothers never stop worrying about their babies.

Finally, I am asked to do Channel 4's *Taskmaster* – 'bout bleedin' time. I've wanted to do it forever, but despite it being made by Avalon, the management company that I have been with for over thirty years, I do not get asked until series fifteen (rude). The truth is, *Taskmaster* was originally on Dave, and Dave didn't want me. It's as simple as that.

I have to wait and wait and wait until the show moves to Channel 4, and finally I am asked. It's worth the wait; on Dave each series was a measly five episodes, now it's ten, and the money is much better than on Dave. Ha! I win. They also offer a clothing allowance because, due to the messiness of the show, you have to have duplicates of everything you wear onscreen. I opt for an orange kimono ensemble with black top, trousers and orange trainers. The kimono is sort of both dressing gown and ninja cape.

If you're not into this show then you won't understand quite what a juggernaut *Taskmaster* is. There are versions in umpteen countries, *Taskmaster* school clubs, merchandise, the works. It's hosted by Greg Davies, who if I had any libido left I would very much fancy, and the brilliant Alex Horne, who is also a musician and the brains behind the whole set-up.

TM is a massive success because everyone who works on it is a fan. I've never seen such backstage commitment to a programme.

I have a complete ball filming the live tasks in the late spring of 2022, even when I crash a barge into a wall, and laugh my head off during the studio records which are done in September.

The show will be aired in the spring of 2023 and my agent thinks it will give my career a bit of a boost! Haha, I'm in my sixties. To be honest, career boost or not, I wouldn't have missed the TM experience for the world. It's one of my favourite telly experiences of all time, and the closest I've ever come to laughter incontinence on film.

The summer of 2022 is record-breakingly hot, Phoebe puffs around in the heatwave, her due date comes and goes, we will know when they are going into King's, because they will be parking on our drive. We are constantly on the lookout for a little blue car. The plan is to park and then leisurely stroll the ten minutes down to the hospital.

Only it doesn't really go like that. The call comes saying they are on their way at 6.20 in the morning. By the time they arrive it's very obvious Phoebe isn't walking anywhere. We get them both in her father's car, Tristram carrying all her kit. They are ashen-faced. I burble the entire four-minute drive to the hospital, get her out and more or less carry her in. At the lift she tells me, very sternly, that this is where I must leave them.

Forty-five minutes later, the baby is born, and by 7.30 that evening they are walking out of the hospital with this new human being. I can't say I approve of this speedy exit; I think it's reducing childbirth to removing an ingrowing toenail.

However straightforward a birth is, it's traumatic. All of a sudden you are responsible for a tiny life.

I try to recognise him, but I can't. He has very tightly shut eyes and a slightly chewed lip. There must be something, he can't be a complete stranger. I am desperate to know him, but he is a little sealed secret in a Babygro. His name is Arlo Jude.

There are a lot of Arlos born in south London in 2022; by the time he gets to school there will be seven in his class.

'A R L O,' my mother spells back at me. 'His name is Arlo, not Arnold?'

'No, not Arnold,' I reply.

When Arlo is four months old and a proper bounce-on-your-knee big bald fabulous baby, we take him to see his great-grandmother.

I'm glad the staff took photos. The baby sits on my mother's knee, ninety-three years separating them, then he sits on my knee. One sock has fallen off and my mother's old hand is holding his little pink toes.

Endings

Geof and I finally do what we have been meaning to do for three years: we spend Xmas 2022 in Lytham. Bigger, more exciting Christmases can wait. We pile the car up, swing by Booths and hunker down in June's flat.

I take Aileen to visit June on Xmas Day and Boxing Day, then again before we leave on the 27th. The visits don't go well. June is progressively crosser and increasingly fed up, she barely opens her presents (I still have one in my wardrobe), she doesn't want to eat, she wants to go to bed. It's upsetting and Aileen is devastated. For some reason, I still think she will be fine; she never liked Xmas much, not once she got older. Christmases were best when we lived at 49 Blackpool Road, cigar smoke and little bowls of crisps and peanuts, Cinzano and lemonades for the girls, my mother offering around mushroom vol au vents.

Back in London we have a belated Xmas lunch with the rest of the family – those who aren't laid out with norovirus – but, mid-afternoon, the nursing home calls my sister's landline. June isn't getting up any more; a woman who never slept beyond 8.30 a.m. is now living under the covers. She has gone into hibernation, she will not eat.

My sister goes north and I follow on 2 January. Ben is in court again, robbery and corruption (joke: he's a criminal defence barrister), so it's Sara and me for the finale.

This is in equal parts desperate, confusing and farcical.

A number of nurses pop in to say goodbye before they finish their shifts. These women know she will not be alive in the morning. We are not convinced.

Neither of us has thought about provisions and the fact that we are both ravenous come the evening of the vigil adds a surreal note to the proceedings. I'm desperate for some cheese.

The kitchens are locked, it's just us and the night staff. 'You must have a banana in your bag,' my sister insists, but I haven't, and we agree that you can't exactly order in a pizza to eat at your dying mother's bedside.

We ransack her room for leftover Xmas goodies and find nothing but an empty drum of Turkish delight. I lick out the powdery residue and I don't even like Turkish delight. Both of us are too terrified to go to the bathroom in case we miss the moment. I may have wee'd in a handbasin, but let's pretend I didn't.

June is not conscious, but we chat away and hold her hand. She is dramatically changed and reminds me of a Käthe Kollwitz charcoal. It's a shocking transformation from just a week ago.

The process of death can be long. There are many times during that night when we think she has taken her last breath, only for her to snore back to life. My mother always did snore. We are tired, but daren't sleep; we take it in turn to snooze, but neither of us manage to truly drop off.

The second of January turns into the third, and some time just after midnight, or was it just after 1 a.m., June dies.

We are weirdly still not convinced. 'Are you sure?' we ask each other. 'Are you absolutely certain?' A nurse on duty comes to the room and certifies the death. We have to do some paperwork before we can leave and finally get back to June's at around 2 a.m.

I think I have some toast. I don't really have much of an appetite any more.

I get into my mother's bed, while my sister settles into the spare bedroom, and start to cry.

My sister comes in and in a very un-Sara-ish way gets into bed to comfort me. I am howling by now, but I feel I need to warn her that I haven't got any pants on. She leaps out of the bed. It was nice while it lasted.

Telling our aunt is the worst part of everything, even worse than everything else.

No one ever tells you about the administration that comes with a death. It should be taught in schools. There are certificates that must be signed within a certain time, people to be notified, accounts to be closed.

Being 'creative' has always given me a legal loophole to get out of any admin shit. I hate it, I don't understand it and I'm too lazy to make the effort to get to grips with anything that requires a witnessed signature.

My brother and sister, both being in the legal profession, do 'forms' as a second language. This is great but occasionally they have conversations when they speak mostly in acronyms. It's like being trapped in a particularly bewildering episode of *Line of Duty*.

My sister is turbo-charged around death. She just gets on with it. I trail behind her, mostly getting in the way. We register the death in the same office where parents are registering newborns, which is weirdly comforting. Just goes on, doesn't it, life.

The funeral is held a couple of weeks later and we underestimate how many egg sandwiches an elderly group of June's mates can stash away and have to order more.

I think I have dealt with this, I think that I'm fine with my mother dying, she was ninety-three and she'd had enough. It's over, the flat is put on the market and the wheels of probate are put into motion.

I cannot believe that very soon I will not have access to June's flat, that I will not have somewhere to stay in Lytham, that I am an orphan.

I remind myself I'm nearly sixty-three and get on with writing a new novel.

I have lied to my publishers about a brilliant idea that I've had and attempt to sell them this half-baked story over lunch.

They give me the benefit of the doubt and encourage me to go ahead. I plough on. I have no idea where I'm going, I like the characters, I like the setting, but I can't get the story.

I'll find it, I tell myself, if I just keep going. I keep going, individual pages are great, there is some lovely writing, it just doesn't add up to anything. This has never happened to me before. It's like endlessly playing a game of patience that will never 'come out'.

Arlo gets bronchiolitis in February; he is poorly enough for King's to send a home hospital team out. The girls are amazing: sometimes they come twice a day.

Inevitably, I catch it, or some version of it. RSV is mentioned. I feel awful, I am in bed for eleven days and suddenly I realise that it's not just a virus, it's everything: it's losing June, which reminds me of losing Derek, and trying to write a book when I'm neither mentally nor physically strong enough to pull this particular rabbit out of the hat.

Hopefully, in the future, I'll yank the bloody thing out by its ears and it will be wonderful. But not now.

I eventually summon up the courage to tell my agent, who is understanding. 'No one has a gun to your head,' he reminds me. He will talk to the publishers.

He does, then he phones me. 'How do you feel about writing an autobiography?'

Onwards . . .

And Now (Postscript)

It's April 2024 and I am sixty-four. I don't mind. What's the alternative?

Phoebe's play *Shed* finally made its debut at Manchester's Royal Exchange in February, almost five years after she won the Bruntwood Prize. It receives a raft of four- and five-star reviews.

My grandson is a toddler, he is the light of my life, he is my silver lining, he is the apple of my eye. He doesn't like sitting next to me when I take him to singing sessions, he moves as far away from me as possible, almost as if he's embarrassed, as if even he knows I can't sing, ha!

Being a nana has given me something I didn't expect. I even make him flapjacks. It's good to be able to do something for my daughter, to give her son the time I didn't cherish enough with her when she was a toddler.

I miss my parents and I miss my childhood, but I can take myself back there. I can feel the hearth rug we had at Blackpool Road under my knees, visualise the fake Delft tiled wallpaper in the kitchen at Rossall Road, see my sister ignoring me at school, my brother inhaling the nozzle from a bicycle tyre and being taken to hospital to have it removed, hear my father whistling when he got home, wherever we lived, and my mother laughing at his jokes.

How lucky I have been.

Now, about that prime-time chat/quiz/art show . . .

Acknowledgements

Thanks to Catherine Burke, Richard Allen-Turner, Serena Brett and Zoe Gullen. Also huge gratitude to all the venues I've ever played, all the tour managers, support acts, fellow Grumpies and, most of all, the audience, because if you didn't show up, I'd just be some woman shouting on stage.

Apologies to my siblings if I remember things differently from you, but as ever, I am right and you are wrong.

Finally, all my love and thanks to Geof and Phoebe. Without you, I am hopeless.

Picture Credits

Jenny Eclair is a stand-up comedian and writer.

Having toured umpteen solo shows, she has also worked extensively in radio and TV, with drama, sitcom, reality telly (including *I'm A Celebrity . . . Get Me Out Of Here!*), presenting roles and panel shows all under her belt. She was also once the face of Vagisan Moisturising Cream.

Jenny is well known for starring in BBC1's *Grumpy Old Women*, produced by Judith Holder, with whom she co-wrote four live international *Grumpy* shows. She and Judith now co-host the podcast *Older and Wider*, a weekly post-menopausal scream for attention with additional swearing.

Jenny competed on series 15 of Channel 4's *Taskmaster* and currently co-hosts the podcast spin-off, *Taskmaster: The People's Podcast*.

She has written six novels, loads of comedy books, a collection of short stories and seven series of BBC Radio 4's much-loved *Little Lifetimes*.

Basically, she's been around the block.